ⓈHORT**ORDER**

MACROMEDIA®
Fireworks 2.0

NANCY MARTIN AND RONNIE SAMPSON

Short Order Macromedia® Fireworks 2.0

Copyright © 2000 by Hayden Books®

International Standard Book Number: 0-7897-2043-4

Library of Congress Catalog Card Number: 99-66440

First Printing: December 1999

01   00   99   4   3   2   1

Printed in the United States of America

Trademarks

Warning and Disclaimer

EXECUTIVE EDITOR
Beth Millett

ACQUISITIONS EDITOR
Karen Whitehouse

DEVELOPMENT EDITOR
Laura Norman

MANAGING EDITOR
Thomas F. Hayes

PROJECT EDITOR
Lori A. Lyons

COPY EDITOR
Sossity Smith

INDEXER
Heather McNeill

PROOFREADER
Maribeth Echard

TECHNICAL EDITOR
Allison Kelsey

INTERIOR DESIGN
Karen Ruggles

COVER DESIGN
Aren Howell

COPY WRITER
Eric Borgert

LAYOUT TECHNICIANS
Liz Johnston
Brad Lenser

PRODUCTION
Dan Harris

OVERVIEW

iv

CONTENTS

ABOUT THE AUTHORS

Nancy Martin has a BFA in Graphic Design and a background in typography and publication design. She began working in new media in 1990.

Ronnie Sampson has a BFA in Painting and Printmaking and a background in graphic design, illustration, and animation. He started working in new media in 1985.

In 1989, Nancy and Ronnie formed Signature Graphics. In 1993, Signature Graphics became Viridian. Their first CD-ROM title, the award-winning Word Tales, was published in 1992 by Time Warner. Since then, they have been writing, developing, and producing CD-ROM titles for the educational and entertainment markets, as well as designing software interfaces, developing new media prototypes, creating Web toys, and writing and designing Web sites. They also provide consulting and conduct multimedia lectures and workshops.

Their Web address is `http://www.sfo.com/~viridian`. They can be contacted by email at `viridian@sfo.com`.

DEDICATION

We dedicate this book to our parents, Robert and Joan Martin, and Dr. Otto and Edith Sampson.

ACKNOWLEDGMENTS

We would like to thank John "JT" Thompson, Macromedia, for recommending us; Karen Whitehouse, Acquisitions Editor, Macmillan Publishing, for the great opportunity; Laura Norman, Development Editor, Macmillan Publishing, for helping us find the book in all of this; Allison Kelsey, Technical Editor, for test-driving all the tasks; Lori Lyons, Project Editor, Maribeth Echard, Proofreader, Liz Johnston, Layout Technician, Macmillan Publishing, and the rest of the staff for sweating the details; John Pierce, Publisher, Macmillan Publishing, for convincing us that we could do this; Doug Benson, Macromedia, for technical expertise; Hirokatsu "Minta" Araki, for technical information; Henry Trieu, for that extra push; Yong Lee and Stella Chang for their patience and support; Maria Lee and Donna Li for helping us keep it together; and each other for proving that married couples do complete each other's sentences.

TELL US WHAT YOU THINK!

As the reader of this book, you are our most important critic and commentator. We value your opinion and want to know what we're doing right, what we could do better, what areas you'd like to see us publish in, and any other words of wisdom you're willing to pass our way.

As a Publisher for Hayden Books, I welcome your comments. You can fax, email, or write me directly to let me know what you did or didn't like about this book—as well as what we can do to make our books stronger.

Please note that I cannot help you with technical problems related to the topic of this book, and that due to the high volume of mail I receive, I might not be able to reply to every message.

When you write, please be sure to include this book's title and author as well as your name and phone or fax number. I will carefully review your comments and share them with the author and editors who worked on the book.

Fax: 317-581-4666

Email: hayden@mcp.com

Mail: John Pierce
         Hayden Books
         201 West 103rd Street
         Indianapolis, IN 46290 USA

INTRODUCTION

Whom This Book Is For

Short Order Macromedia Fireworks 2.0 is for anyone interested in learning to use Fireworks to meet the challenges of designing and producing graphics for the World Wide Web. Using illustrated tasks, tips, and notes, this book will help you gain the skills and insights you need to become a more effective and productive Web artist—in short order.

About Macromedia Fireworks 2.0

Fireworks is the Swiss Army knife of Web graphics programs. It offers tools for creating vector graphics, pixel art, text layouts with typographic controls, 3D effects, and GIF animations. Plus, it offers comprehensive tools for Web graphics optimization and export, including JavaScript behaviors and automatic HTML generation. You can design, animate, add interactivity, optimize, and export Web-ready graphics all from one program.

Fireworks integrates all this functionality into a powerful, easy-to-use interface in which you can create graphics using Bézier paths with bitmap attributes. Your graphics remain editable, even if you apply 3-D Live Effects or painterly brush strokes to them in the Document window.

The same applies to text you create in Fireworks' Text Editor. You can edit text content or change its attributes at any time, no matter how much you have transformed it.

You can even paint and edit on a pixel-level as you would in a bitmap-editing program such as Photoshop. Many Fireworks tools have dual modes—you can use the same tool on a path or a bitmap. Fireworks' image-creation tools offer you convenience and flexibility.

Your saved Fireworks files are always editable, too. Anytime you need to update or revise your art, open the saved PNG files, and all your paths, text, and bitmap objects are ready to edit. And if you placed art on layers or animated a rollover button or banner ad using frames, all of that information remains intact, ready for your revisions.

Where Fireworks really shines, though, is in its Web optimization and exporting capabilities. Use Fireworks' Export Preview function to optimize Fireworks PNG files or any standard graphics format files. Fireworks offers real-time previews of your Web optimization choices with side-by-side comparisons of up to four export settings. You don't have to switch to a Web browser to preview your files. Fireworks' wizards and optimization tools can help you compress your files to their smallest optimal size while retaining image quality, resulting in faster, better-looking Web sites. You can increase your efficiency even more by batch processing multiple files to custom settings that you define.

Fireworks also offers dedicated Web tools such as hotspot objects to create URL links in image maps, behaviors to generate automatic JavaScript rollovers, and a slice tool to cut images into pieces. Fireworks then generates the HTML code to reassemble the pieces in a Web page table and adds the associated URL links.

Fireworks offers something for everyone in the Web graphics business.

What You Can Do with Macromedia Fireworks 2.0

Fireworks is designed for creating Web and screen graphics. Its image-creation environment is based on the RGB color model for optimal screen, not print, reproduction. It also offers tools designed specifically to streamline Web graphics preparation, such as adding URL links and JavaScript behaviors to images. Some of the things you can do with Fireworks are

- Create fully editable 3D buttons and other graphics using Fireworks' Live Effects, which include drop shadows, bevels, glows, and embosses.

- Use typographic controls and apply Live Effects to text that stays editable.

- Modify and update elements easily because they remain vector objects and editable text.

- Edit brush strokes and textured fills that are objects, not bitmaps.

- Get the smallest/best-quality image files by using the comparative preview function, optimize function, custom palettes, and the Export Wizard.

- Increase your Web graphics productivity with batch processing.

- Create image maps (with hyperlinked hot spots), add their hyperlinks, and export the map and its HTML together.

- Combine different file types in a single image using slicing and automatic HTML tables.

- Automate the creation of JavaScript rollovers and their associated HTML, including indirect rollovers, message bar displays, and toggle group rollovers.

- Create GIF animations for illustrations and ad banners.

- Convert multipage or multilayer graphics files to GIF animations.

What's New in Fireworks 2.0

Fireworks 2.0 offers significant improvements over the previous release. Based largely on user feedback, Macromedia has refined and added features to keep pace with the needs of Web professionals. Some of the new features are

- The capability to import images directly from a scanner or digital camera.

- Hot-spot and slice tools are incorporated into the Toolbox.

- Editable Export palettes.

- New Web objects and JavaScript behaviors.

- Convenient VCR controls in the Document window.

- Onion-skinning to aid in drawing animations.

- Tool and operation panels can be grouped and arranged to save space while remaining convenient.

- Applying multiple 3D Live Effects is easier.

- Fills, strokes, effects, and type attributes can be saved as reusable styles.

- You can quickly crop documents to their smallest possible size with the Trim Canvas feature.

- Objects on layers can be shared across frames.

- Web objects are easily accessible and editable on their own layer.

- Path operations, such as Union, Intersect, and Simplify, provide one-step object manipulation.

- Expanded batch processing capabilities include find and replace, reusable batch scriptlets, and a project log to track changes.

- Customizable HTML output styles available in popular Web-authoring formats.

There are many more new features and capabilities in Fireworks 2.0, and future versions promise still more. As you dig deeper into this multifaceted program, you will discover new ways to add sizzle to your Web pages.

How Fireworks Fits into Your Workflow

As a combination program, Fireworks doesn't offer all the depth of narrow-focused graphics programs such as FreeHand or Photoshop. You might prefer to continue creating art in your favorite programs and use Fireworks to efficiently process your images for the Web. Fireworks' powerful Web-focused tools and functions are highly compatible with many popular graphics programs. You also can edit or create art from scratch within Fireworks. Just use the parts of Fireworks that you need.

You can incorporate Fireworks into your Web-development process in a number of ways:

- If your Web page layout program doesn't have good image-mapping capabilities, use Fireworks' Web tools to create accurate hot spots—even over complex, irregularly shaped areas. Set up your URL links and add JavaScript behaviors, and then let Fireworks generate all the necessary HTML for you to simply cut and paste into your Web document.

- If your current graphics process involves a combination of vector and pixel-editing programs for art creation, then a third program, such as DeBabelizer, for optimization and export, and finally a browser for previewing the results; switch to Fireworks' Web-focused optimization with its dynamic, side-by-side previews. You can skip the back-and-forth between the browser and DeBabelizer and have at least one fewer program to juggle as you work.

- If you are using Photoshop just for adding 3D effects, you can skip the rasterizing process entirely and open your vector graphics directly in Fireworks. Add 3D depth to your graphics with Live Effects, which have the added bonus of remaining editable, so you can easily alter or update your vector graphic at any time—the effect will automatically adjust, or you can switch effects just as quickly.

- If you are exporting GIFs directly from vector graphic software and wish you had more control over the results, use Fireworks' export optimization tools instead and control your GIF's palette, dithering, background transparency, and file size. Save and reuse your customized settings, even batch process graphics to a wide variety of formats or globally search and replace colors, URLs, or text to easily update your Web graphics.

How to Use This Book

Our overall goal in creating this book was to make it clear, convenient, and concise. To that end, we have divided the information into brief, step-by-step tasks with helpful tips, notes, and illustrations. The tasks are grouped into chapters that cover all the operations you can perform in Fireworks. Because each task is designed as a standalone exercise, you do not have to follow them sequentially.

The most effective way to use this book is to complete the tasks at your computer as you read them. They are written so that you can substitute your own projects for the examples as you go.

Tips and notes provide information to supplement each task. They offer optional ways to achieve effects, suggest shortcuts and timesavers, clarify important points, and give background information on Fireworks.

We have included hundreds of illustrations to guide you visually through this exploration of Fireworks. Screenshots with callouts will help familiarize you with the components of Fireworks' interface.

Like Fireworks itself, this book is written for both Macintosh and Windows users. Directions for Macintosh appear in parentheses and directions for Windows, in brackets—for example, (delete)[backspace].

About Short Order

If you are looking for a solution for optimizing and exporting graphics to the Web, use Fireworks' optimization and export tools. You can import art in a wide variety of formats and export the best-looking, fastest-loading graphics in the most efficient way possible. Use Chapters 1, 2, and 3 to optimize and export your Web graphics immediately.

With Fireworks now in your tool arsenal, use Chapters 4 through 11 to create your graphics as well as optimize them for the Web. Fireworks borrows many of its graphics-creation tools from other popular drawing and painting programs, so your learning curve here will be pleasantly short. Fireworks combines drawing, typographic, and painting tools into the same application, so you can use them all on the same document without switching to dedicated programs for each function.

Use Chapters 12, 13, and 14 to produce image maps, 3D rollover buttons, and sliced graphics with Fireworks' Web-focused tools and features such as JavaScript behaviors. You will save time, while producing optimal interactive Web graphics.

If you want to animate your graphics, use Chapters 15 and 16. Turn layered art into animated GIFs, use in-between objects to create motion, set up believable motion with onion-skinning, and fine-tune your animations for optimal playback over the Web. Animate text and set up easy-to-manipulate symbols and instances for more complex animations.

If you want to use Fireworks as your primary graphics program, use Chapter 17 to take Fireworks beyond the Web. Export to a variety of formats, print graphics, and edit Fireworks files in other programs.

Fireworks will become indispensable to you as you incorporate it into your workflow. *Short Order Macromedia Fireworks 2.0* will help you make that transition as quickly and painlessly as possible.

As a quick, convenient guide to all the things you can do with this powerful program, *Short Order Macromedia Fireworks 2.0* makes understanding and using Fireworks easier than ever.

CHAPTER 1

In this chapter you learn how to...

Open Bitmaps and Vector Graphics

Open Text Files

Scan or Upload Digital Images

Create a New Document

Import Bitmaps and Vector Graphics

Import Fireworks Files

Import Text

Drag and Drop into Fireworks

Copy and Paste into Fireworks

I f you create graphics for the Web by using traditional graphics programs such as Adobe Photoshop, Illustrator, CorelDRAW, or Macromedia FreeHand, you probably wish the programs were as powerful and easy to use for Web graphics as they are for creating print graphics. Also on your wish list might be a way for one program to handle both bitmap and vector graphics from creation to Web optimization so that you wouldn't have to switch programs in the middle of your production process.

OPENING, IMPORTING, AND CREATING DOCUMENTS IN FIREWORKS

Fireworks is that program. It's a hybrid: It can read, edit, and produce both bitmap images and vector graphics for the Web. You can continue to use your traditional programs and import your graphics into Fireworks for further editing and Web optimization, or you can start from scratch and create your Web graphics using Fireworks' familiar graphics tools.

Fireworks supports many different file formats, both bitmap and vector based, and enables you to edit them much as you would in their native programs. It can even open files that contain layers while keeping their layers intact.

With its bimodal workspace, Fireworks enables you to work with both bitmap and vector objects. Image edit mode is similar to an image-editing program: You can paint and manipulate graphics on a pixel level. Object mode is similar to a drawing program: You can draw and edit vector paths.

Opening Bitmaps

To use Fireworks' Web optimization features or hybrid graphics-editing tools, you can start with graphics you've already created in other programs. If you have existing bitmap files you want to optimize or add vector graphics to, open them in Fireworks. Fireworks can read many bitmap file formats, such as Adobe Photoshop versions 3 and later (1.1), BMP, GIF, JPEG, PICT, PNG, TIFF, Targa, and Macromedia xRes LRG.

When you open a bitmap file, a black and blue striped border surrounds the image, signifying that you are in image edit mode (1.2). Working in Fireworks' image edit mode is similar to working in Photoshop and other image-editing programs. You can scan in photographs, paint images, and edit pixels directly.

 O T E

If you open a Photoshop file that contains alpha channels but no layers, Fireworks applies all the alpha channels to the image as it opens. If you open a layered file, Fireworks ignores the alpha channels.

 I P

If you have a graphics file that you want to use as a template for other graphics, and you don't want to risk overwriting it when you save a new graphic, check Open As Untitled in the Open File dialog box when opening the "template" file to open an untitled copy of your file.

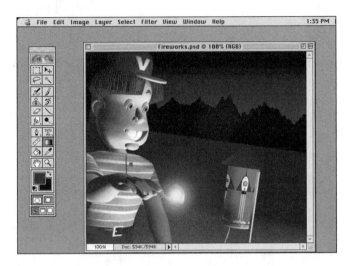

1.1

1.2

1.3

1.4

GIFs, JPEGs, and PNG files open with an added empty Layer 1. You can use it to add objects to your file, delete it, or ignore it. It doesn't increase your file size if it's empty.

1. To open an existing bitmap, choose File→Open and select the file you want to open.

2. If you opened a layered Photoshop file (1.3), double-click an image object to enter image edit mode for the selected object.

   If you opened a single-layer Photoshop file or other bitmap, your image is now ready for editing in Fireworks (1.4).

 T I P

If you want to open a layered Photoshop file as a flattened image without eliminating the layers in the original file, set your default preferences in both Photoshop and Fireworks before opening the file in Fireworks. In Photoshop 5, under File→Preferences→Savings Files, turn on Include Composited Image with Layered File before saving a file. In Photoshop 4, under File→Preferences→Saving Files, turn on 2.5 Compatibility before saving a file. Then in Fireworks, under File→Preferences→General, turn on Use Flat Image If Available before opening a compatible Photoshop file.

Opening Vector Graphics

You can open vector graphic files from Adobe Illustrator versions 3 and later (1.5), Macromedia FreeHand 7 or 8, and CorelDRAW 7 or 8 (uncompressed) in Fireworks. Opening vector graphics offers a few more options than bitmap graphics, such as setting a physical size and image resolution before opening the file. Imported vector graphics are fully editable.

If you use the multiple-page layout feature of a program such as FreeHand to create artwork for GIF animations or rollover buttons, you can open those files as frames in Fireworks. Fireworks will open the file and place each page on a separate frame. You also can open a single page from a multipage document.

If you are opening a vector graphics file that contains layers, you can choose to retain your file's layer structure, flatten the image into one layer, or convert the layers into frames. Use the Convert to Frames option if you created the artwork for an animated GIF or rollover on layers in a vector graphic program.

If your graphic contains grouped objects, color blends, or tiled fills, you can choose to have them rasterized as bitmap images when Fireworks opens the file.

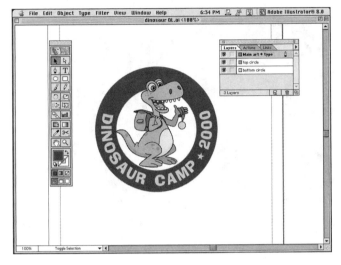

1.5

 O T E

Frames in Fireworks are not the same as frames in an HTML document. Fireworks frames are animation frames. Each frame is the same size and represents a single cel in an animation or a single state in a rollover button.

Layers in Fireworks are similar to layers in Illustrator or FreeHand. Each layer is a transparent field through which objects on the other layers are visible. Fireworks adds a top layer, called the Web layer, to every document opened or created in Fireworks. This layer is reserved for Web objects, such as hot spots and slices, and cannot be deleted.

 I P

Opening a graphics file that was saved in CMYK color mode for print causes a pronounced color shift. Convert CMYK color files to RGB color before opening them in Fireworks.

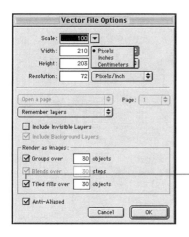

1.6

1.7

If you want to smooth the edges of imported vector graphics, turn on Anti-Aliased. The graphics will remain editable as vectors.

To import all the pages as frames, select Open Pages As Frames from the Frames pop-up menu.

If you placed objects or text on master pages in a multipage CorelDRAW document, Fireworks copies those elements onto each frame when you choose Open Pages As Frames.

1. To open an existing vector graphic, choose File→Open and select the file you want to open.

2. To resize the graphic, enter a percentage or a measurement in pixels, inches, or centimeters in the Vector File Options dialog box (1.6).

3. Set the image resolution to 72 pixels/inch if your graphic is destined for the Web or computer screen.

4. To import a single page, select Open a Page from the Frames pop-up menu (1.7). Select the page in the Page Number pop-up.

continues

 I P

Fireworks has trouble maintaining imported text attributes—such as kerning, alignment, and text box placement—from other graphics file formats. It's best to set your text in Fireworks. To use existing vector files that contain formatted text, rasterize the files or convert the text to outlines first. You won't be able to edit the text in Fireworks, but it retains its original appearance.

(N) O T E

Fireworks cannot open EPS (Encapsulated PostScript), compressed CDR (CorelDRAW), or CMX files. Filenames for uncompressed CorelDRAW files must end with the .cdr extension.

Opening Vector Graphics continued

5. To retain a file's layers, select
Remember layers from the
Layers pop-up menu (1.8). To
change layers to frames, select
Convert Layers to Frames from
the Layers pop-up menu. To
flatten a vector graphic, select
Ignore Layers from the Layers
pop-up menu.

6. If you want Fireworks to rasterize complex groups, blends,
and tiled fills, click the Groups,
Blends, and Tiled Fills check
boxes in Render As Images to
turn on preferences. Then,
select a threshold number for
the number of objects or steps
a selection must contain before
Fireworks rasterizes it during
import.

7. When you have finished
setting parameters, click OK
to close the dialog box and
open the graphic (1.9).

**To import objects on
layers that were turned off,
click the Include Invisible
Layers check box.**

**To import objects from a
document's background
layer, click the Include
Background Layers
check box.**

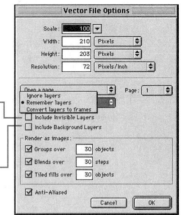

1.8

1.9

 **O T E**

*Fireworks cannot import blends from
Illustrator. Instead, objects that contain
blends open as solid-color fills.*

*Fireworks imports only the beginning and
end objects of a blend from CorelDRAW. The
objects open as a group. Fireworks cannot
open tiled fills from CorelDRAW.*

Opening Text Files

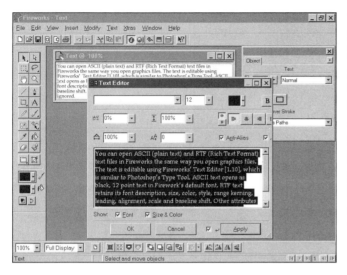

1.10

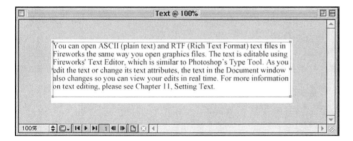

1.11

You can open ASCII (plain text) and RTF (Rich Text Format) text files in Fireworks the same way you open graphics files. The text is editable using Fireworks' Text Editor, which is similar to Photoshop's Type tool. As you edit the text or change its text attributes, the text in the Document window also changes so you can view your edits in real time. For more information on text editing, please see Chapter 11, "Setting Text."

1. To open an ASCII or RTF text file, choose File→Open and select the file you want to open.

2. To edit the text or its attributes, double-click the text block to access the Text Editor (1.10).

3. When you finish editing, click OK to close the Text Editor and return to the Document window with the text block selected (1.11).

 O T E

ASCII text opens as black, 12-point text in Fireworks' default font. RTF text retains its font description, size, color, style, range kerning, leading, alignment, scale, and baseline shift. Other attributes, such as extra paragraph spacing and indents, are ignored.

Scanning or Uploading Digital Images

After connecting a scanner or digital camera to your computer and configuring it, you can scan or upload digital images directly into Fireworks 2 by using the TWAIN module or Photoshop Acquire plug-in (Macintosh only) that comes with your device's software.

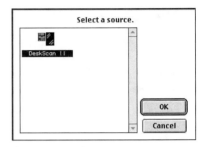

1.12

1. To import from a scanner or digital camera, choose File→Scan→TWAIN Source and select the TWAIN module or Acquire plug-in for your scanner or camera (1.12).

2. Choose File→Scan→TWAIN Acquire and follow the instructions for the TWAIN module or Acquire plug-in selected to scan in your image.

3. Your new untitled Fireworks document (1.13) is now ready for editing.

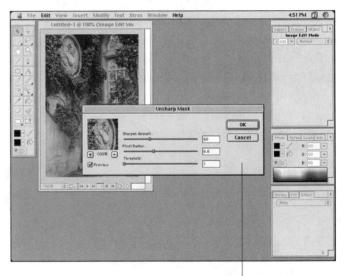

1.13

Choose Xtras→Sharpen→Unsharp Mask to sharpen edges within the image. Sharpen Amount changes the contrast between pixels. Pixel Radius changes the number of pixels surrounding the edge pixels that get sharpened. Threshold changes how far apart different pixels must be to be considered edge pixels and so sharpened by the filter.

 O T E

Before scanning, copy the TWAIN module or Photoshop Acquire plug-in (Mac only) for your scanner or camera into the Fireworks\Settings\ Xtras folder, and then restart Fireworks.

Creating a New Document

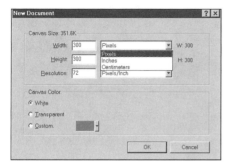

1.14

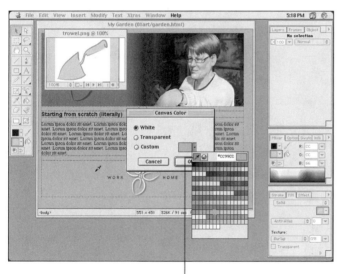

1.15   **To match the canvas color to a color in an open document that is visible on your desktop, use the Eyedropper to click the color you want to match.**

(N) O T E

After opening or creating a file in Fireworks, save it as a Fireworks file. Fireworks files are saved in a proprietary PNG format, which retains a document's vector graphics and text editability along with any export parameters you select. To save your file in a different format, such as GIF, PICT, or JPEG, you must export the file.

Starting fresh in Fireworks is similar to creating a new document in other graphics programs. You choose your document's size, resolution, and background color to begin. You can edit any of these parameters later from the Document view. Documents can be up to 6,000 pixels wide by 6,000 pixels high.

1. To create a new document, choose File→New.

2. In the New Document dialog box, set the width and height of your document in pixels, inches, or centimeters using the pop-up menus (1.14).

3. Set the resolution to 72 pixels/inch if your graphic is destined for the Web or computer screen.

4. Set the canvas color to white, transparent, or custom.

   To choose a custom color, click the color well and select a color in the system color picker. Click OK to return to the New Document dialog box.

   To choose a color from your default palette, click the pop-up arrow next to the color well to select a swatch from the default color palette (1.15).

5. Click OK to create your new, untitled document. Your document consists of a layer for art and a Web layer for adding hot spots and slices.

Importing Bitmaps

In Fireworks, importing a file is different from opening a file. Importing is for placing a file into another document on a specific layer at specific coordinates. Bitmap file formats you can import include Adobe Photoshop versions 3 and later, BMP, GIF, JPEG, PICT, PNG, TIFF, Targa, and Macromedia xRes LRG. Imported bitmaps are placed as image objects and are selected so you can work with them immediately upon import.

Importing a layered Photoshop file removes the layers with each layer becoming an image object. To import a single layer or an alpha channel from Photoshop, copy and paste or drag and drop the layer or channel into your Fireworks document.

1. To import a bitmap into an open document, choose File→Import from the open document's window, and then select the file you want to import.

2. In the Document window, select the layer you want the imported file on and click the import cursor where you want the upper-left corner of the graphic to be (1.16). If you want to resize the file when importing, click and drag the import cursor instead.

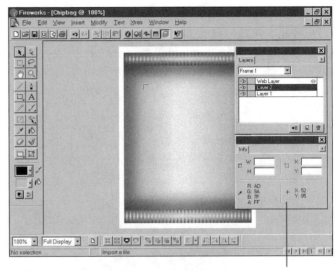

1.16

Use the Info panel X- and Y-coordinates to assist you in placing an imported graphic.

 **O T E**

Any files that you open or create in Fireworks can be saved in Fireworks' PNG format, which retains the bitmap and/or vector information in the file for later revisions and updates.

 I P

Fireworks can render common layer blend modes, but not Photoshop exclusive modes such as dissolve, overlay, soft light, hard light, color dodge, color burn, and exclusion, or Photoshop adjustment layers. Flatten the image in Photoshop before opening it in Fireworks to retain these effects.

Importing Vector Graphics

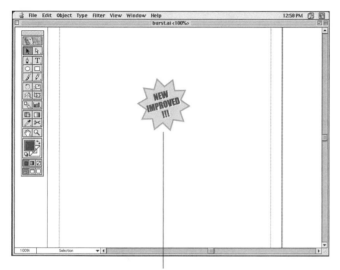

1.17   **Convert text to outlines before importing into Fireworks.**

If you want to place a vector graphics file in a Fireworks document, import it. You can place it on a specific layer in the document at specific coordinates. You can import vector graphic files from Adobe Illustrator versions 3 and later (1.17), Macromedia FreeHand 7 or 8, and CorelDRAW 7 or 8 (uncompressed). Imported vector paths are editable and are selected so you can adjust them immediately after import.

1. To import a vector graphic, choose File→Import from an open document's window, and then select the file you want to import.

2. If you want to resize the graphic, enter a percentage or a measurement in pixels, inches, or centimeters in the Vector File Options dialog box.

3. Set the image resolution to match the image resolution of the open document (1.18).

continues

1.18   **To import objects from a document's background layer, check Include Background Layers.**   **To import objects from layers that were turned off, check Include Invisible Layers.**

 **O T E**

Fireworks merges layers when importing and cannot convert layers to frames when importing vector graphics.

Importing Vector Graphics continued

4. If you want Fireworks to rasterize complex groups, blends, and tiled fills, click the Groups, Blends, and Tiled Fills check boxes in Render As Images to turn on preferences. Then, select a threshold value for the number of objects or steps a selection must contain before Fireworks rasterizes it during import.

5. If you want to smooth the edges of imported graphics, turn on Anti-Aliased. The graphics will remain editable as vectors.

6. When you have finished setting parameters, click OK.

7. In the Document window, select the layer you want the imported file on and click the import cursor where you want the upper-left corner of the graphic to be (1.19). If you want to resize the file when importing, click and drag the import cursor instead (1.20).

1.19

Use the Info panel (Window→Info) to aid in placing the Import cursor.

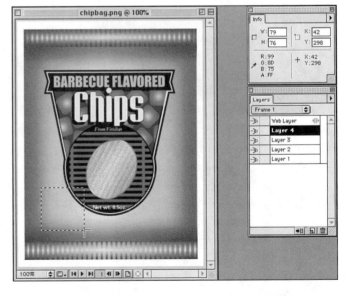

1.20

(T) I P

If you don't know the image resolution of the open document, click Cancel to return to the Document window, and then (click and hold)[click and release] the Page icon at the bottom of the Document window to check the document's current resolution.

Importing Fireworks Files

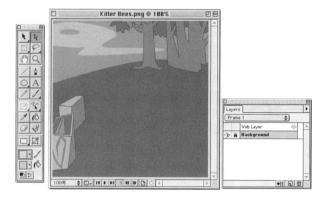

1.21

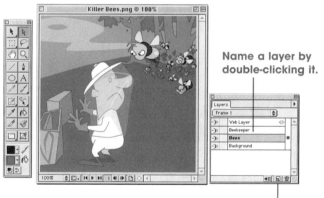

Name a layer by double-clicking it.

1.22

Add layers by clicking New/Duplicate layer.

Add a saved Fireworks file to an open Fireworks document by importing it. Fireworks merges layers in the saved file when importing, but the imported objects remain separate and editable and are selected when imported so you can adjust them immediately after import. If the file consists of multiple frames, only the first frame is imported.

1. To import a saved Fireworks file, choose File→Import from an open document's window (1.21), and then select the file you want to import.

2. In the Document window, select the layer you want the imported file on and click the import cursor where you want the upper-left corner of the graphic to be (1.22). If you want to resize the file when importing, click and drag the import cursor instead.

Any hot spot and slice objects are imported onto the Web layer of the current document.

Importing Text

Import ASCII and RTF text files into Fireworks the same way you import graphics. The text is editable using Fireworks' Text Editor, which is similar to Photoshop's Type Tool. For more information on text editing, please see Chapter 11, "Setting Text."

1. To import an ASCII or RTF text file into an open document, choose File→Import from the open document's window, and then select the file you want to import.

2. In the Document window, select the layer you want the imported text on and click the import cursor where you want the upper-left corner of the text to be (1.23). If you want the text to be a specific width, click and drag the import cursor instead. The text block resizes to maintain its line breaks (1.24).

3. To edit the text or its attributes, double-click the text block to access the Text Editor.

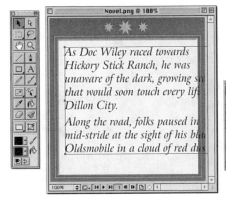

1.23

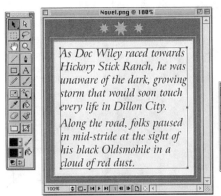

1.24

(N) O T E

ASCII text imports as black, 12-point text in Fireworks' default font. RTF text retains its font description, size, color, style, range kerning, leading, alignment, scale, and baseline shift. Other attributes such as extra paragraph spacing and indents are ignored.

Dragging and Dropping into Fireworks

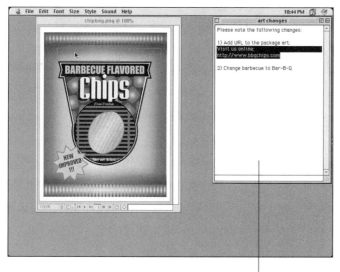

1.25

Dragging and dropping RTF text results in a large aliased bitmap selection that is no longer editable as text. Use ASCII text instead.

 I P

If you are dragging and dropping from frames that contain multiple objects, group the objects on each frame first by choosing File→ Select All, and then Modify→Group on each frame. The frames will be easier to separate after placing them in the new document.

 I P

To drag and drop part of a bitmap object from one Fireworks document to another, double-click it with the Pointer Tool to enter image edit mode, and then click and drag the Marquee tool around the desired selection. Switch to the Pointer Tool to click and drag the selection to the other Fireworks document window.

If you have a Fireworks file that contains art on different frames and you want to add it to another Fireworks document, importing brings in only the first frame. Use drag and drop instead to bring the frames in one by one. Fireworks centers the dragged object(s) automatically in the new document. Position them after dragging and dropping all the frames.

If you like to work with different programs open on your desktop, you can also drag and drop objects, images, and text into Fireworks documents from open files in Adobe Photoshop versions 4 and 5, Adobe Illustrator 7 and 8, Macromedia FreeHand 7 and 8, Macromedia Flash 2 and later, Microsoft Office 97, Microsoft Internet Explorer 3 and later, Netscape Navigator 3 and later, SimpleText (Mac only), and CorelDRAW 7 and 8.

1. To drag and drop into an open Fireworks document, select a destination layer in the open document by clicking it in the Layers panel.

2. Select a graphic or text in an open application and drag it onto an open Fireworks document (1.25).

3. Release the mouse when a dotted outline appears on the destination window. The dragged selection will appear in the center of the destination document.

Copying and Pasting into Fireworks

You can copy objects from CorelDRAW 7 and 8, FreeHand versions 7 and 8, Illustrator versions 3 and later, and Photoshop versions 4 and 5, plus objects saved as PNG, PICT (Macintosh), DIB (Windows), and BMP (Windows), or ASCII text, and paste them into Fireworks. Depending on which Fireworks mode you are in, pasting in Fireworks gives different results.

Working in object mode is similar to working in a drawing program: Pasted vector graphics and text retain their editability. Pasted bitmap graphics become rectangular image objects. Fireworks pastes these objects in the center of the active document.

Working in image edit mode is similar to working in an image-editing program: Both vector graphics and bitmap images paste as pixel selections surrounded by a dotted line with alpha channel transparency to maintain their original appearance. Fireworks pastes these objects in the upper-left corner of the highlighted bitmap object.

1. Copy a bitmap image, a vector graphic, or text from another program (1.26).

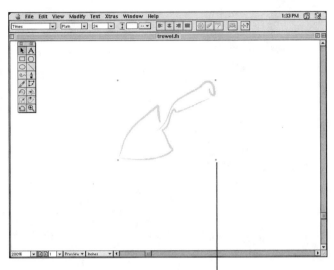

1.26

If you are copying more than one object, group them first.

1.27

You also can copy and paste RTF text into open Fireworks documents; however, you lose all text formatting.

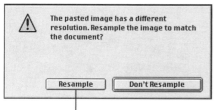

2. Open a Fireworks document.

3. To paste in object mode, choose Edit→Paste (1.27). If you copy a bitmap image that has a different resolution from the document you are pasting it into, Fireworks asks whether you want to resample the image (1.28). Choose Don't Resample to paste the object at its original pixel dimensions. Choose Resample, and Fireworks adds or subtracts pixels to match the new document's resolution.

1.28 **When changing pixel depth in a bitmap image, resampling adds or subtracts pixels to retain image quality. Resampling up to a higher resolution retains image quality, but details can become blurry. Downsampling to a lower resolution causes data loss, especially subtle transitions, causing more contrast in images.**

4. To paste in image edit mode, double-click a bitmap object so that it is surrounded by a blue double-dotted line, and then choose Edit→Paste (1.29).

1.29 **In image edit mode, you can move the selection, but after you deselect it by clicking elsewhere with the Pointer tool or choosing Edit→Deselect, the selection merges with the current bitmap object. It is no longer a separate object.**

 **O T E**

Fireworks 2.02 offers four different interpolation methods for resampling images. The default is Bicubic. To reduce unwanted artifacts, try Bilinear or Soft. For a high-contrast result, try Nearest Neighbor. To change methods, choose File→Run Script, select a .jsf file in Fireworks 2/Scaling Options, and click Open.

CHAPTER 2

If you have ever waited for a Web page full of graphics to load, you know why you want optimized graphics. Visuals deliver a richer experience than plain hypertext, but if your images are slow to appear, your audience loses interest. You need to create attractive graphics that display quickly. Optimized graphics balance image quality and file size for fast downloads.

OPTIMIZING ART FOR THE WEB

If your current method of optimizing requires working between several programs and proofing the results in a browser, you will appreciate how Fireworks streamlines the process. Create artwork in your favorite programs or use the familiar tools in Fireworks, and then optimize your graphics with real-time previews of the results. Make side-by-side comparisons of the results of different optimization settings. When you like what you see, export your graphic, knowing that it will appear in Web browsers as you intend.

In addition to side-by-side, real-time previews, Fireworks optimization offers a full range of customization choices and timesaving features. These range from the virtually hands-off approach of letting the Export Wizard make all the choices for you, to the ultimate control of importing and editing custom palettes, designating transparency, and setting JPEG compression. If you are processing a volume of graphics, you can further increase your productivity by saving and reusing your custom palettes and optimization settings across your project.

Exporting a Graphic with the Export Wizard

If you want help optimizing your images for export, use the Export Wizard. You don't have to determine the best way to optimize an image; instead, the Wizard asks questions about how your file will be used and presents optimal graphics formats in the Export Preview window. In addition to displaying the graphic as it will look when exported with the suggested parameters, the Preview window also displays estimated file size and download time. All you have to do is name the file and select a location to export it.

2.1

1. With your graphic open in the Document window (2.1), choose File→Export Wizard.

2. In the Export Wizard dialog box (2.2), answer the questions about how you plan to use the file. Click Continue.

3. In the Analysis Results dialog box, the Export Wizard describes its recommended optimization settings. Click Exit to see its suggestions.

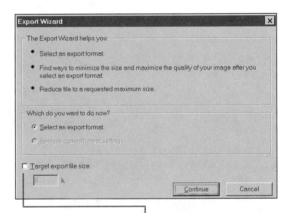

2.2 **If you have a file size restriction for your Web graphic, select Target Export File Size and enter a size in kilobytes.**

 I P

*If you prefer to set your own export para-
meters, use the Export Wizard to check
your settings and make suggestions. In
the Export Preview window (File→Export),
click the Magic Wand button and select
Analyze Current Format Settings.*

Highlighted preview window is the Wizard's preferred option. Select a different option by clicking it.

File size

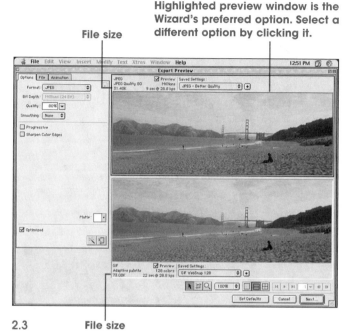

2.3   File size

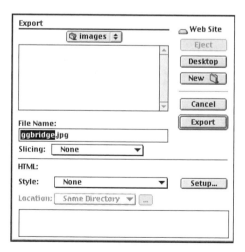

2.4

4. If the Wizard has more than one suggestion, it splits the preview screen to show you the options with the smaller image on top **(2.3)**. If you like the Wizard's selection in the Export Preview window, click Next. If you want to adjust the settings, please skip to the relevant file type optimization section later in this chapter.

5. In the Export dialog box, Fireworks provides a default filename with the appropriate file extension **(2.4)**. Type a new filename (if desired), select its destination, and click Export. Your original document is unchanged unless you save your exported file with the same name.

(N)OTE

Exporting a file is different from saving a file. Exporting (File→Export or File→Export Wizard) creates a copy of the original file, which can be saved in any of the export file formats (GIF, JPEG, PNG, and so on). Saving (File→Save) from the Document window saves the graphic as a Fireworks PNG file only. A saved Fireworks PNG file maintains all its layers and vector graphics. An exported file, no matter what the format, is always a single-layer, bitmapped graphic.

Choosing a Graphics File Format

Instead of using Firework's Export Wizard, set export parameters yourself and preview the results in Fireworks' Export Preview window. Fireworks exports graphics for the Web, screen, or print. GIF, JPEG, or PNG are formats specifically designed to compress images for fast transfer across the Web, but they do it in different ways. Choose a format based on your graphic's design and purpose.

GIF (Graphics Interchange Format) supports up to only 256 colors, but offers lossless (no reduction in quality) image compression. It approximates colors beyond its 256 limit by dithering. GIF also offers simple transparency: Colors can be designated 100% opaque or 100% transparent (2.5).

JPEG (Joint Photographic Experts Group) is designed to compress photographs and other images that contain complex or subtle color transitions (2.6). It supports millions of colors by using lossy compression, which means it discards image information as it compresses. By controlling how much JPEG compression is applied, you can balance the amount of detail lost against how small (in kilobytes) you need the file to be. JPEG does not support transparency.

2.5

2.6

2.7

PNG (Portable Network Graphic) is the newest and most versatile of the Web graphic formats. It has a more sophisticated compression scheme for flat color than GIFs do. It can support up to 32-bit color (24-bit plus an alpha channel), yet it offers lossless compression to retain an image's fine color details better than JPEG does. Plus PNGs offer alpha channel transparency, which means that pixels can be partially transparent, making the edges of a PNG blend smoothly into a background (2.7).

The trade-off is that not all browsers fully support the PNG format yet, and you can get some unintended results. Use PNG formats when you want to manipulate your alpha channel graphics in other programs, such as Adobe Photoshop 5, or Macromedia's Director 7 and Flash 4, before adding them to your Web site.

Table 2.1

If Your Image	Use	Cautions
Has large areas of flat color	GIF	If an image contains blends, gradients, anti-aliasing or non-Web-safe colors, GIF optimization could result in larger files than JPEG optimization.
Has transparent areas	GIF	Anti-aliased edges will show unless the image is optimized to the background color it will appear on.
Is a photograph, gradient image, or other continuous tone image	JPEG	Images can be only rectangular with no transparency
Has feathered edges, anti-aliasing, or varied opacity settings, and you want to place it on different backgrounds	PNG	Not supported by all browsers; only partially supported by other browsers.

Optimizing and Exporting GIFs

When optimizing GIFs for the Web in Fireworks, select a Web-focused palette, and then adapt it by reducing its colors and editing individual colors in the palette. Save your edited palettes to use with other documents. You also can dither to approximate colors outside the Web-safe range, designate transparent colors for placing images over backgrounds, and interlace graphics for faster appearance in Web browsers.

2.8

1. With your graphic open in the Document window, choose File→Export **(2.8)**.

2. Select GIF in the Format pop-up menu in the Export Preview Options panel **(2.9)**.

3. Select a palette from the Palette pop-up menu.

You also can load or save a custom palette using the Options panel pop-up menu.

 T I **P**

For the fastest, smallest GIFs when you don't need to optimize them yourself, choose File→Export Special→Export As Image Well from the Document window. You skip the Export Preview window and just name and save your GIF. Image Well images are used in Lotus Notes Domino Designer, but if you aren't using Domino Designer, you can still use this option as an automatic Web graphics generator.

2.9 **Web-safe colors are marked by a diamond in the center of the color's swatch.**

Not all palette types can be imported into Fireworks. Photoshop CLUTs (Color Look-Up Tables) and ACTs are compatible.

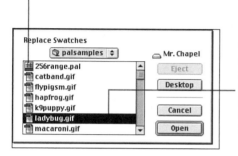

2.10

To use the palette of an 8-bit graphic created in another program, select the graphic file itself and its palette loads.

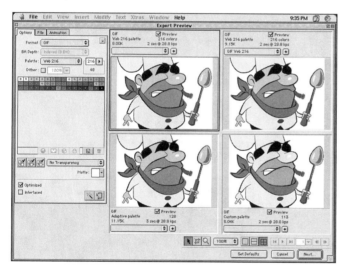

2.11

- Choose Web 216 to use only the 216 colors common to both the Macintosh and Windows platforms.

- Choose Adaptive to create a custom palette using the actual colors in the image. If your PNG contains fewer than 256 colors, you also can choose the Exact palette.

- Choose WebSnap Adaptive to create a palette in which colors that are close in value to Web-safe colors snap to [convert to] those colors.

- Choose Custom to add your own palette from another program or another image. In the (Replace Swatches)[Open] dialog box, locate the desired palette and select it **(2.10)**.

continues

 I P

To compare up to four different export settings at a time, select one of the Split View choices at the bottom of the preview window . To change the export settings of any view, click its window **(2.11)**. *Then alter the settings.*

If the image is larger than its preview window, use the Pointer to pan around the image. All previews in split views are magnified the same, and they all pan simultaneously. To quickly access the Pointer when using another tool, hold down the spacebar.

(T) I P

To create a fast-loading, low-source version of a slow-loading, complex graphic, choose Black & White or Grayscale from the GIF Palette pop-up menu. If you choose Grayscale, also reduce the number of colors in the palette to make a smaller file.

Optimizing and Exporting GIFs continued

4. To set the maximum number of colors, enter a number in the Numbers of Colors entry field or select a number in its pop-up menu (2.12).

5. To approximate colors that are not in the selected palette or to smooth out banding, check Dither (2.13). Then enter a percentage in the Dither Amount field or use its pop-up slider. The higher the percentage, the smoother the dithering is and the larger the file size.

Reducing the number of colors reduces a GIF's file size. The number below the entry field indicates the number of colors the GIF currently contains.

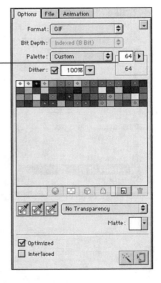

2.12

 O T E

If you set the number of colors to lower than the actual number of colors in an image, some colors are eliminated, beginning with the least-used colors. Any parts of your image containing those colors convert to the closest color remaining in the palette.

T I P

To create smaller GIF files, use an adaptive palette and turn off dithering. Turning off dithering causes the greatest reduction in file size, especially if the file is composed primarily of flat areas of color. Unless you need GIF transparency, JPEG might be a better choice for complex color graphics.

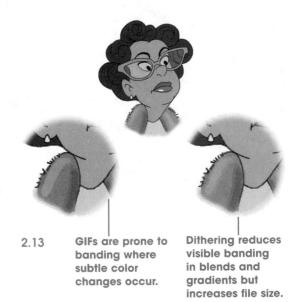

2.13 **GIFs are prone to banding where subtle color changes occur.**

Dithering reduces visible banding in blends and gradients but increases file size.

Remove all color edits at once
using the Options pop-up menu.   **Edited color**

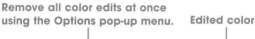

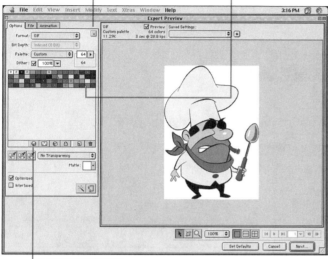

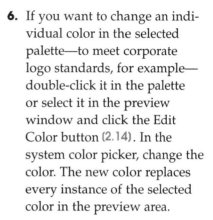

2.14   **To revert to the original color,
select the edited color swatch
and click Edit Color again.**

Transparent color

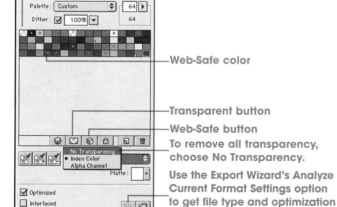

Web-Safe color

Transparent button

Web-Safe button

To remove all transparency,
choose No Transparency.

Use the Export Wizard's Analyze
Current Format Settings option
to get file type and optimization
suggestions.

2.15

6. If you want to change an individual color in the selected
palette—to meet corporate
logo standards, for example—
double-click it in the palette
or select it in the preview
window and click the Edit
Color button (2.14). In the
system color picker, change the
color. The new color replaces
every instance of the selected
color in the preview area.

7. To make a color transparent,
select it by clicking it in the
palette or preview window
and click the Transparent
button (2.15). To revert to
the original color, select the
transparent color and click
the Transparent button again.

continues

OTE

*Editing or otherwise altering a color replaces
all instances of that color in the exported
image, but it does not change the original
image. The Fireworks PNG file of the original image retains the editing information,
so if you export the image again, your edits
appear again in the Export Preview.*

IP

*(Ctrl-click)[Right-click] a color in the palette
to access the shortcut menu of color-editing
options.*

Optimizing and Exporting GIFs continued

8. To convert a color to Web-safe, select it by clicking it in the palette or preview window and click the Web-Safe button. The color will change to its closest Web-safe equivalent. To revert to the original color, select the altered color in the palette or preview window and click the Web-Safe button again.

9. To lock individual colors so that they are not removed or changed when changing palettes or reducing the number of colors in a palette, select the color in the palette or preview window, and click the Lock Color button **(2.16)**. To unlock a locked color, select it in the palette or preview window and click the Lock Color button again.

Unlock all colors at once by using the pop-up menu.   **Locked color**

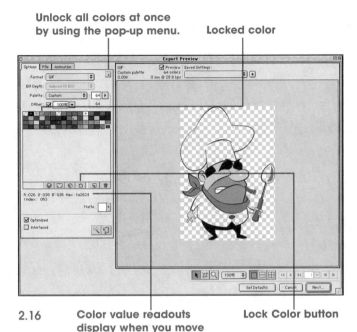

2.16   **Color value readouts display when you move the cursor over the image.**   **Lock Color button**

(N)OTE

Locking a color does not prevent you from editing it or otherwise manipulating it. It only prevents Fireworks from changing or removing it if you switch palettes or reduce colors, with some exceptions. If you switch to another palette after locking colors, the locked colors are added or discarded depending on the new palette:

- *In Adaptive and WebSnap Adaptive palettes, locked colors are forced into the new palette.*

- *In Web 216 palettes, up to 40 locked colors are added to the palette. Additional locked colors are discarded.*

- *In a Custom palette, locked colors are added until the total number of colors in the palette equals 256. Additional locked colors are discarded.*

(T)I P

Selecting a range of colors in a palette deselects any individual color selected. So, to edit a range of colors and other selected colors simultaneously, select the range first.

A gray-and-white checker-board denotes which parts of the exported GIF will be transparent.

2.17

Index transparency

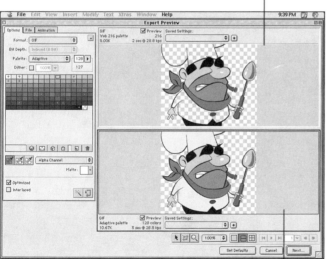

2.18

Alpha Channel transparency

10. By default, a GIF has no transparency. To make the document's canvas color transparent, select (Index Color)[Index Transparency] in the Transparency pop-up menu (2.17).

11. To change the Index color, use the Select Transparency tool to click the desired color from the color palette or the preview image .

- Use the Add to Transparency tool to make additional colors transparent.

- Use the Subtract from Transparency tool to revert colors from transparent.

- To remove all transparency settings, select No transparency in the Transparency pop-up menu.

continues

(N) O T E

In GIFs, use Alpha Channel transparency instead of Index Color transparency when you are silhouetting an image that includes the background color and you don't want transparent holes in your image (2.18).

Optimizing and Exporting GIFs continued

12. To avoid a halo around a transparent GIF when it is placed
on a Web page (2.19), select the
Web page's background color
in the Matte pop-up Web-safe
palette or color picker.

13. To have Fireworks create the
smallest file with the fewest
colors based on the options
you have selected, check
Optimized.

14. To create an interlaced image,
check Interlaced. Interlacing
makes your image load progressively in Web browsers, which
makes it appear to load faster.

2.19

(T) I P

*Match a Web page's background color by
opening the page in a browser, and then
(clicking) [click-holding until over the
desired color] on its background with the
Matte pop-up Eyedropper tool (2.20).*

(T) I P

*To reuse a transparent GIF on different Web
page background colors, create it on a transparent background, and then select a Web-
safe color background using the Matte pop-up
palette and export the graphic. Export it
again using another background color from
the Matte palette to a different name.*

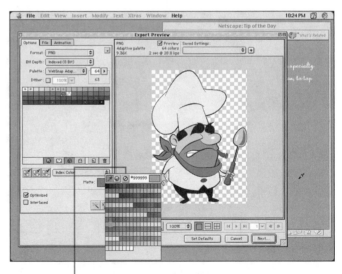

2.20　　**Click None to have no matte
background color defined.**

To use a saved export setting, select it from the pop-up menu.

Save Settings button

2.21

2.22

15. To save your export settings for reuse, click the + button above the preview window **(2.21)**, type a name for the custom settings in the Preset Name dialog box, and click OK. To delete an export preset, remove or delete its file from the Fireworks\Settings\Export Settings folder.

16. When you have finished setting your optimization parameters, click Next.

17. In the Export dialog box, Fireworks provides a default filename with the GIF file extension. Type a new name if desired, select its destination, and click Export. Your original document is unchanged unless you save your exported file with the same name.

 **O T E**

Changing an image's background color in Export Preview does not affect the original image **(2.22)***.*

 I P

To export a file using its previous export settings, choose File→Export Again from the Document window. You skip the Export Preview dialog box and can rename the file and choose a new location in the Export dialog box.

Optimizing and Exporting JPEGs

When optimizing JPEGs for the
Web, use Fireworks' Export Preview
sliding scales for setting variables to
retain image quality while achieving
the fastest load times possible.
Compare different settings in real-
time previews to easily choose the
optimal settings for any image.

1. With your graphic open in the
   Document window, choose
   File→Export.

2. Select JPEG in the Format pop-
   up menu in the Export
   Preview Options panel (2.23).

3. To set the degree of compression that meets your speed
   versus quality needs, enter a
   percentage in the Quality field
   or use its pop-up slider.

4. Hard edges in images do not
   compress well in JPEGs. To
   reduce file size by blurring
   edges, select a number in the
   Smoothing pop-up slider
   (2.24). Higher numbers
   produce more blurring.

5. If your image has text or other
   fine details, check Sharpen Color
   Edges to preserve the sharpness
   of these areas. Sharpen Color
   Edges increases your file's size.

 **O T E**

JPEG compression offers you a trade-off:
Smaller files mean less color detail versus
larger files offering better image definition.

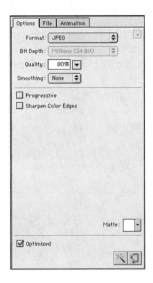

2.23

No Smoothing   **Level 2 Smoothing**

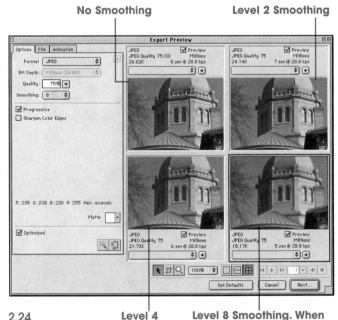

2.24

Level 4
Smoothing

Level 8 Smoothing. When
smoothing hard edges to
reduce file size, check
that important details
don't become blurry.

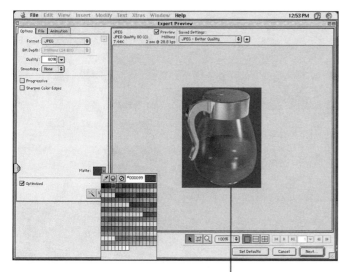

2.25

Use a Web-safe color for your Web page's background and choose the same color in the Matte pop-up palette to make a JPEG look silhouetted.

Some image-editing programs cannot open progressive JPEGs. If you plan to manipulate the JPEG further in other programs, save the progressive download option until you have finished.

To use a saved export setting, select it from the Saved Settings pop-up menu. To delete an export preset, remove or delete its file from the Fireworks\Settings\Export Settings folder.

6. To make a JPEG that progressively loads in a Web browser, check Progressive. Progressive JPEG files are smaller than regular JPEGs, also helping to speed the download.

7. If you created your image on a transparent background, select a background color using the Matte pop-up palette, eyedropper tool, or system color picker **(2.25)**.

8. To have Fireworks automatically create the smallest file using optimized compression tables, select Optimized. As a general rule, leave this turned on. It works in combination with whatever other options you select.

9. To save your export settings for reuse, click the + button above the preview window, type a name for the custom settings, and click OK.

10. When you have finished setting your optimization parameters, click Next.

11. In the Export dialog box, Fireworks provides a default filename with the JPG file extension. Type a new name if desired, select its destination, and click Export. Your original document is unchanged unless you save your exported file with the same name.

Optimizing and Exporting Eight-Bit PNGs

Eight-bit PNGs offer better flat-color compression than GIFs, resulting in smaller file sizes (2.26). PNG is not supported by all browsers, however, so double-check your results in your intended browser because Fireworks cannot always accurately predict how your grahics will display. If you limit your intended platform to the latest browsers using special plug-ins, you can take advantage of some of PNG's capabilities. Until it is a more widely accepted format, use 8-bit PNGs for importing into other Fireworks' files for further manipulation, such as scaling or bitmap editing. Your original art file is untouched, the graphic imports as one object, and you can choose index or alpha channel transparency.

PNG index transparency transitions more smoothly to a background than GIF transparency, which is especially noticeable when scaling or otherwise transforming the image. Alpha channel transparency separates the image from its background when exporting, which is preferred when the image contains the same color as the background and you don't want transparent holes in the image.

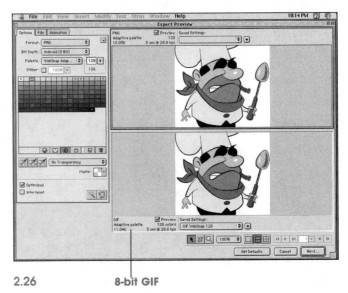

2.26   **8-bit GIF**

2.27

1. With your graphic open in the Document window, choose File→Export.

2. Select PNG in the Format pop-up menu in the Export Preview Options panel (2.27).

3. Select 8-bit color depth from the Bit Depth pop-up menu.

To set the maximum number of colors in the palette, enter a number in the Numbers of Colors entry field or use its pop-up menu.

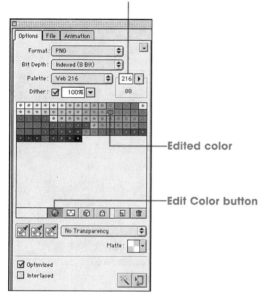

Edited color

Edit Color button

2.28

4. Choose a palette from the Palette pop-up menu.

   - Choose Web 216 to use only the 216 colors common to both the Macintosh and Windows platforms.

   - Choose Adaptive to create a custom palette using the actual colors in the image. If your PNG contains fewer than 256 colors, you also can choose the Exact palette.

   ● Choose WebSnap Adaptive to create a palette in which colors that are close in value to Web-safe colors snap to [convert to] those colors.

   ● Choose Custom to add your own palette from another program or another image. In the (Replace Swatches)[Open] dialog box, locate the desired palette and select it.

5. To approximate colors that are not in the selected palette, check Dither. Then select a percentage in the Dither Amount field.

6. To edit a color, double-click it in the palette or select it in the preview window and click the Edit Color button **(2.28)**. Then change the color in the system color picker. To revert to the original color, select the edited color and click the Edit Color button again.

 I P

To select a range of colors, select the first color in a range on the palette. Hold Shift while clicking the last color in the range. To select multiple colors, click the first color. Hold (Command)[Ctrl] as you select additional colors on the palette.

continues

Optimizing and Exporting Eight-Bit PNGs continued

7. To make a color transparent, select it in the palette or preview window and click the Transparent button **(2.29)**. To revert to the original color, select the transparent color in the palette or preview window and click the Transparent button again.

8. To convert a color to Web-safe, select it in the palette or preview window and click the Web-Safe button. To revert to the original color, select the altered color in the palette or preview window and click the Web-Safe button again.

I P

To save your custom palettes to use with other Fireworks documents, or in other applications that support Photoshop palettes, choose Save Palette from the Options panel pop-up menu. Name the palette and select a destination folder, and then click Save.

I P

*In Fireworks, load saved palettes into the Swatches panel in the Document view to use in creating art **(2.30)** or load them into the Export Options panel when exporting other documents. In Photoshop, use Replace Swatches in the Swatches window pop-up panel to substitute a Fireworks palette for the current palette.*

Color-editing options also are accessible in the Options pop-up menu.

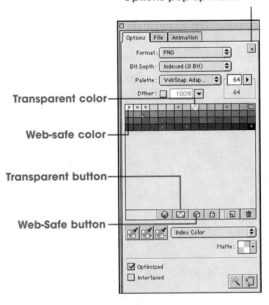

Transparent color

Web-safe color

Transparent button

Web-Safe button

2.29

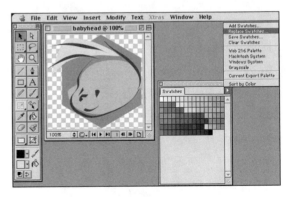

2.30

Locked color   **Unlock all colors at once by using the Options pop-up menu.**

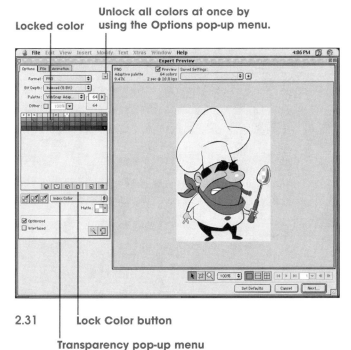

2.31   **Lock Color button**

Transparency pop-up menu

2.32   **Alpha channel transparency swatch**

9. To lock individual colors so that they are not removed or changed when changing palettes or reducing the number of colors in a palette, select the color in the palette or preview window, and click the Lock Color button (2.31). To unlock a locked color, select it and click the Lock Color button again.

10. To make the document's canvas color transparent, select (Index Color)[Index Transparency] in the Transparency pop-up menu.

To prevent areas in your graphic that are the same color as the background from becoming transparent, choose Alpha Channel from the Transparency pop-up menu (2.32).

11. To change the index transparency color, use the Select Transparency tool to click the desired color from the color palette or the preview image.

● To add transparent colors to index transparency, use the Add to Transparency tool to select colors in the palette or preview window.

● To subtract colors, use the Subtract from Transparency tool to select colors in the palette or preview window.

continues

Optimizing and Exporting Eight-Bit PNGs continued

- To remove all transparency settings, select No Transparency in the Transparency pop-up menu.

12. To change the PNG's background color, select a color in the Matte pop-up Web-Safe palette or color picker (**2.33**). Background color changes do not affect alpha channel graphics.

13. To have Fireworks create the smallest file with the fewest colors based on the options you have selected, check Optimized.

14. To have Fireworks create an image that loads progressively in Web browsers, check Interlaced (**2.34**).

15. To save your export settings for use later on, click the + button above the preview window, type a name for the custom settings, and click OK.

16. When you have finished setting your optimization parameters, click Next.

17. In the Export dialog box, Fireworks provides a default filename with the PNG file extension. Type a new name, select its destination, and click Export. Your original document is unchanged unless you save your exported file with the same name.

2.33   **When using index transparency, select the background color the graphic will be placed on. Fireworks recolors the graphic's edge pixels to make a seamless transition to the background.**

2.34   **Interlaced doesn't reduce file size, but because the image starts appearing on the Web page before it finishes loading, it seems to load faster.**

Optimizing and Exporting 24-Bit and 32-Bit PNGs

Choose 32-bit color depth for complex color images that include an alpha channel.

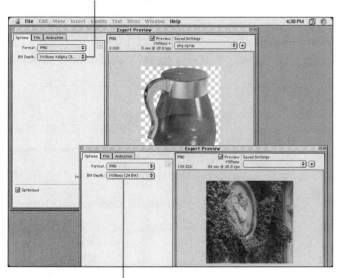

2.35   **Choose 24-bit color depth for continuous tone rectangular images that don't require transparency.**

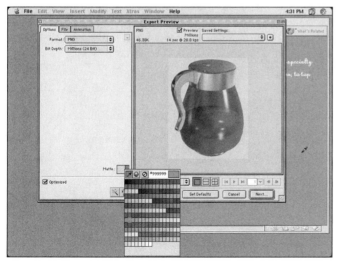

2.36

PNG provides lossless compression in continuous tone images, resulting in better image quality than JPEG compression does, but at a larger file size. If image quality is paramount, and large downloads are not a problem, then choose 24-bit PNG over JPEG, depending on which browser(s) you are supporting. Not all browsers support PNG, so always preview PNGs in their destination browser(s).

PNG also offers multilevel alpha channel transparency, which allows you to make complex masks for semitransparent and irregularly shaped continuous tone images. The resulting PNG blends smoothly into a background. However, even fewer browsers support alpha channels, so this option is best used when you want to manipulate a PNG in something such as Adobe Photoshop 5 or animate it in Macromedia Director 7 or Flash 4.

1. With your graphic open in the Document window, choose File→Export.

2. Select PNG in the Format pop-up menu in the Export Preview Options panel.

3. Select a color depth from the Bit Depth pop-up menu (2.35).

4. To change a 24-bit PNG's background color, select a color in the Matte pop-up Web-Safe palette or color picker, or use the Matte Eyedropper tool (2.36).

continues

Optimizing and Exporting 24-Bit and 32-Bit PNGs continued

5. To save your export settings for use later on, click the + button above the preview window, type a name for the custom settings, and click OK.

6. When you have finished setting your optimization parameters, click Next.

7. In the Export dialog box, Fireworks provides a default filename with the PNG file extension **(2.37)**. Type a new name, select its destination, and click Export. Your original document is unchanged unless you save your exported file with the same name.

2.37

Original image with alpha channel mask

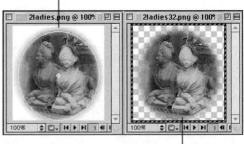

To use a saved export setting, select it from the Saved Settings pop-up menu. To delete an export preset, remove or delete its file from the Fireworks\Settings\Export Settings folder.

*When exporting PNGs, be sure to rename them so that you don't replace the original art file with the exported copy **(2.38)**. Otherwise, all the layers, editable vector art, and text are lost in the conversion to a bitmapped image.*

2.38

Exported bitmapped image

Changing File Size and Dimensions

You also can select a target file size in the Export to Size Wizard.

2.39

To distort a graphic, uncheck Constrain so that the width and height fields do not update simultaneously when scaling.

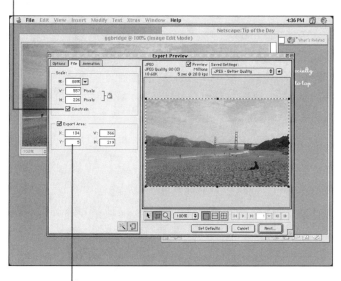

2.40   **Enter coordinates to select an exact area of an image for export.**

You can adjust your file size in the Export Preview before exporting. If you want a specific file size, use the Export-to-Size Wizard or the Export Wizard. They optimize your files while constraining them to a stated file size. Depending on your file type, they attempt to meet your request by reducing the number of colors in an image, using dithering and/or optimization, or modifying image quality and smoothing. Enlarge or reduce your graphic's size when exporting with the Scale settings in the File panel.

To export a portion of an image, use the Crop tool in the Preview window or the Export Area settings in the File panel to define the size and position of an export area within a document.

1. To export a graphic to a targeted file size, click the Export-to-Size button 🔲. Enter a desired file size in the Export to Size Wizard dialog box **(2.39)** and click OK.

2. To scale a graphic, enter a percentage or choose one from the pop-up slider in the File panel **(2.40)**. The width (W) and height (H) in pixels update automatically.

continues

Changing File Size and Dimensions continued

3. To crop for exporting, select the Crop tool at the bottom of the Export Preview area. Drag the handles on the dotted marquee surrounding the image to select the area you want to export **(2.41)**.

2.41

 O T E

Cropping in the Preview window or selecting an export area does not affect the original image. However, cropping or export area settings are retained in the Export Preview. If you export the image again, your cropping parameters will appear again.

(T) **I P**

You also can export a section of a graphic from the Document window by click-dragging the Export Area tool *from the Pointer tool set in the Toolbox across the area you want to export, and then adjust the selection by dragging the marquee handles* **(2.42)**. *Double-click inside the selection to export it. Optimize and save your selection. If you change your mind after you have selected an area in the Document window, double-click outside the area, select another tool, or press Esc. Using the Export Area tool does not affect the original image.*

2.42

Optimizing a Graphic from Dreamweaver

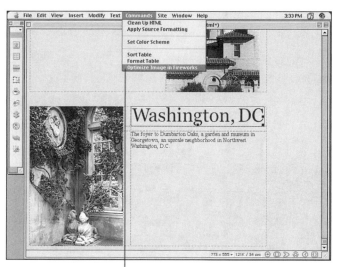

2.43   **The Optimize in Fireworks command only opens Fireworks' Export Preview screen. You cannot edit a graphic with this command; you can only optimize it.**

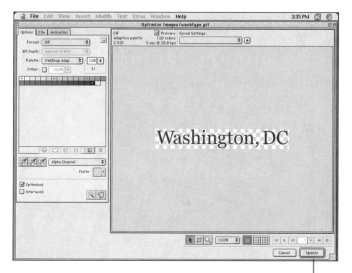

2.44   **Updating a graphic replaces the original graphic. You cannot rename the file.**

In Macromedia's Dreamweaver 2 visual Web page editor, you can quickly access Fireworks' Export Preview to optimize graphics that weren't originally created or optimized in Fireworks.

1. In Dreamweaver 2, select the graphic you want to optimize.

2. Choose Commands→Optimize Image in Fireworks (2.43). This launches Fireworks' Export Preview and displays the following message: Editing [file name]. Do you wish to use an existing Fireworks document as the source of "[file name]"?

3. If you have a source Fireworks PNG file for the graphic, click Yes, locate the PNG file, and click OK. If no Fireworks PNG file exists, click No.

4. Optimize the graphic in the Export Preview window and click Update (2.44) to save the changes and return to Dreamweaver. The updated graphic replaces the original file.

©HAPTER 3

If you are maintaining a Web site and need to periodically update the graphics, you can automate some of the work with Fireworks' batch processing functions. Fireworks offers two types of batch processing: global search and replace in Fireworks PNG files and other vector graphic files, and batch export optimization of any file type Fireworks can read.

BATCH PROCESSING IMAGES FOR THE WEB

Global search and replace can speed up mundane editing tasks, such as changing the color of all the buttons in a site to fit a new color scheme or updating their URL links to new pages. You can also globally replace text and its attributes, such as fonts, styles, and sizes. You can track all your changed files in the Project Log and use the log to manage future searches or batch exports.

With batch exporting, you can export a group of files by using a common set of optimization parameters or unique settings for each file. You can quickly generate thumbnails for a visual table of contents by scaling and exporting a group of images in one operation. Fireworks' export scaling can be done by a fixed percentage or to a fixed width or height, while leaving the original image unchanged.

Finally, you can save your batch processing operations as reusable scriptlets that you can share with other users and run directly from your desktop.

Batch Replacing in Fireworks Files

Batch replacing in Fireworks saves time and ensures consistency across a series of files. You can globally edit or update text, font attributes, object colors, or URL links in a group of Firework's PNG files with Batch Find and Replace. Manage batch replacements further by keeping track of the changed files in the Project Log panel, saving backups of the originals, and saving your editing actions as cross-platform scriptlets to use again.

3.1

1. Choose File→Batch Process in the Document window (3.1).

2. To search and replace elements in open Fireworks files, choose Current Open Files in the Files to Process pop-up menu in the Batch Processing dialog box (3.2).

   To search and replace elements in Fireworks files from disk, choose Custom in the Files to Process pop-up menu or click the … (ellipsis) button. In the

3.2   **To save your batch replace parameters as a script to reuse later, click the Script button. In the Save Script dialog box, name the file and save it.**

For efficiency, move all the files you want to process into one folder on your hard drive. When Fireworks saves backups as it batch processes files, it creates an Original Files folder to save the originals in. The Original Files folder is created in the folder your processed files are in. If your files are in several places, Fireworks will create Original Files folders every place it processes files from.

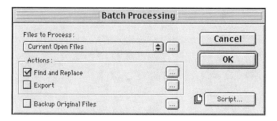

3.3

3.4

(Open Multiple Files)[Open] dialog box, select a file and click Add. Repeat this with the rest of the files you want to batch process. Click (OK)[Done] to return to the Batch Processing dialog box.

3. In the Actions section of the Batch Processing dialog box, choose Find and Replace or click its ... (ellipsis) button **(3.3)**.

4. In the Batch Replace dialog box, select Text, Font, Color or URL from the Attributes pop-up menu.

5. With Text selected, enter the text you want to search for in the Find field **(3.4)**. Enter the revised text in the Change To field. Click the appropriate check box to restrict your search to whole words, to match the case (upper and lower) as typed, or to use regular expressions to find text that meets specific conditions.

continues

O T E

Regular expressions are patterns you use to find special characters or character combinations. For example, if you want to search and replace all instances of the names "Tom" and "Dick" and change them to "Harry," enter **Tom | Dick** *in the Find field and* **Harry** *in the Change to field. Check RegExp and click OK. For a chart of regular expressions, go to* http://developer.netscape.com/docs/ manuals/communicator/jsguide/regexp.htm.

(T) I P

If you have an instance you don't want changed when doing a global find and replace of an element in a group of files, open the file it appears in and lock the layer it is on. Find and Replace ignores elements that are on locked layers.

Batch Replacing in Fireworks Files continued

6. With Font selected **(3.5)**, choose a specific font or the generic Any Font to replace in the Find pop-up menu. You can also search for a font style, such as bold or italic, and a font size or range of sizes to change in the other Find pop-ups. Choose replacements in the Change To pop-ups.

3.5

7. With Color selected **(3.6)**, click the Find pop-up arrow and use the Eyedropper tool above the default palette to click the color in an open document that you want to change. Choose which color instances you want to change, such as Fill, Stroke, or Effect, in the Apply To pop-up menu. Select the new color in the Change To color picker or pop-up palette.

Click the Find color square to select a color in the system color picker.

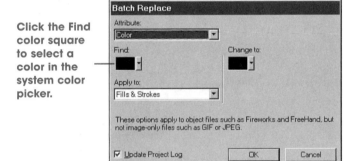

3.6

(N)OTE

Batch processing can change only one attribute at a time. To change multiple attributes, check Update Project Log to save a list of the changed files, and then repeat the batch process by selecting Project Log (All Files) in the Files to Process pop-up menu and choosing a different attribute each time.

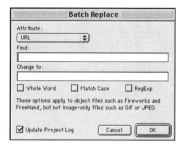

3.7

3.8

8. With URL selected (3.7), enter a URL or part of a URL you want to change in the Find field. Enter the replacement information in the Change To field. Click the appropriate check box to restrict your search to whole words, to match the case (upper and lower) as typed, or to use regular expressions.

9. To keep track of files that have changed, click the Update Project Log check box. Click OK to return to the Batch Processing dialog box.

10. To save an unchanged copy of the files, select Backup Original Files in the Batch Processing dialog box or click the ... (ellipsis) button. In the Save Backups dialog box (3.8), select Overwrite Existing Backups to have new backup copies replace old backup copies. Select Incremental Backups to save incremental backup copies by adding a number to the filenames each time a batch is run. Click OK to return to the Batch Processing dialog box.

continues

Ⓝ O T E

When you replace URLs by batch processing, you must export the changed file(s) to generate HTML documents that include the new URLs.

Batch Replacing in Fireworks Files continued

11. When you finish setting parameters, click OK in the Batch Processing dialog box to process the files. When the batch is finished, click OK in the Batch Progress dialog box **(3.9)** to return to the Document window.

3.9

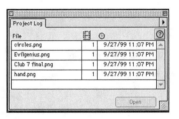

3.10

 I P

*To proof the files you have changed, open the Project Log **(3.10)** and double-click a file to open it and view the Find and Replace changes.*

 I P

*To search and replace within an individual document or to search for a specific instance within a group of files, choose Window→Find & Replace to use the Find & Replace panel **(3.11)**. Like batch processing, you can find and change text, font attributes, object colors, and URL links in a group of files, and specify whether you want to replace or back up originals. If you use this method, however, you can also limit your search to the current open document, a specific frame within the document, or a selected object in the document. You can choose to globally replace all, or you can find each instance individually.*

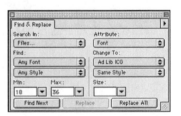

3.11

Batch Replacing in Vector Files

Open Multiple Files

Preview   Illustrator Art

Mr. Cha...

Africa 5.ai
Africa.ai
arrow.eps
Chef1b.eps
crookeps.eps
Cupid.eps
Dogbite
Evil Genius
Frank

Eject
Desktop
Cancel
OK
Add
Add All
Remove

Format : Adobe Illustrator
Size : 77.30 K

baby.fh-1
Chips label.ai
Chef1.eps
Chef.png

☐ Open as Animation

3.12

Vector File Options   ? ✕

Scale: 100

Width: 141   Pixels

Height: 136   Pixels

Resolution: 72   Pixels/Inch

File Conversion:

Open a page   Page: 1

Remember layers

☐ Include Invisible Layers

☑ Include Background Layers

Render as images:

☑ Groups over   30   objects

☑ Blends over   30   steps

☑ Tiled fills over   30   objects

☑ Anti-Aliased

OK   Cancel

3.13

Use Batch Find and Replace to change text, font attributes, or object colors in files created in Adobe Illustrator, Macromedia FreeHand, or CorelDRAW. To search and replace in vector files, you must open them in the Fireworks Document window and save them as PNGs. Keep the original files or overwrite them with the new PNG versions. Then track them in the Project Log panel, save backups of PNG files, and make scriptlets of your Find and Replace actions to use again.

1. Choose File→Open Multiple from the Document window. In the Open Multiple Files dialog box, add files to open (3.12). When all files are added to the multiple file list, click OK.

2. In the Vector File Options dialog box that opens for each file (3.13), adjust the file's dimensions and resolution, if needed, and select pages, layers and rendering options if the document is complex. Click OK.

3. With all the files open, choose File→Batch Process.

continues

Ⓝ **O T E**

Batch Replace does not work on bitmap formats such as Adobe Photoshop, BMP, GIF, JPEG, PICT, TIFF, Targa, or Macromedia xRes LRG.

Batch Replacing in Vector Files continued

4. Choose Current Open Files in the Batch Processing dialog box **(3.14)**.

5. In the Actions section of the Batch Processing dialog box, choose Find and Replace or click its ... (ellipsis) button.

6. In the Batch Replace dialog box, select Text, Font, or Color from the Attributes pop-up menu **(3.15)**.

7. With Text selected, enter the text you want to search for in the Find field. Enter the revised text in the Change To field. Click the appropriate check box to restrict your search to whole words, to match the case (upper and lower) as typed, or to use regular expressions to find text that meets specific conditions.

8. With Font selected **(3.16)**, choose a specific font or the generic Any Font to replace in the Find pop-up menu. You can also search for a font style,

Batch processing can change one only attribute at a time. To change multiple attributes, check Update Project Log to save a list of the changed files, and then repeat the batch process by selecting Project Log (All Files) in the Files to Process pop-up menu and choosing a different attribute each time.

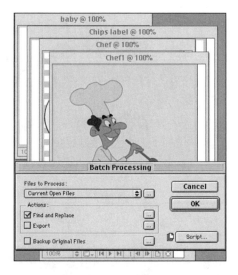

3.14

Fireworks cannot search and replace URLs in non-Fireworks files.

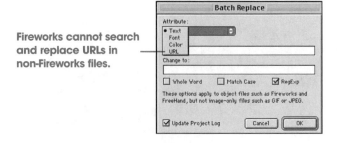

3.15

If you don't know the font name you want to replace, choose the generic Any Font. If you don't want to replace all fonts, use the Find & Replace panel instead.

If you don't know the point size you want to change, select an approximate range.

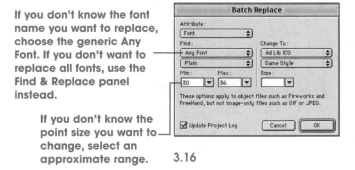

3.16

To select a color in an open document, click it with the palette's Eyedropper tool.

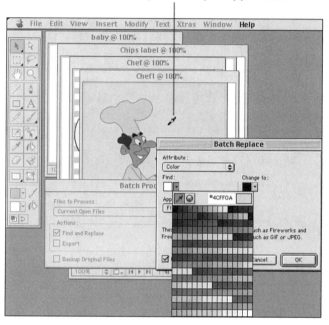

3.17

such as bold or italic, and a font size or range of sizes to change in the other Find pop-ups. Choose replacements in the Change To pop-ups.

9. With Color selected, click the Find color square to select a color in the system color picker, or click the pop-up arrow to use the default palette (3.17). Choose which color instances you want to change, such as Fill, Stroke, or Effect, in the Apply To pop-up menu. Select the new color in the Change To color picker or pop-up palette.

10. Click OK to return to the Batch Processing dialog box.

11. To save an unchanged copy of the files, select Backup Original Files in the Batch Processing dialog box or click the ... (ellipsis) button. In the Save Backups dialog box, select Overwrite Existing Backups to have new backup copies replace old backup copies. Select Incremental Backups to save incremental backup copies by adding a

continues

 **O T E**

If you want Fireworks to keep track of files that have changed, click the Update Project Log check box in the Batch Replace dialog box.

Batch Replacing in Vector Files continued

number to the filenames each time a batch is run. Click OK to return to the Batch Processing dialog box.

12. When you finish setting parameters, click OK in the Batch Processing dialog box to process the files (3.18).

13. In the Documents Must Be Saved Before Batch Processing message box (3.19), click OK to have Fireworks save the files and continue batch processing.

14. In the Save Document dialog box that appears for each file, Fireworks provides the file's default name with the PNG file extension (3.20). Type a new filename (if desired), select its destination, and click Save.

15. When the batch is finished, click OK in the Batch Progress dialog box to return to the Document window.

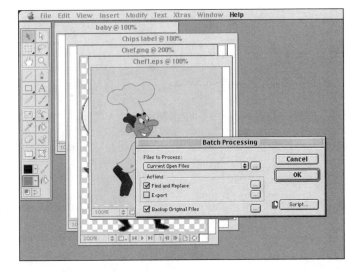

3.18

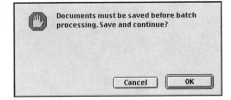

3.19

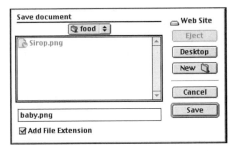

3.20

 I P

If you want to save your batch processing parameters as a script to reuse later, click the Script button in the Batch Processing dialog box. In the Save Script dialog box, name the file and save it.

Batch Processing Files for Export

3.21   **Vector graphics must first be saved in Fireworks' PNG format to be batch processed.**

In addition to global search and replace in Fireworks' files, you can also streamline export optimization of any file type Fireworks can read, including scanned images, with Fireworks' export batch processing (3.21).

You can customize export parameters in the Export Preview window for individual files or for the group, or you can select one of the default settings. You can add a prefix or a suffix to the exported files' names, scale the exported files, and create backups of the files and cross-platform scriptlets to use again.

1. Choose File→Batch Process in the Document window.

2. To batch export files open in the Document window, choose Current Open Files in the Files to Process pop-up menu in the Batch Processing dialog box.

   To batch export files from disk, choose Custom in the Files to Process pop-up menu or click the ... (ellipsis) button. In the (Open Multiple Files)[Open] dialog box, select the files. Click (OK)[Done].

continues

 I P

Batch processing can be slow. If you are processing a large number of files, run a test batch first of a small number of files at your desired settings and check the exported files.

Batch Processing Files for Export continued

3. In the Actions section of the Batch Processing dialog box (**3.22**), choose Export or click its ... (ellipsis) button.

4. In the Batch Export dialog box, select export settings for the batch.

Choose Use Settings from Each File from the Export Settings pop-up menu if you have set export defaults for your files.

5. Under File Name in the Batch Export dialog box, select Add Prefix or Add Suffix to add text to the filename before the file extension for the exported files. Use Original Name when you want to replace files while batch processing.

6. If you want to resize your files, select Scale to Size (**3.23**) to scale to an exact width and/or height and enter a value in pixels for the measurements or select a preset from the pop-up menu.

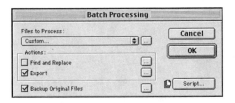

3.22

You can scale the images proportionally to a specific width or height by entering the measurement in one field and selecting Variable from the pop-up menu for the other field.

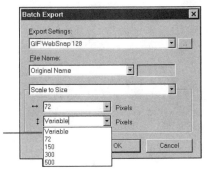

3.23

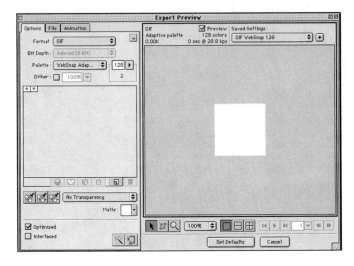

3.24

*Choose Custom in the Export Settings pop-up menu to open the Export Preview window (**3.24**) where you can assign new export settings. Click Set Defaults to return to the Batch Export dialog box.*

3.25

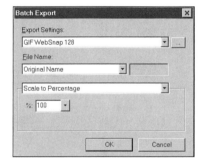

3.26

7. Select Scale to Fit Area (3.25) to scale to fit within a specific area and enter values in pixels in the Max Width and Max Height fields or use the pop-up sliders to choose maximum dimensions.

8. Select Scale to Percentage (3.26) to scale by a percentage and enter a value in the % field or use the pop-up slider.

9. Click OK to store the batch processing parameters.

10. To back up batch processed files, select Backup Original Files in the Batch Process dialog box or click the … (ellipsis) button. In the Save Backups dialog box, select Overwrite Existing Backups to have new backup copies replace old backup copies. Select Incremental Backups to save incremental backup copies by adding a number to the filenames each time a batch is run. Click OK.

11. When you finish setting parameters, click OK in the Batch Processing dialog box to process the files.

 **O T E**

Fireworks' Batch Processing doesn't always render GIF trans-
parency correctly. Export transparent GIFs individually to maintain
correct transparency.

Creating Image Thumbnails

Because large graphics take longer to download than small ones, setting up a table of contents that hyperlinks thumbnails of images (small versions) to their full-sized versions on separate Web pages is a handy way to present an online portfolio (3.27), your company organizational chart, or your family tree. Your audience will get some idea of what they will see before they click a thumbnail link to the actual image.

1. Choose File→Batch Process in the Document window.

2. To create thumbnails from originals open in the Document window, choose Current Open Files in the Files to Process pop-up menu in the Batch Processing dialog box (3.28).

   To create thumbnails from disk, choose Custom in the Files to Process pop-up menu or click the ... (ellipsis) button. In the (Open Multiple Files)[Open] dialog box, select the files to batch process. Click (OK)[Done] to return to the Batch Processing dialog box.

3. In the Actions section of the Batch Processing dialog box, choose Export or click its ... (ellipsis) button to select export settings.

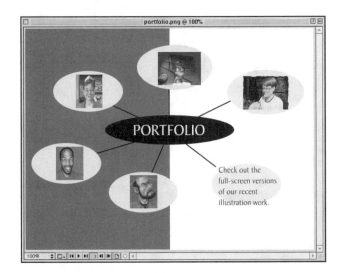

3.27

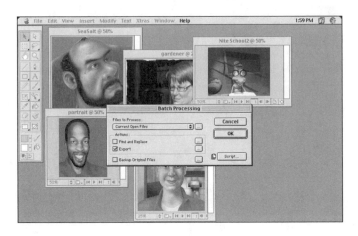

3.28

3.29

Select Custom to open the Export Preview window where you can assign new overall export settings for the thumbnails.

3.30

Create uniform-looking thumbnails by scaling them all to a specific width or height, and choosing Variable from the pop-up menu for the other dimension.

3.31

4. In the Batch Export dialog box, select Use Settings from Each File from the Files to Process pop-up menu (3.29) if you want your thumbnails to have the same file type, palette, and compression settings as the originals you are scaling them from.

5. Under File Name in the Batch Export dialog box, select Add Prefix or Add Suffix to add text to the filename before the file extension to differentiate the thumbnails from the full-size images (3.30).

6. To scale the thumbnails, select Scale to Size to scale to an exact width and/or height and enter a value in pixels for the measurements or select a preset from the pop-up menu (3.31).

continues

T I P

If you want to save your thumbnail batch processing parameters as a script to reuse on other batches, click the Script button in the Batch Processing dialog box. In the Save Script dialog box, name the file and save it.

Creating Image Thumbnails continued

7. Select Scale to Fit Area to scale each thumbnail proportionally to fit within a specific area and enter values in pixels in the Max Width and Max Height fields or use the pop-up sliders to choose dimensions for a maximum area for each thumbnail to fit.

8. Select Scale to Percentage to scale thumbnails proportionally by a percentage and enter a percentage in the % field or select one on the pop-up slider.

9. Click OK to store the batch processing parameters and return to the Batch Processing dialog box.

10. When you have finished setting parameters, click OK in the Batch Processing dialog box to process the thumbnails.

3.32

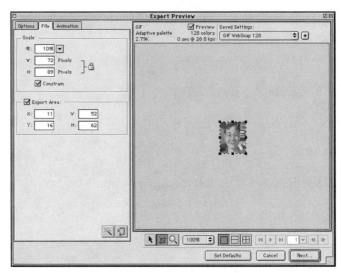

3.33

 I P

Check your thumbnails after batch processing for readability. If an image has shrunk too small to be readable, use the Export Area tool [icon] in the Document window to drag-select a section of the original (3.32) to shrink to a thumbnail and then double-click. Use the File panel in the Export Preview to size the thumbnail, set optimization parameters in the Options panel, and click Next to export (3.33).

Batch Processing from the Project Log Panel

Project Log panel pop-up menu

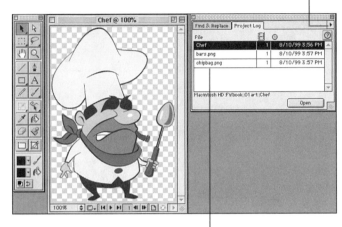

3.34

Open any file listed in the Project Log by double-clicking it.

If you want to run a set of files through multiple find-and-replace operations or export files you have changed using Batch Replace or the Find and Replace panel, turn on Update Project Log in the Batch Replace dialog box before you start running the first batch. Fireworks tracks the changed files and lists them in the Project Log panel.

Choose Window→Project Log to check the list, and then add or delete files using the Project Log panel pop-up menu (3.34). You can batch process the entire list or only selected files. To select multiple files for batch processing, (Command-click)[Ctrl-click] them in the Project Log panel.

Choose File→Batch Process, and in the Batch Processing dialog box, choose Project Log (All Files) or Project Log (Selected Files) from the pop-up menu (3.35). Then proceed to process the batch as in the earlier tasks (3.36).

3.35

3.36

 I P

If you want a hard copy of the Project Log, find the Project_Log.htm file in the Fireworks\ Settings folder on your desktop and open it in a browser to view or print the Project Log.

Using Batch Scriptlets

Reuse your batch process settings by saving them as cross-platform scriptlets. If you are working in a multiuser setting, you can ensure consistency when updating graphics for a site by distributing a revision scriptlet to everyone who is editing graphics. No matter where changes are made or who does them, all the revisions made with the scriptlet will be correct.

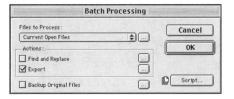

3.37

1. To create a batch processing scriptlet without processing any files, choose File→Batch Process in the Document window.

2. In the Actions section of the Batch Processing dialog box, choose Find and Replace or Export or click an … (ellipsis) button (3.37). Then set up the actions you want the scriptlet to perform.

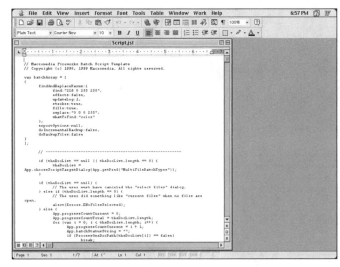

3.38

Batch processing scriptlets are written in JavaScript and can be edited in a simple text editor (3.38).

If you want your scriptlet to back up original files, select Backup Original Files in the Batch Process dialog box or click the … (ellipsis) button to choose the backup method.

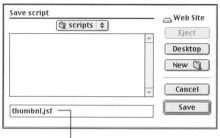

3.39   **Save scriptlets with a .jsf (JavaScript file) extension.**

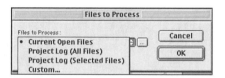

3.40

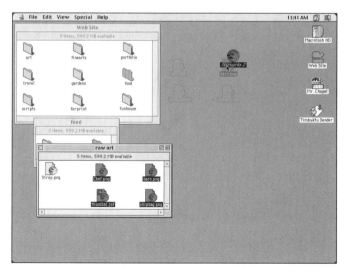

3.41

3. To create the scriptlet, click the Script button in the Batch Processing dialog box. In the Save Script dialog box (**3.39**), name the file and save it. Click Cancel in the Batch Processing dialog box to return to the Document window without running the script.

4. To run the scriptlet, choose File→Run Script from the Document window. Locate the scriptlet on your hard drive and open it.

5. In the Files to Process dialog box (**3.40**), select the files you want to process with the scriptlet and click OK.

 I   P

*You can also run scriptlets from the desktop by dragging them together with the files you want to process onto the Fireworks program icon (**3.41**). Fireworks launches and runs the script on the selected files. If you drag more than one scriptlet with the files to process, Fireworks automatically processes the files with each of the scriptlets.*

CHAPTER 4

In this chapter you learn how to...

Manage Palettes

Mix Colors

Create Custom Palettes

Fireworks offers two tools for creating and managing colors: the Color Mixer and the Swatches panel. Create and edit colors in the Color Mixer. If you want to reuse, import, or save colors, use the Swatches panel.

CREATING, EDITING, AND MANAGING COLORS

When creating graphics, you are not limited to the colors in the Swatches panel. Fireworks enables you to work in 24-bit (millions of colors). This means that when you open a pre-existing graphic in the Document window, it ignores the current Swatches panel and maintains all its colors. Only when you export the image as an 8-bit graphic will its colors shift or dither down to 8-bit color or less.

To create your own custom palettes, start with an existing palette and edit the colors, or build an entirely new palette. Sample colors from a graphic in the Document window, or use the Color Mixer to create colors. Then add the colors to the Swatches panel.

Because it is a 24-bit environment, Fireworks might use non-Web-safe colors to create certain effects, such as anti-aliasing, feathering, gradients, glows, and transparency, even if you are using a restricted palette to create graphics. These effects will dither or color-shift when you export them to an 8-bit or less format. To avoid these problems, don't use these features when creating graphics. If you want to use them, export your graphics using an adaptive palette or as JPEGs or 24-bit PNGs.

Managing Palettes

Fireworks' default palette is the Web 216 palette, which contains all the cross-platform Web-safe colors, but you can switch to another preset palette, such as the Mac or Windows palette, import a palette from another program or 8-bit graphic, or use the current Export palette.

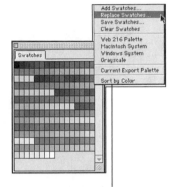

The Document window Swatches palette is different from the Export palette. The Swatches palette is like an artist's palette; use it to add color to graphics and to save colors you created in the Color Mixer. If you switch to another palette, it doesn't affect the open graphic in the Document window; it just changes the premixed colors available to add to the graphic. The Export palette is more restrictive. It contains the colors that the graphic maps to when exported. If the graphic contains colors not included in the Export palette, those colors switch or dither to colors in the Export palette.

4.1 **To arrange the current palette by color, choose Sort by Color.**

Fireworks can open CLUTs (Mac only), ACTs (Windows only), or palettes from 8-bit graphics.

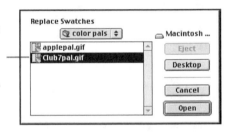

4.2

1. To switch to another palette, choose Window→Swatches, and then choose one of the default palettes or Replace Swatches in the Swatches panel Options pop-up menu (4.1).

2. In the Replace Swatches dialog box, locate the color palette or GIF image file that contains colors you want to add (4.2), and click OK.

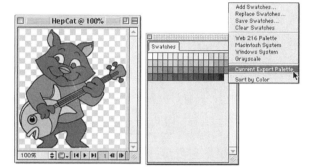

4.3

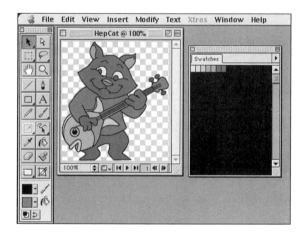

4.4

3. To append a palette to the current palette in the Swatches panel, choose Add Swatches in the Options pop-up menu, and then locate the color palette or GIF image file that contains colors you want to add.

4. To revert a palette to its original swatches, select the palette name in the Swatches panel Options pop-up menu.

5. To use the current custom palette from the Export Preview, choose Current Export Palette in the Swatches panel Options pop-up menu (4.3).

 O T E

Changing colors in the Swatches panel does not change colors that are already in objects in a document (4.4).

 I P

To avoid unpleasant surprises in an exported graphic, create the artwork in an 8-bit or smaller palette. Use Fireworks' default palette, which contains all the cross-platform Web-safe colors, switch to another preset palette, import a palette, or create your own custom palette.

Mixing Colors

Create custom colors in the Color Mixer using Hexadecimal, RGB, CMY, HSB, or Grayscale color models. The Color Mixer displays colors both visually and as numeric values, so you can create and edit colors both ways. If you want to reuse a custom color, add it to the Swatches palette.

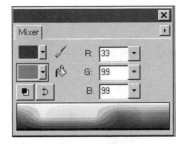

4.5

The Color Mixer contains two color wells: one for coloring strokes, such as the outline of a vector object or the path created by the Paint Brush tool, and one for coloring fills, either the interior of a vector object or an area in an image object filled by the Paint Bucket tool. A third color well, for coloring Live Effects (Fireworks' editable special effects such as glows and drop shadows), is accessible on the Live Effects panel and can be edited by using the Color Mixer, also.

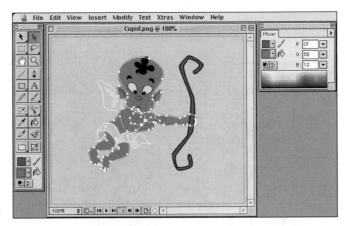

4.6

1. To create a color using the Color Mixer, choose Window→Color Mixer to display the Color Mixer (4.5).

2. Select the object or objects in which you want to change colors (4.6). If you do not want to edit colors in existing objects, choose Edit→Deselect.

 **O T E**

Objects that are selected when colors are edited update automatically, and any object drawn after editing colors includes the new colors.

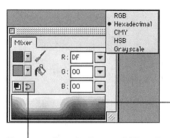

When using Hexadecimal color, color bar choices are restricted to the Web 216 palette.

To swap the stroke and fill colors, click the Swap Colors button.

4.7

4.8

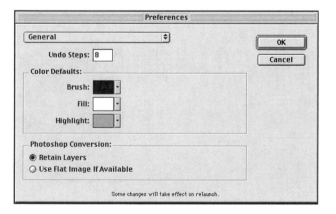

4.9

3. Select the Stroke color well or Fill color well in the Color Mixer to choose the destination for the new color.

4. Choose a color model from the Color Mixer Options pop-up **(4.7)**.

● Choose the default color model, Hexadecimal, for Web graphics.

● Choose RGB (Red, Green, Blue) for computer screen graphics.

● Choose CMY (Cyan, Magenta, Yellow) for print graphics.

● Choose HSB (Hue, Saturation, Brightness) for creating tints or tones of a color.

● Choose Grayscale for images with gray tones only.

continues

(T) I P

To create a color for a Live Effect that uses color, such as the drop shadow or glow, choose Window→Effect; then select the effect in the Effect category pop-up menu in the Effect panel and click its color well **(4.8)**.

(N) O T E

To reset to the default colors of black and white, click the Default Colors button . *If you want to change the defaults, choose File→Preferences→General and select new default colors* **(4.9)**.

Mixing Colors continued

5. To pick a color visually from the color bar, move the cursor over the color bar, and click-drag when it changes into an eyedropper cursor. Release when the Eyedropper is on the desired color **(4.10)**.

6. To change the color in a color well to a different one in the current Swatches panel, click the pop-up arrow next to the color well and select a swatch.

7. To define a color with the system color picker, double-click the color well.

8. To copy a color from anywhere on your desktop, use the Eyedropper tool from the pop-up palette to (click)[click to select, and then click and hold until over] the desired color **(4.11)**.

9. To add a new color to the current Swatches palette, choose Window→Swatches and move the cursor beyond the end of the visible palette in the Swatches panel **(4.12)**. Click when the cursor changes into a paint bucket.

To change a color numerically, enter values in the color component fields or use their pop-up sliders.

As you click-drag, the color well and color component fields update.

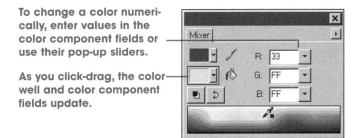

4.10

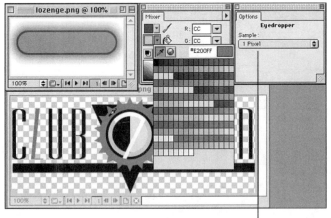

4.11

To sample an exact color, set the Eyedropper tool to 1 Pixel. To sample a blend of the pixels in an area, choose 3×3 Average or 5×5 Average.

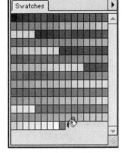

4.12

(N) O T E

To switch palettes, choose Window→Swatches, and then select another palette in the Swatches panel Options pop-up menu.

Creating Custom Palettes

4.13

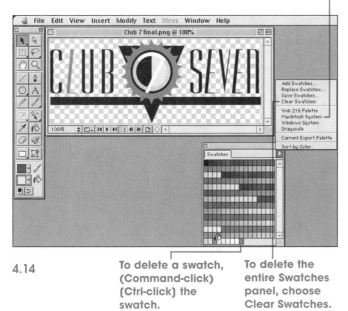

To switch palettes, select another palette.

4.14

To delete a swatch, (Command-click) (Ctrl-click) the swatch.

To delete the entire Swatches panel, choose Clear Swatches.

 O T E

Edit→Undo does not undo swatch additions, edits, or deletions.

T I P

Use palettes when creating graphics to control which colors are available. For example, if you have a group of five corporate colors, you can create a palette with only those colors so that they might be quickly and precisely selected when drawing.

As you select or create custom colors for your graphics, save them in custom palettes you can easily access in other graphics and share with other users. You can modify an existing palette whether a Fireworks preset palette, an imported palette, or the current palette from the Export Preview, to create a new palette. Or start from scratch and build a palette with only the colors you need (4.13).

1. To add a color to the current Swatches palette, create one in the Color Mixer or use the Eyedropper tool to select one in an open document.

2. Choose Window→Swatches and move the cursor beyond the last swatch in the Swatches panel. Click when the cursor changes into a paint bucket.

3. To replace a swatch with another color, create or select the new color. Then shift-click the swatch in the Swatches panel you want to change (4.14).

4. To save the swatches as a custom palette, choose Save Swatches in the Swatches panel Options pop-up menu. In the Export Swatches dialog box, name the file, select its destination, and click OK.

CHAPTER 5

Drawing in Fireworks is similar to using other drawing programs, such as Adobe Illustrator and Macromedia FreeHand. It offers Bézier path drawing tools and some standard shape tools, such as rectangles and ovals. It also has click-and-drag rounded-corner rectangles, starbursts, and triangles for quick Web graphics creation.

DRAWING AND COLORING VECTOR SHAPES

In addition to flat color fills and strokes, Fireworks offers customizable patterns, textures, and gradient blends. Unlike other drawing programs, your custom patterns can be bitmaps. With Fireworks, you can combine bitmaps and vectors in the same object.

You can even create 3D effects that look like bitmaps, but are better because they are always editable. Firework's Live Effects are customizable common graphics effects such as bevels and drop shadows, which remain live (editable). Whenever you change an object, its Live Effects automatically update.

Save your custom patterns, textures, gradients, brushes, and Live Effects as styles to use in other documents or to share with other users.

Drawing Rounded-Corner Rectangles, Starbursts, and Triangles

Rounded-corner rectangles are common button shapes that Fireworks offers as an option for the Rectangle tool. You select the degree of corner roundness first, and then draw the rectangle.

Another efficiency-enhancing tool in Fireworks is the Polygon tool. Use it to draw triangles, pentagons, hexagons, and other equal-sided polygons with up to 360 sides. Draw starbursts with up to 360 points and any degree of sharpness, from 0° for sharp points to 100° for a straight-sided circle effect.

1. To draw a rounded-corner rectangle, double-click the Rectangle tool button in the Toolbox to select the tool and open the Tool Options panel.

2. In the Tool Options panel, enter a percentage or use the pop-up slider to define the degree of corner roundness (5.1).

3. To draw the rectangle, click in the drawing area with the Rectangle tool where you want a corner of the rectangle and drag to its opposite corner (5.2). To create a square, hold the Shift key while clicking and dragging.

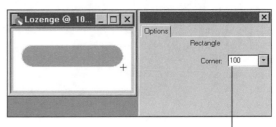

5.1

To make a lozenge-shaped button, set the corner roundness to 100%.

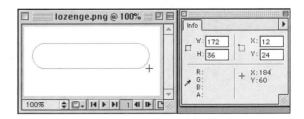

5.2

To draw a specific size shape, choose Window→Info before click-dragging. As you drag the shape, watch the X and Y dimensions and release the mouse button at the desired measurements.

 I P

To change a document's background color, choose Modify→ Document→Canvas Color. To choose a custom color, click the color well in the Canvas Color dialog box to use the system color picker or click the pop-up arrow to use the default palette. To match the canvas color to a color in an open document on your desktop, use the Eyedropper tool above the palette to click the color. Click OK to update the background.

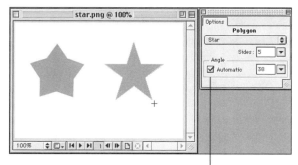

5.3

To create traditional stars, check Automatic before dragging the shape.

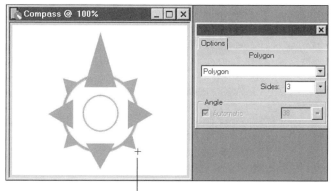

5.4

To create triangles, other polygons, or stars that line up along 45° axes, hold the Shift key while dragging the Polygon tool.

5.5

4. To draw a starburst, triangle, or polygon, select the Polygon tool from the shapes pop-up group in the Toolbox , and then double-click the Polygon tool button to open the Tool Options panel.

5. To create a star, select Star from the pop-up menu in the Tool Options panel **(5.3)**. Enter values or use the pop-up sliders for the number of points and their degree of sharpness.

6. To create a triangle or other polygon, select Polygon from the pop-up menu in the Tool Options panel. Enter a value or use the pop-up slider for the number of sides.

7. To draw the star, triangle, or polygon, click in the drawing area with the Polygon tool where you want the center point of the shape and drag outward **(5.4)**.

(T) I P

To draw from a center point, hold the (Option)[Alt] key while dragging.

(T) I P

*To visually align vector shapes, choose View→Rulers, and then click-drag guides from the rulers onto the canvas. Choose View→Guide Options→Edit Guides to customize guide settings **(5.5)**.*

Coloring Vector Objects

It's easy to add colors, patterns, or gradients to vector objects. For solid colors and gradients, the default palette is the Web-safe palette, but you can switch palettes and add new colors from the system picker or from your desktop to match any non-Web-safe color you need.

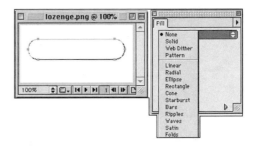

5.6

If your graphics will be exported as GIFs or 8-bit PNGs, any non-Web-safe colors will be automatically remapped to their nearest Web-safe equivalents or dithered when exported. To control how a custom color fill will look in 8-bit, make it a Web dither before exporting. A Web dither fill is a dither pattern of the two Web-safe colors that are closest in value to the custom color.

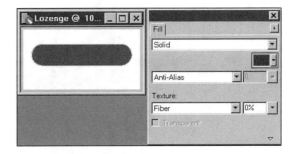

5.7

Fireworks also gives you bitmap pattern fills and textures to add to vector objects. You can use third-party patterns and textures, as long as they are saved in Fireworks' PNG format.

1. To change a selected vector object's fill from the default, choose Modify→Fill. In the Fill panel, select a fill from the Fill category pop-up menu (5.6).

2. Choose None for a transparent fill or Solid (5.7) for a flat-color fill. Double-click the Fill color well to select a color in the system color picker, or click its pop-up arrow to use the Swatches palette.

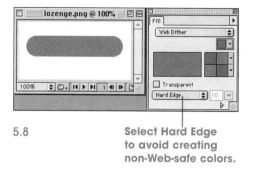

5.8

**Select Hard Edge
to avoid creating
non-Web-safe colors.**

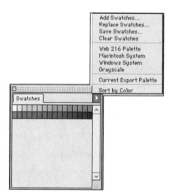

5.9

Choose Web Dither (5.8) for a
Web-safe dithered fill to match
a non-Web-safe color. Double-
click the Fill color well to select
the non-Web-safe color in the
system color picker, or select
the color on your desktop with
the Eyedropper tool above the
pop-up Swatches palette. If
you want to change either one
of the dither colors, double-
click its Fill color well to select
a color in the system color
picker, or click its pop-up
arrow to use the Swatches
palette. Check Transparent to
make the lighter Web Dither
fill color invisible.

continues

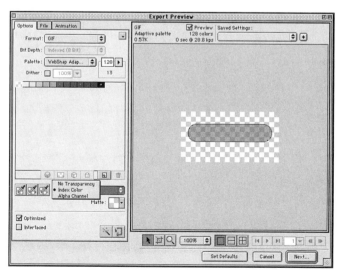

5.10

 I   P

*To switch to a different palette, choose
Window→Swatches and then select a
different palette in the Swatches panel
Options pop-up menu* **(5.9)**.

 I   P

*To maintain transparency when exporting,
choose GIF or PNG format in the Export
Preview Options panel. Then select Index
or Alpha Channel transparency* **(5.10)**.

Coloring Vector Objects continued

Choose Pattern (5.11) to fill the object with a bitmap pattern. Select the pattern in the Fill Name pop-up. It includes a preview of the selected pattern.

Choose one of the gradients (5.12) to fill the object with an editable gradient blend. Select a preset color combination in the Fill Name pop-up menu.

3. Choose Hard Edge, Anti-Alias, or Feather for the fill's edge type. If you choose Feather, set the amount by entering a value in pixels in the Amount of Feather field or using its pop-up slider (5.13).

You can use third-party textures and patterns that reside elsewhere on your system other than in the Fireworks\Settings folders by choosing File→Preferences→Folders and clicking the ... (ellipsis) button to browse to the folder that contains the files. The files must be in PNG format and will be accessible when you relaunch Fireworks.

To preview a fill before applying it to an object, click the triangle at the bottom of the Fill panel and uncheck Auto-Apply. Check changes in the preview window. Click Apply to add the fill to the selected object.

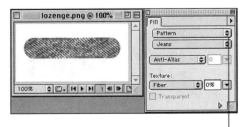

5.11   **Add new patterns by saving them as PNG files in the Fireworks\Settings\Patterns folder.**

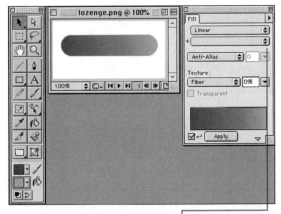

5.12   **Choosing a gradient blend without a preset color combination results in a blend using the colors in the Stroke and Fill color wells.**

**Feathering is applied equally to
both sides of an object's path.**

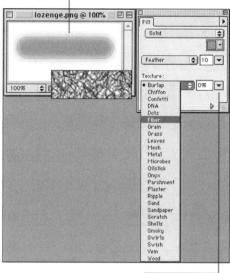

5.13   **Lower values result in subtle
textures. Higher values result in
contrasting textures.**

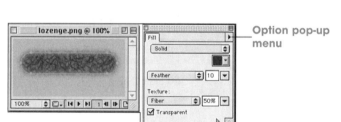

Option pop-up
menu

5.14

4. Modify solid, pattern, or gradient fills by selecting a texture in the Texture Name pop-up menu and entering a percentage in the Amount of Texture field or by using its pop-up slider. The Texture Name pop-up includes a preview of the selected texture.

5. Check the Transparent box to make the background visible through the texture (5.14).

 I P

Add your own textures by saving them as grayscale PNG files in the Fireworks\ Settings\Textures folder.

Ⓝ O T E

Save gradients for reuse in the same document by choosing Save Gradient As in the Fill panel Options pop-up menu. To use a saved gradient fill in another document, copy and paste an object that contains the fill into the new document. It will appear in the new document's Fill Name pop-up menu.

Outlining Vector Objects

Vector graphics can be outlined by any type of brush stroke, from one-pixel, aliased lines to bitmapped calligraphic brush strokes. Fireworks offers a large set of strokes that you can customize by changing their size, edge softness, and texture.

1. To change a selected vector object's outline, or stroke, choose Modify→Stroke. In the Stroke panel (5.15), select a style in the Stroke category pop-up menu. Choose None for no outline.

2. If you choose a style other than None, select a brush shape from the Stroke name pop-up menu (5.16).

3. Double-click the Stroke color well to select a color in the system color picker or click the pop-up arrow to use the Swatches palette.

4. Use the Edge Softness slider to blur the stroke (5.17).

5. Set the width of the stroke by entering a value in the Tip Size field or using the pop-up slider.

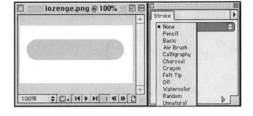

5.15

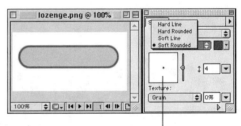

5.16

Tip Preview displays the selected stroke's tip.

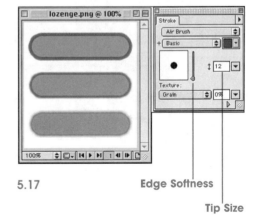

5.17

Edge Softness

Tip Size

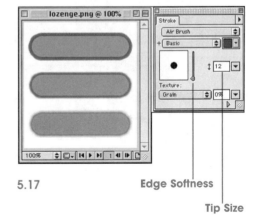 **O T E**

Save strokes for reuse in the same document by choosing Save Stroke As in the Stroke panel Options pop-up menu. Name the stroke in the Save Stroke dialog box and click OK.

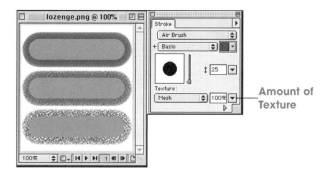

5.18

Opaque fills cover any part of a stroke inside an object's path. Partially transparent fills blend with any part of a stroke inside an object's path.

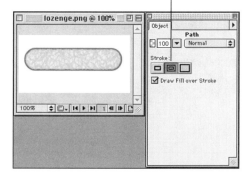

5.19

Amount of Texture

6. Modify the stroke by selecting a texture in the Texture Name pop-up menu (5.18).

7. Set the stroke's transparency by entering a percentage in the Amount of Texture field or using its pop-up slider.

8. To adjust the stroke's position on the object, double-click the object with the Pointer tool to bring up the Object Inspector (5.19). Under Stroke, choose Inside, Centered, or Outside to move the stroke in relation to the object's edge. Check the Draw Fill over Stroke box to have the fill cover the stroke inside the object.

 I P

To see the effect of adjusting the stroke's position, turn off the drawing path's visibility by choosing View→Hide Edges.

 O T E

To use a saved stroke in another document, copy and paste an object that contains it into the new document. The stroke will appear in the new document's Stroke Name pop-up menu in the Stroke panel.

Making Vector Objects Three-Dimensional

Turn vector objects into 3D buttons
with Fireworks' Live Effects.
Common effects such as bevels and
drop shadows are available in the
Effects panel, and when applied, are
always editable.

1. To add 3D effects to the button,
   choose Modify→Effect with
   the object selected. In the Effect
   panel (5.20), select an effect in
   the Effect category pop-up
   menu.

2. Choose Inner Bevel or Outer
   Bevel (5.21) for a standard 3D
   button. Select the bevel type in
   the Effect Name pop-up menu.

   Choose Drop Shadow (5.22) to
   float the button above the
   background. Select Basic or
   Soft in the Effect Name pop-up
   menu.

   Choose Emboss (5.23) to make
   the object a 3D mask for other
   objects and the background.
   Select Inset or Raised in the
   Effect Name pop-up menu.

   Choose Glow (5.24) to add
   a ring of color around the
   button. Select Basic or Halo in
   the Effect Name pop-up menu.

3. Set the width of bevels,
   embossing, or glows by
   entering a value in pixels in
   the Width field or using its
   pop-up slider.

5.20

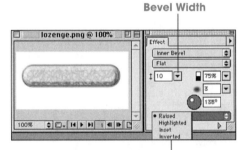

Bevel Width

5.21   **The Button Presets pop-up
menu offers four default
treatments for rollover
button states.**

**Set the shadow's distance
from the object in pixels.**

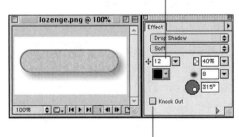

5.22   **Check to make the object
casting the shadow invisible.**

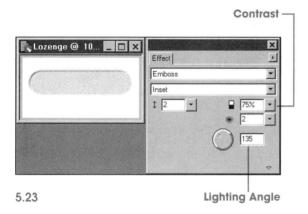

Contrast

Lighting Angle

5.23

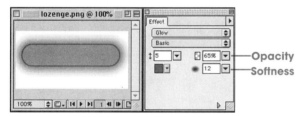

Opacity
Softness

5.24

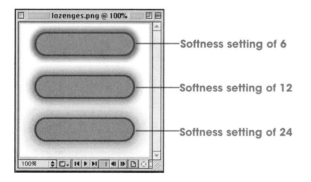

Softness setting of 6

Softness setting of 12

Softness setting of 24

5.25

4. Set the lighting intensity in bevels and embosses by entering a percentage in the Contrast field or by using its pop-up slider. Set the transparency of shadows and glows by entering a percentage in the Opacity field or by using its pop-up slider.

5. Select a color for outer bevels, shadows, and glows by double-clicking the color well to use the system color picker or click its pop-up arrow to use the Swatches palette.

6. Modify the effect's edges by entering a value in pixels in the Softness field or by using its pop-up slider (5.25).

7. Change the lighting angle in bevels, shadows, or embossing by entering a value in degrees in the Angle field or spinning the Lighting wheel.

continues

 I P

To copy all fill, stroke, and effect attributes from one object to another, select the object with the desired attributes and choose Edit→Copy. Then select the second object and choose Edit→Paste Attributes.

Making Vector Objects Three-Dimensional continued

8. Choose Multiple (5.26) in the Effect Name category to apply multiple effects to the button. Check the box next to each effect you want to apply. Each time you check an effect, make specific settings for that particular effect in the dialog box that opens.

9. If you have extra white space around the button, choose Modify→Document→Trim Canvas to have Fireworks trim the canvas to the button and its effects (5.27).

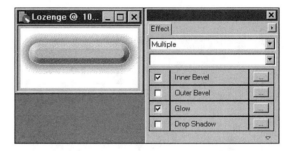

5.26

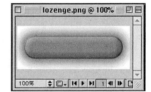

5.27

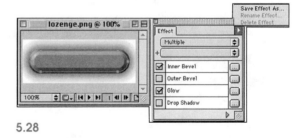

5.28

NOTE

Save single or multiple effects for reuse in the same document by choosing Save Effect As in the Effect panel Options pop-up menu (5.28). To use a saved effect in another document, copy and paste an object that contains the effect into the new document. It will appear in the new document's Effect Name pop-up menu in the Effect panel.

Adjusting Pattern and Gradient Fills

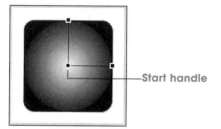

—Start handle

5.29

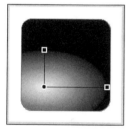

5.30

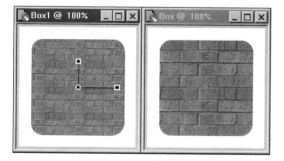

5.31

After applying a pattern or gradient fill to a vector object, adjust the fill's direction, scale, color, and skew. If you want a linear gradient that changes from top to bottom instead of from left to right, rotate the fill interactively. Instead of a gradient that covers the entire object, shorten the gradient's range to cover only part of the object. Distort a pattern fill by stretching or squeezing it. Use skewing to change the pattern's direction and distort it at once.

1. To adjust a selected object's pattern or gradient fill, choose the Paint Bucket tool.

2. To move the fill within the object, drag the round start handle that appears in the object (5.29).

3. To change the distance a gradient covers, drag a square end handle that appears on or near the object in or out on a straight line (5.30).

4. To change the size of a pattern, Shift-drag a square end handle in or out on a straight line (5.31).

continues

Adjusting Pattern and Gradient Fills continued

5. To distort a pattern, drag a square end handle in or out on a straight line **(5.32)**.

6. To skew the fill, drag a square end handle at an angle **(5.33)**.

7. To rotate the fill, move the Paint Bucket tool over the line connecting the start and end handles. When the cursor changes into a circular arrow, click and drag to change the fill's orientation **(5.34)**.

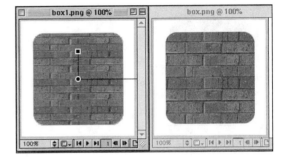

5.32

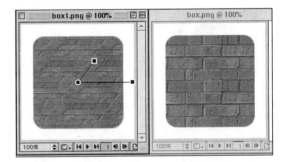

5.33

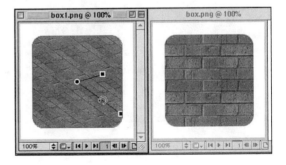

5.34

 I P

To remove pattern and gradient edits, double-click inside the object with the Paint Bucket tool.

Editing Gradient Fills

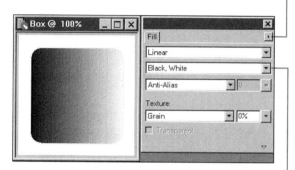

Options pop-up menu

5.35   Instead of picking colors in the Toolbox, you can select a preset color combination in the gradient colors pop-up menu.

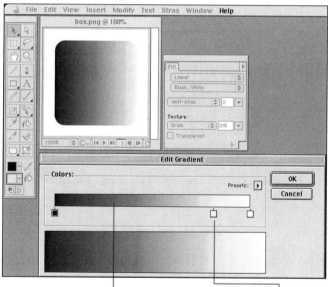

5.36   To add a new gradient color well, click in an empty space below the color ramp.

To delete a color well, drag it away from the color ramp.

To give vector objects the look of chrome or airbrushed contours, create custom color gradients or edit existing color gradients using the Fill panel. Save your custom gradients to use again within the same document or add to other documents.

1. To create a new gradient, select a vector object to fill, and then double-click the Brush color well in the Toolbox to select a starting color in the system color picker or click the Brush color pop-up arrow to use the Swatches palette.

2. Double-click the Fill color well in the Toolbox to select an end color in the system color picker or click the Fill color pop-up arrow to use the Swatches palette.

3. Select one of the preset gradients from the Fill category pop-up menu in the Fill panel (5.35) to set the gradient's direction.

4. To change the gradient's colors and range, choose Edit Gradient in the Fill Options pop-up menu.

5. In the Edit Gradient dialog box, click and drag a color well below the color ramp to change the distance of the blend (5.36).

continues

Editing Gradient Fills continued

6. To change a color in the gradient, double-click its color
well and select a color in the
Swatches palette (5.37).

7. When you have finished
adjusting the gradient's color
ramp, click OK.

8. To save the gradient within the
open document, choose Save
Gradient As in the Fill panel
Options pop-up menu (5.38).
In the Save Gradient dialog
box, name the fill and
click OK.

9. To use a saved gradient fill in
another document, copy and
paste an object that contains
that fill into the new document. The gradient name will
appear in the new document's
gradient color combinations
pop-up menu.

 I P

*If you plan to reuse the same gradient often
in other documents, save it as a Style. With
an object containing the gradient selected,
choose Window→Styles. In the Styles panel
Options pop-up menu, choose New Style. In
the Edit Style dialog box, name the style and
click OK.*

 O T E

*Use the Fill panel Options pop-up menu to
rename or delete any of the gradient color
combinations in the current document.*

**Click the Color Wheel to
access the system color picker.**

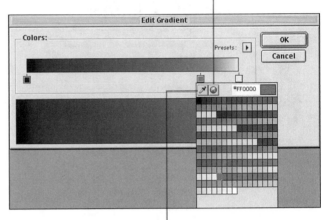

5.37

**Use the Eyedropper tool to
sample any visible color.**

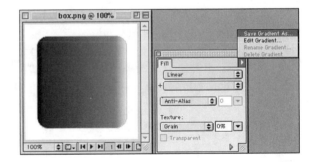

5.38

Defining and Using Styles

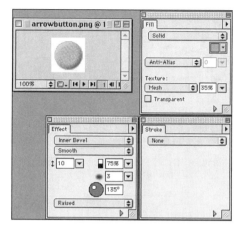

5.39

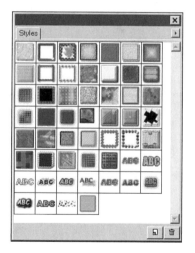

5.40

If you want to reuse your custom fills, strokes, and effects in other documents, save them as styles in the Styles panel. A style can include any combination of fill, stroke, and effect attributes. It can even include type specifications for text. Instead of copying and pasting objects that contain your formatting into new documents and then applying each attribute individually to new objects, you can simply apply a saved style to any object in any document and the object instantly updates to include whatever attributes are included. Multiple styles can be applied to an object.

1. To set a new style, create an object with the stroke, fill, and effect settings you want (5.39).

2. Choose Window→Styles to open the Styles panel (5.40).

3. With the object selected, click the New Style button at the bottom of the Styles panel .

continues

(T) I P

Fireworks comes with a default library of styles, but to avoid having your site look like everyone else's, edit the preset styles or delete them. You also can import more styles from the Fireworks CD and Macromedia's Web site.

Defining and Using Styles continued

4. In the Edit Style dialog box
(5.41), enter a name for the
style and check the properties
you want to apply with the
style. Click OK.

5. To apply the style to a selected
object, click its preview tile in
the Styles panel (5.42).

6. To edit a style, double-click it
in the Styles panel and make
changes in the Edit Style
dialog box.

7. To export a style, select it in the
Styles panel and choose Export
Styles from the Styles panel
Options pop-up menu (5.43).
To export multiple styles, hold
the Shift key as you select
styles. In the Export Selected
Styles As dialog box, name the
.stl file, choose a location for it,
and click Save (5.44).

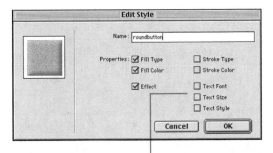

5.41 **Properties left unchecked will not be
applied to an object with the style.**

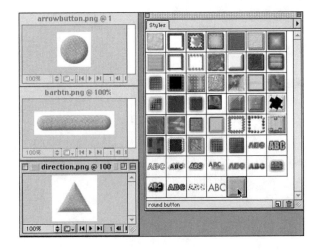

5.42

N O T E

*Fireworks doesn't track which styles are
applied to which objects. If a style is later
edited, objects that used that style don't
automatically update. You must apply the
revised style manually to update the objects.*

T I P

*You can't alter individual style attributes, such as the fill color or
stroke width, with Edit Style. You can only choose which style properties to include in the style. For example, include fill and effect
attributes, but not stroke attributes of a style, so that when you apply
it to other objects, those objects retain their stroke attributes, but copy
the fill and effects of the style. To alter individual style attributes, you
must create a new style using the Fill, Stroke, and Effect panels, and
save it in the Styles panel. Then delete the old style.*

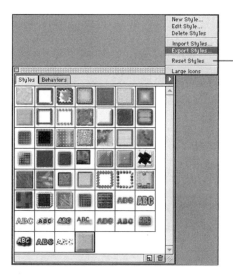

5.43

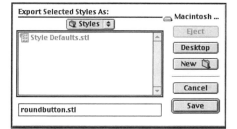

5.44

To reset styles to Fireworks' default library, choose Reset Styles from the Styles panel Options pop-up menu.

8. To import styles, choose Import Styles from the Styles panel Options pop-up menu. In the Open File dialog box, locate an .stl file and click Open. All the styles in the file will be appended to the bottom of the Style panel.

9. To delete a style, select it in the Styles panel and click the Delete Style button at the bottom of the Styles panel. To delete multiple styles, hold down the Shift key as you select styles, and then click the Delete Style button.

 I P

You don't have to create a style to share style attributes with another document or user. Copy an object that has the desired attributes and paste it into a new document. Any style attributes attached to the object appear in the appropriate Fill, Stroke, or Effect panel.

T I P

You can easily maintain visual consistency throughout a site or other project, even when more than one user is creating graphics, by exporting and importing styles for your graphics between users.

CHAPTER 6

U se Bézier path tools and automatic editing tools to create unique graphics. Fireworks' path tools are similar to those in other drawing programs: Draw paths by plotting points, and then customize them with fills, strokes, and Fireworks' Live Effects.

DRAWING AND EDITING VECTOR PATHS

In addition to the control offered with Bézier paths, you can use Fireworks' more intuitive tools, such as the Brush, Pencil, Freeform, and Reshape Area tools, to create and edit path objects without plotting points. If you prefer to use a digital pen and tablet instead of a mouse, these tools can be adjusted to respond to pressure input. If you don't use pressure-sensitive input devices, you can alter the weight of a stroke on a path manually to mimic the look of brush-and-ink illustrations.

Fireworks also offers automatic operations to smooth paths, change open paths into closed outline shapes, and create larger or smaller copies of objects that trace around the original object.

If you're a power user, create your own custom brush strokes and save them as styles to use in other documents. Alter the weight of a stroke on a path to mimic the look of brush-and-ink illustrations. Use a combination of path tools to create 3D spheres and other objects, which, like all Fireworks path objects, are always editable.

Drawing Paths

To create custom lines and shapes, use the Pen tool to draw paths by plotting points (6.1). Create straight or curved path segments by placing corner or curve points. Paths consist of up to three elements: anchor points, which are placed wherever the path ends or changes; path segments, which connect the points; and point handles on curve points only, which control the position and shape of curved path segments adjacent to a point.

1. To draw by plotting points, select the Pen tool in the Toolbox and click to establish a beginning point.

2. To create straight path segments, click the Pen tool to form corner points (6.2) where the path changes direction.

3. To draw a simple curved path segment from a corner point, click-hold the Pen tool where you want the curve's end point and drag (6.3) in the opposite direction of the desired curve. As you drag, handles appear on the point. To constrain curve handles to a 45° angle, hold the Shift key while dragging the point handle.

 **O T E**

When drawing paths, the fill defaults to none and the stroke defaults to the settings in the Stroke panel.

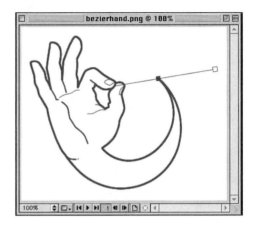

6.1

As you draw or edit points, Fireworks shows a preview of the path.

The currently active point is hollow.

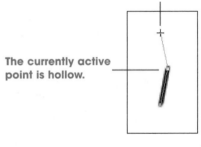

6.2

The length of the curve handle determines the curve's depth. Its angle determines the curve's slope.

6.3

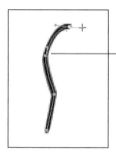

As you drag the end point, one of the beginning point's handles disappears. The remaining handle shows that point's direction.

6.4

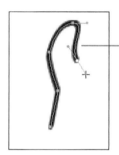

Dragging in a direction that is less than 90° different from the starting curve's direction results in an S-curve.

6.5

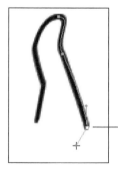

The two curve handles on a curve corner point are independent of each other.

6.6

To draw another simple curved path segment after creating a curve point, click-hold the Pen tool where you want the curve's end point and drag in the opposite or perpendicular to the direction you dragged the first curve point (6.4).

To draw an S-curve path segment, click-drag the Pen tool to create a starting curve point, and then click-hold the mouse where you want the curve's end point and drag in the same direction as you dragged the starting curve point (6.5).

To draw a curve corner, start from either a curve or corner point, and then click-drag the Pen tool to start a new curve point. Without releasing the mouse, hold (Option)[Alt] while dragging the curve handle on the curve point (6.6).

continues

 I P

To draw simple straight lines, click-drag with the Line tool. Constrain the line to 45-degree angles by holding Shift while dragging. To add to the path, click an end point with the Pen tool and continue drawing.

 I P

Use curve corner points when you want to change the direction of a curve, such as when you want to created a scalloped edge.

Drawing Paths continued

4. To end an open path, double-click the Pen tool. If the last point was dragged to create curve handles, move the Pen tool back over the point until a small arrow appears next to the cursor **(6.7)** and double-click.

To close a path instead, click the starting point when a solid square appears next to the cursor **(6.8)**.

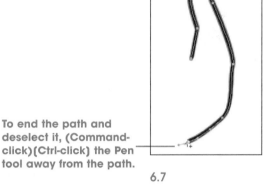

To end the path and deselect it, (Command-click)(Ctrl-click) the Pen tool away from the path.

6.7

(N) O T E

The Pen cursor includes an open box before starting a new path .

The Pen cursor includes an arrow when it's over a point indicating that click-dragging here results in a curve point .

The Pen cursor includes a solid square when it's over an end point indicating that clicking here results in a closed path .

6.8

(T) I P

Draw freeform paths with the Brush or Pencil tool by click-dragging a path in one stroke **(6.9)**. *Fireworks plots the points in the path for you. Constrain lines to horizontal or vertical absolutes by Shift-click-dragging. To end an open path, release the mouse button. To close a path, return to the path's starting point and release when the cursor contains a black square. The Brush tool defaults to the Stroke panel settings. The Pencil tool defaults to a one-pixel, hard-edged line.*

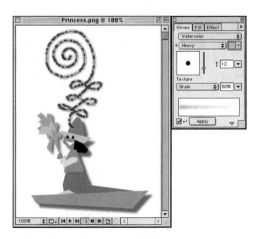

6.9

Editing Vector Objects Point-by-Point

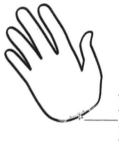

To temporarily access the Subselect tool while using the Pen tool, hold down (Command)(Ctrl).

6.10

Selected points look hollow.

6.11

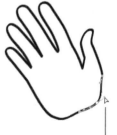

6.12   To constrain curve handles to their original angle, (Option-Shift) (Alt+Shift)-click-drag a point's handle.

For maximum control when customizing vector objects, edit the individual points that make up the objects' paths. In addition to moving points, you can adjust curves by using point handles, convert curve points to corner points and vice versa, and add or delete points.

1. To move a point in a path, use the Subselect tool to click and drag the point (6.10).

   To move more than one point at a time, use the Subselect tool to Shift-click the individual points or drag a selection area around the points (6.11). Then click and drag on one of the points.

2. To adjust a path segment's curve, use the Subselect tool to click an adjacent point, and then drag its handle (6.12).

continues

 O T E

Corner points are where two straight path segments meet. Create a corner point by clicking with the Pen tool. Curve points are where the path bends. Create a curve point by click-dragging with the Pen tool. Curve-corner points are where a curved segment meets another curved segment or a straight segment. Create a curve-corner point by click-dragging a curve, and before releasing the mouse, hold (Option)[Alt] while dragging to make the two curve point handles independent from each other.

Editing Vector Objects Point-by-Point continued

3. To convert a corner point to a curve point, click it with the Pen tool and drag out the handles (6.13).

   To convert a curve point to a corner point, click it once to select it, and then double-click it with the Pen tool.

   To convert a corner or curve point to a curve corner point, click it once to select it, and then click and drag a handle. After a handle appears, hold (Option)[Alt] and move the handle independently of the point's other handle (6.14).

4. To insert a point into an existing path, click the path with the Pen tool (6.15).

6.13

6.14

 T I **P**

To alter portions of a selected path without adjusting points, use the Redraw Path tool from the Brush tool pop-up group in the Toolbox. Click the Redraw Path tool on the segment you want to alter, and then drag the new path and release. Fireworks plots the necessary points to create the new path.

The Pen cursor changes into a cross with an insert caret when it's over a selected path.

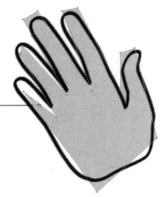

6.15

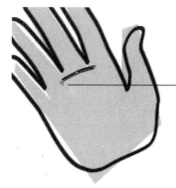

The Pen cursor changes into a cross with an X when it's over a point of a selected path.

6.16

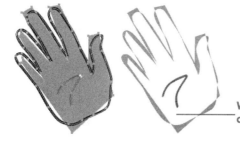

When you join shapes or closed paths, any areas that overlap are deleted.

6.17

To access the Knife tool, you must first select a path object.

6.18

5. To extend an existing open path, select it and click an end point with the Pen tool and continue drawing (6.16).

6. To connect paths or combine objects into a composite, use the Subselect tool to select the paths' endpoints you want to join or select the objects and choose Modify→Join (6.17). The composite object will have the style attributes of the bottom image.

7. To split a selected path, drag the Knife tool across it to slice it into two or more paths (6.18).

  O T E

To delete a point, select it with the Subselect tool and press (Delete)[Backspace].

 **O T E**

To split a composite object into its source objects, select the composite and choose Modify→Split.

Pushing and Pulling Vector Objects

Manually adding points and altering point handles can be a slow, laborious process. If you don't need that level of control, use the Freeform tool instead to push or pull any part of the path. It automatically adds and adjusts the path's points for you as you click-drag. If you use a pressure-sensitive input device, you can adjust the tool's size with pressure as you click-drag.

Check Pressure to control tool size with a pressure-sensitive pen.
Check Preview to see the results of using the Freeform tool as you drag it.

6.19

1. To push or pull a selected path, choose the Freeform tool from the reshape tool group.

2. Double-click the Freeform tool button to open the Tool Options panel (6.19) and enter a value in pixels in the Size field or use the pop-up slider.

3. To push a segment, click outside the selected line and drag into it (6.20).

4. To pull a segment, move the cursor onto the center of the segment to be pulled, and then click-drag to reshape the path (6.21).

The Freeform tool changes into an open circle when it is clicked outside a path.

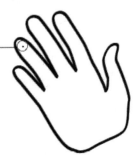

6.20

6.21 The Freeform tool changes into an open arrow with an S next to it when it is over a selected path.

(T) I P

If you are not using a pressure-sensitive pen, you can decrease the Freeform tool size interactively by pressing 1 or the left cursor key while holding the mouse button. To increase its size, press 2 or the right cursor key while holding the mouse button.

Reshaping Vector Objects

Check Strength to control the strength of the effect with a pressure-sensitive pen.

6.22 **Check Size to control tool size with a pressure-sensitive pen.**

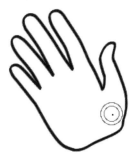

6.23

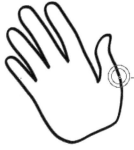

Lower strength percentages make a smoother transition between reshaped segments and the rest of the path. Higher percentages make sharper transitions.

6.24

For a more subtle reshaping action than the Freeform tool's, choose the Reshape Area tool. Instead of just one blunt cursor, the Reshape Area tool offers a two-step graduated cursor. The inner circle is the tool at full strength, the outer circle is the maximum area affected, and the strength of the tool fades between the two circles.

1. To push or pull a selected path, double-click the Reshape Area tool from the reshape/scrub tool group to open the Tool Options panel.

2. Enter a value in pixels in the Size field or use the pop-up slider to set the overall tool size (6.22). Enter a value in the Effect Strength field or use the pop-up slider to set the size of the inner circle of the tool.

3. To push a segment, click outside the selected line and drag into it (6.23).

4. To pull a segment, move the cursor onto the center of the segment to be pulled, and then click-drag to reshape the path (6.24).

(T) I P

To decrease the Reshape Area tool size interactively, press 1 or the left cursor key while holding the mouse button. To increase its size, press 2 or the right cursor key while holding the mouse button.

Mimicking Pressure-Sensitive Brush Strokes

You can mimic the effect of using a pressure-sensitive pen with the Path Scrubber tool (6.25). The Path Scrubber tools affect only paths that have pressure-sensitive brush strokes and only to the extent of the selected stroke's parameters, such as brush size and ink opacity. Pressure-sensitive strokes are depicted as tapering or fading in the previews at the bottom of the Stroke panel and the Edit Stroke panel. Strokes that are not pressure-sensitive are unaffected by the Path Scrubber tools.

6.25

1. To edit a stroke's appearance on a path, select the path with the Pointer tool (6.26).

2. Choose the + or - Path Scrubber tool in the Edit Line pop-up group in the Toolbox and double-click it.

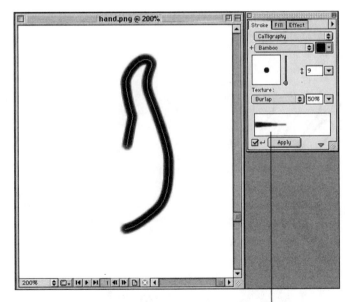

6.26

A preview stroke that tapers or fades demonstrates the sensitivity settings that apply if you're using a pressure-sensitive pen.

(N) O T E

The Path Scrubber tools alter paths drawn in the Document window. To change a brush stroke's default settings or create your own brush strokes, see "Designing Custom Brush Strokes" in Chapter 10, "Customizing Tools and Materials."

6.27

Enter a value from one to ten to set the strength at which the tool increases or decreases its pressure and speed characteristics while scrubbing.

3. In the Tool Options panel (6.27), check Pressure to affect the stroke's pressure characteristics while scrubbing. Check Speed to affect the stroke's speed characteristics while scrubbing.

4. To pinch (compress) a path, move the – Path Scrubber tool across the path (6.28).

5. To swell (expand) a path, move the + Path Scrubber tool along the path (6.29).

For a clear view of the Path Scrubber tool's effect, turn off the drawing path's visibility (View→Hide Edges).

6.28

To switch temporarily between + and – Path Scrubber tools, hold (Option)(Alt).

6.29

Ⓣ I P

A stroke cannot expand or darken beyond its maximum default setting. To imitate calligraphy, use the - Path Scrubber tool across the entire path to compress it before using the + Path Scrubber tool to swell particular areas.

Ⓣ I P

If you want strokes to expand and contract as you draw, choose a stroke that tapers off in the Stroke panel preview window. Select the Brush tool and use a pressure-sensitive pen to draw. If you use a mouse instead, you can achieve the same results by pressing the left-arrow key while drawing with the Brush tool to taper the stroke off, or by pressing the right-arrow key to expand the stroke.

Editing Vector Objects Automatically

You can automatically alter a vector object with Fireworks' Alter Path commands. Smooth paths by removing points with the Simplify command, convert the stroke on an open path into a closed shape with the Expand Stroke command, and create expanded or contracted copies of closed shapes with the Inset Path command. Inset Path is different from scaling an image because it traces the original path at a set distance and simplifies it, instead of scaling the object from a single point.

1. To smooth a selected vector path, choose Modify→Alter Path→Simplify, and then enter an amount in the Simplify dialog box field or use the pop-up slider (6.30) and click OK.

2. To change a path into a closed outline shape, choose Modify→Alter Path→Expand Stroke, and then enter an amount in pixels in the Width field of the Expand Stroke dialog box or use the pop-up slider (6.31).

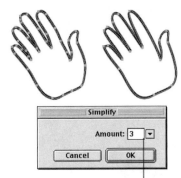

6.30 **Higher Simplify values eliminate more points and result in more distortion.**

The outline object defaults to the style attributes of the original path.

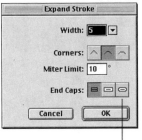

6.31 **Choose a shape for end caps on the path.**

 I P

If you use the Brush tool or Pencil tool to draw paths, use the Simplify command to eliminate unneeded points that were plotted automatically.

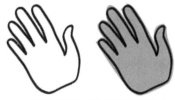

Create rough cut-out fills for outline shapes with inset paths by filling the inset with a solid color, no stroke, and then pasting the original outline shape over the inset shape.

6.32

Choose a corner shape and set corner sharpness with the Miter Limit. Click OK when you finish making your selections.

3. To make an expanded or contracted copy of a closed shape, choose Modify→Alter Path→Inset Path. In the Inset Path dialog box, choose whether the new object will follow inside or outside the original object's path (6.32). Set the distance in pixels away from the original path in the Width field or use the pop-up slider. Choose a corner shape, and then set corner sharpness in the Miter Limit field. Click OK.

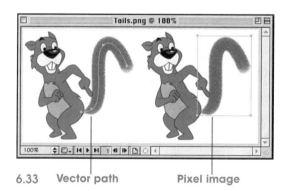

6.33   **Vector path**   **Pixel image**

 O T E

Only paths drawn in object mode can be edited as paths. Using the Brush, Pen, Line, or Shape tool in image edit mode, which is denoted by a black and blue striped border around the document, paints pixels onto the open image and can be edited only as pixels, not paths (6.33).

CHAPTER 7

In this chapter you learn how to...

Transform Vector Objects

Align, Arrange, and Group Objects

Combine Vector Objects

Clip an Image to a Shape

Blend Color Objects

Make Line Art Dimensional

Manage Objects with Layers

Simple shapes are a great timesaver and point-by-point drawing gives you the ultimate in control, but you can also build interesting forms easily by transforming and combining objects. Objects can be interactively or numerically scaled and rotated, so you can fine-tune as you transform or work to a numerical specification. Objects can also be slanted, distorted, flipped, and combined into unique shapes.

MANIPULATING AND ORGANIZING OBJECTS

Use Fireworks' transformation operations to increase your productivity: Build one side of a graphic, and then mirror it to complete the other half by cloning and flipping. Create the steps in an animation by cloning and transforming an object multiple times. Make kaleidoscope images by repeatedly scaling, rotating, and flipping simple objects.

Use Fireworks' automatic operations to arrange, align, and group vector objects and bitmap images. Cut bitmap images into interesting shapes by clipping them inside vector objects. Create color-blended objects interactively with object-level blending that is similar to Photoshop's layer-blending modes.

Use a combination of path tools to create 3D spheres and other objects, which like all Fireworks path objects, are always editable. Organize multiple objects on layers to separate different button states, changing elements from static ones in updatable graphics, or other logical subgroups.

Transforming Vector Objects

Vector objects can be transformed into unique shapes with the Scale, Skew, and Distort tools. Although they are similar to tools in other drawing and painting programs, Fireworks' versions are simple and intuitive: no Shift or (Option)[Alt]-click and drag. The cursor changes as you move it around the selected object(s), and that determines which operation is performed as you inter-actively edit.

In addition to the tools in the Toolbox, Fireworks offers more transformation operations under the Modify menu. Use numeric transfor-mations to size or rotate objects a specific amount, and flip objects to create mirror images.

1. To resize a selected vector object proportionally, choose the Scale tool 🔲 and click-drag a corner handle (7.1).

   To stretch a selected object verti-cally or horizontally, choose the Scale tool and click-drag a top, bottom, or side handle (7.2).

2. Double-click to apply the effect.

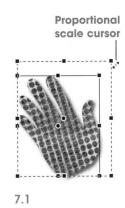

Proportional scale cursor

7.1

Vertical Scale cursor

Scale attributes turned on   **Horizontal Scale cursor**   **Scale attributes turned off**

7.2

Ⓣ I P

Move transformed objects by click-dragging the cursor inside a selected object when the cross arrows cursor 🕂 *appears.*

7.3   Copy, color, skew, and scale
an object to create a shadow.
Then paste the original on top
of the shadow.

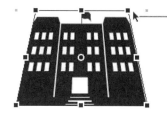

Use corner skewing to create
one-point perspective.

7.4

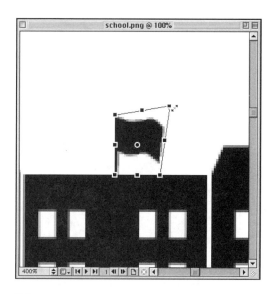

7.5

3. To slant a selected object along
   one axis, choose the Skew tool
    from the Transform tools
   pop-up and click-drag a side,
   top, or bottom handle (7.3).
   Double-click to apply the effect.

4. To apply perspective to a
   selected object, choose the
   Skew tool from the Transform
   tools pop-up and click-drag a
   corner handle (7.4). Double-
   click to apply the effect.

5. To freely reshape a selected
   object, choose the Distort tool
   from the Transform tools
   pop-up and click-drag any
   handle (7.5). Double-click to
   apply the effect.

6. To rotate a selected object,
   choose any transform tool, and
   then move the cursor outside the
   object and click-drag when the
   circle arrow cursor appears.

continues

(N) O T E

*To resize a selected object numerically,
choose Modify→Transform→Numeric
Transform. In the Numeric Transform dialog
box pop-up, choose Scale to resize by a percentage or Resize to size to a dimension, and
enter a value in the Width or Height field.
Check Constrain Proportions to scale the
width and height proportionally. Check Scale
Attributes to size the object's style attributes
proportionally. Click OK.*

Transforming Vector Objects continued

To rotate the object around an axis different from the object's center, drag the center point to a different location, and then rotate **(7.6)**. To return the center point to the object's center, double-click the point.

7. Double-click to apply the effect.

8. To rotate a selected object a set amount, choose Modify→ Transform and then select Rotate 180°, Rotate 90° CW (clockwise), or Rotate 90° CCW (counterclockwise) **(7.7)**.

9. To flip a selection, choose Modify→ Transform and then select Flip Horizontal or Flip Vertical **(7.8)**.

 I P

Copy and paste when you want to perform intermediate edits, such as coloring and skewing a shadow. For one-step copying and pasting, select an object and choose Edit→ Clone. To make a copy offset from the original, choose Edit→Duplicate.

 **O T E**

To rotate a selected object by a degree, choose Modify→Transform→Numeric Transform. In the Numeric Transform dialog box pop-up, choose Rotate and enter a degree in the Angle field or spin the degree wheel. Check Scale Attributes to have the object's fill, stroke, and effects rotate with it. Click OK.

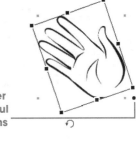

Changing an object's center point before rotating is useful for animating simple motions such as a hand wave.

7.6

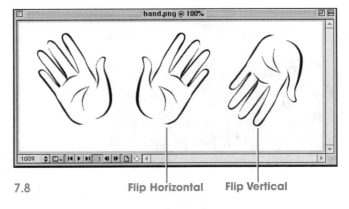

Rotate 180°

Rotate 90° cw

7.7

Rotate 90° ccw

7.8

Flip Horizontal   Flip Vertical

Aligning, Arranging, and Grouping Objects

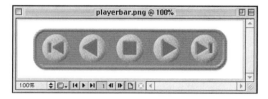

7.9

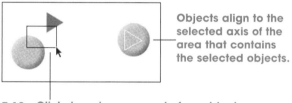

Objects align to the
selected axis of the
area that contains
the selected objects.

7.10   **Click-dragging over part of an object
with the Pointer tool selects it.**

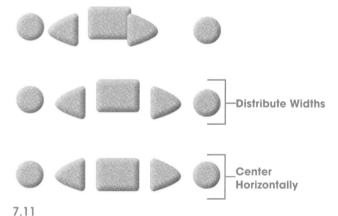

—Distribute Widths

—Center
Horizontally

7.11

Whenever you get more than one
object on the screen at a time, you
need to arrange them in relation to
one another. Even a simple navigation bar with VCR-type buttons can
quickly become complex (7.9). As
you create the individual pieces that
make up the buttons and the bar,
organize them by arranging,
aligning, and grouping them.
Grouping refers to binding individual objects together so that they
retain their individual style attributes, but move, resize, and otherwise transform together.

1. To assemble a compound
   object, create or import the
   individual pieces in any order
   in one file.

2. To align selected objects to one
   another (7.10), choose Modify→
   Align and then select Left,
   Right, Top, Bottom, Center
   Horizontally, or Center
   Vertically.

3. To evenly space selected
   objects along an axis (7.11),
   choose Modify→Align and
   then select Distribute Widths
   (horizontal) or Distribute
   Heights (vertical).

continues

Ⓣ I P

*If an object you want to move is covered by
another object, use the Select Behind tool from
the Pointer tool group in the Toolbox* *.*

Aligning, Arranging, and Grouping Objects continued

4. To change the stacking order of a selected object or group of objects, choose Modify→ Arrange and then select: Bring to Front, Bring Forward, Send Backward, Send to Back **(7.12)**.

5. To group selected objects together **(7.13)**, choose Modify→ Group.

6. To select an object within a group, click it with the Subselect tool **(7.14)**.

To adjust visual centering, use the keyboard's arrow keys to nudge a selected object one pixel at a time.

7.12

To select an object behind another object within a group, hold (Option)(Alt) as you click the group with the Select Behind tool.

To ungroup objects, select the group and choose Modify→Ungroup.

7.13

To inset the arrow, copy it, choose Emboss in the Effect panel, and then paste. The original arrow pastes exactly in place over its embossing.

7.14

 **O T E**

Objects are stacked on a layer in the order in which they are created. Even if they do not overlap, the most recently created object will be on top in the stacking order.

 I P

On Windows, you also can use the Front/Back and Forward/Backward buttons on the Modify toolbar to arrange objects.

Combining Vector Objects

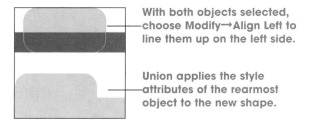

With both objects selected, choose Modify→Align Left to line them up on the left side.

Union applies the style attributes of the rearmost object to the new shape.

7.15

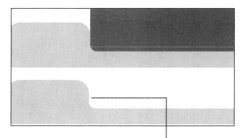

7.16   Punch knocks the topmost object out of the object(s) behind it, leaving their style attributes unchanged.

Intersect applies the style attributes of the rearmost object to the new shape.

7.17

Crop deletes the topmost object (here a copy of an object) and leaves the style attributes of the remaining objects unchanged.

7.18

Fireworks offers four easy ways to merge two or more vector objects to create more unique shapes. Union combines them into a single object. Intersect combines only the areas of the shapes that overlap into a single object. Punch uses the front object to knock out any parts of objects behind it. Crop uses the front object to remove any parts of objects outside itself.

1. To create a compound shape from two or more closed vector objects, draw and arrange the objects to overlap, and then select them by click-dragging over them with the Pointer tool.

2. Choose Modify→Combine→ Union to combine the shapes into a single shape (7.15).

3. Choose Modify→Combine→ Punch to delete the front object and any parts of objects that are behind it (7.16).

4. Choose Modify→Combine→ Intersect to create a shape that includes only areas that overlap (7.17).

5. Choose Modify→Combine→ Crop to delete the front object and any parts of shapes that are outside the front object's area (7.18).

Clipping an Image to a Shape

Fireworks' Modify operations, Union, Punch, Intersect, and Crop, don't work with bitmaps, or image objects. If you want to place a photograph inside an oval window, for example, use Firework's Paste Inside operation. You can, however, fill any vector object, whether it's a simple closed path, a compound shape, or text, with another object or image, by making the vector object a mask that clips the other object or image to its shape.

1. In an open document that contains the image to be clipped, draw or import a closed vector object to be the window, or mask object. Position the mask object over the part of the image you want to clip (7.19).

2. With the mask object selected, choose Solid black in the Fill panel, and then choose None in the Stroke and Effect panels.

3. With the image selected, choose Edit→Cut (7.20).

7.19   **If the document is surrounded by a blue and black striped border, click the Stop button to exit image edit mode before drawing the vector object.**

7.20

(N)OTE

To remove the cut object from the mask object, choose Modify→Ungroup.

7.21

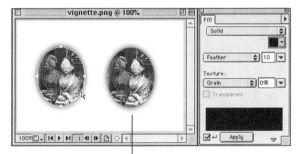

7.22   **The mask is feathered,
but the photograph is not.**

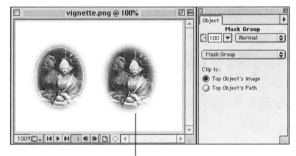

7.23   **With the photograph clipping to the
feathered mask's image, it fades
smoothly into the background.**

4. Select the mask object and
choose Edit→Paste Inside.
The cut object pastes inside
the selected object in the same
position from which it was
cut (**7.21**).

5. To edit or reposition either
object, select it with the
Subselect tool, and then make
edits or move the object.

6. To make the shape a vignette
that fades into the background,
select the mask object with the
Subselect tool (**7.22**). In the Fill
Panel, change its fill edge to
feather and set a feather
amount.

7. Double-click the cropped
object with the Pointer tool to
open the Object Inspector.
Under Clip To, choose Top
Object's Image (**7.23**).

 O T E

*When you paste an object inside a vector
object, choose Clipping to Top Object's
Image to make the top object an alpha mask
so that its fill becomes a grayscale screen
through which the other object is seen; or
choose Clipping to Top Object's Path to
make the top object's path a border within
which the other object is 100% visible and
outside of which it's invisible.*

Blending Color Objects

Create unique color treatments where objects overlap with blending modes and transparency. Blending modes determine how the color or colors of a selected object (the blend color) interacts with the color or colors of objects behind it (the base color), including the document's canvas.

Default opacity of 100% is completely opaque. Opacity of 0% is completely transparent.

7.24

1. To set the transparency of an object, double-click the object to open the Object Inspector, and then enter a value in the Object-level Opacity field or use the pop-up slider (7.24).

2. To set a selected object's blending mode, select a blend type in the Blending Mode pop-up menu in the Object Inspector.

   - Choose Normal, the default, to apply no blending effect to the selected object.

   - Choose Multiply to combine the blend color with the base color, resulting in darker colors.

   - Choose Screen to combine the inverse of the blend color with the base color, resulting in lighter colors (7.25).

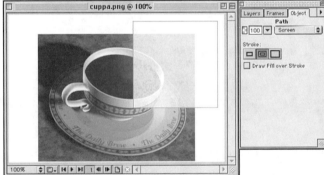

7.25

 I P

Transparency and color blend effects produce colors that are not Web-safe. Choose an adaptive palette when exporting as a GIF or 8-bit PNG to minimize dithering.

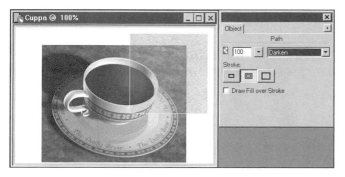

7.26

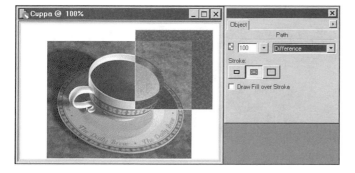

7.27

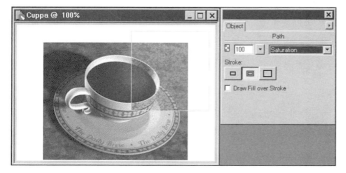

7.28

- Choose Darken to select the darker of the blend color and base color as the result (7.26).

- Choose Lighten to select the lighter of the blend color and base color as the result.

- Choose Difference to subtract the color with less brightness from the color with more brightness (7.27).

- Choose Hue to combine the hue value of the blend color with the luminance and saturation of the base color.

- Choose Saturation to combine the saturation of the blend color with the luminance and hue of the base color (7.28).

- Choose Color to combine the hue and saturation of the blend color with the luminance of the base color, for coloring monochrome images and tinting color images.

continues

 O T E

Fireworks' blending modes differ from Photoshop's in one important way: In Photoshop, everything on a layer has the same blending mode. In Fireworks, objects that reside on the same layer can have different opacity and blending modes.

Blending Color Objects continued

- Choose Luminosity to combine the luminance of the blend color with the hue and saturation of the base color **(7.29)**.

- Choose Invert to invert the base color **(7.30)**.

- Choose Tint to use the blend color to tint or tone the base color. Lighter blend colors result in lighter tints. Darker blend colors result in darker tones.

- Choose Erase to remove the blend and base colors to reveal the canvas color.

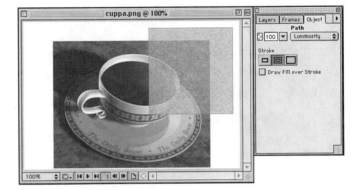

7.29

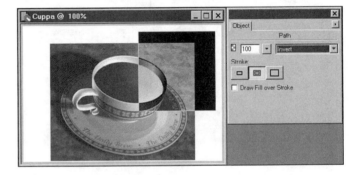

7.30

 I P

To create a duotone from a grayscale image, draw an object to cover the image and fill it with the duotone's second color. Set the object's blend mode to Tint and adjust its opacity.

T I P

To set the opacity or blending mode of multiple objects, group the objects (Modify→ Group), and then modify them in the Object Inspector. If you ungroup the objects, they will return to their original opacity and blending modes.

Making Line Art Dimensional

If you are making a sphere, choose Radial for the fill type.

Set the shape's stroke to None.

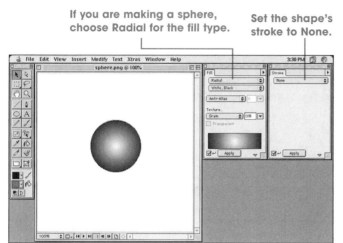

7.31

7.32

7.33   If you are exporting the shape as a GIF, add some texture to reduce banding.

Fireworks' Live Effects are great for making 3D buttons, but you also can make 3D spheres and more complex objects using custom gradient and pattern fills, textures, mask groups, blend modes, and some of Fireworks' automatic operations. Add finishing touches, such as highlights, with the brush tool set to airbrush.

1. Create a vector shape. In the Fill panel (Window→Fill), choose a gradient in the fill category and White, Black in Fill Name. Set the texture amount to 0% (7.31).

2. Select the Paint Bucket tool to turn on the fill's edit handles and move the start circle handle to where you want a highlight and the square handle(s) to where you want the darkest shading (7.32).

3. Choose Edit→Clone.

4. In the Fill panel, choose Solid in Fill Category and choose a color in the Fill color well or pop-up palette (7.33).

5. To add shading to the object, choose Edit→Clone again.

continues

Blending Color Objects continued

6. Choose Modify→Alter Path→Inset Path. Select Outside for Direction; set Width at 10 **(7.34)**.

7. In the Fill panel, choose None in Fill Category.

8. In the Stroke panel, select Air Brush in the Brush Category pop-up menu and choose a dark color in the Stroke color well or pop-up palette. Set the shading depth in the Tip Size pop-up slider **(7.35)**.

9. Double-click the shading path to open the Object Inspector and set the stroke to draw inside the path.

10. Move the shading path close to the side of the object opposite the light source **(7.36)**. Adjust the path, if needed, to shade the object correctly.

7.34

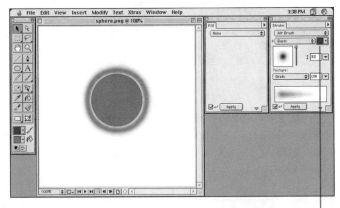

7.35

Instead of choosing black, pick a color that is a dark shade of the object's solid color.

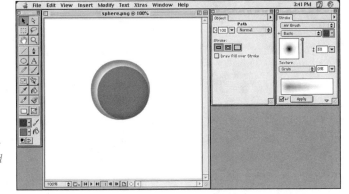

7.36

(T) I P

If your shape is smaller than 70 pixels wide, use a Live Effect instead of Inset Path to add dimension. Select the solid color clone, choose Smooth Inner Bevel in the Effect panel, and set the bevel width to half the shape's width.

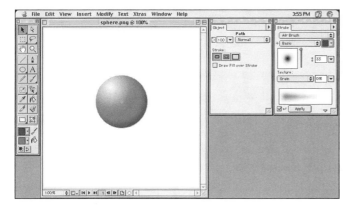

7.37

11. Cut the shading path, select the solid-color object and choose Edit→Paste Inside. Adjust the shadow, if necessary, by selecting the path with the Subselect tool.

12. Choose Modify→Arrange→ Send to Back.

13. Click-drag to select all and choose Modify→Mask Group (7.37).

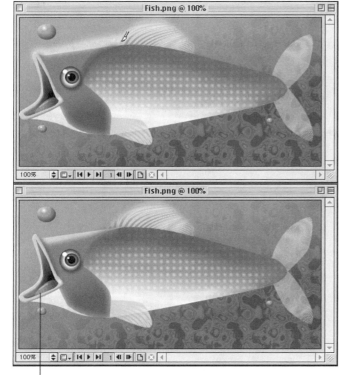

7.38 | **For more control creating highlights and shading, use the Pen tool.**

(N) O T E

If you are making an irregular shape (7.38), add custom highlights and shading with the Brush tool set to Air Brush in the Stroke panel. Set the stroke's color and width, choose View→Hide Edges, and then click-drag highlights or shading with the Brush tool. Cut the new path(s), select the object, and choose Edit→Paste Inside.

Managing Objects with Layers

To further organize your work beyond arranging objects in relation to one another, use layers to separate multiple graphics. Fireworks' layers (transparent fields through which objects on other layers are visible) are similar to layers in other drawing programs, with one addition: Fireworks adds a top layer, called the Web layer, to every document opened or created in Fireworks. This layer is reserved for Web objects, such as hot spots and slices, and cannot be deleted.

1. To organize graphics on layers, choose Window→Layers in an open document to open the Layers panel. Two default layers are listed in the Layers panel—the Web Layer and a layer for art (7.39).

2. To name a layer, double-click it in the Layers Panel, and then name it in the Layer Options dialog box (7.40).

3. To rearrange layers, select one and drag it to another place in the list (7.41).

 **N** O T E

Aligning, punching, cropping, or color-blending objects work the same whether they are on the same layer or different layers. Rearranging the stacking order of objects is restricted to single layers only. Grouping or combining using the Union or Intersect commands moves objects that are on different layers to the top layer.

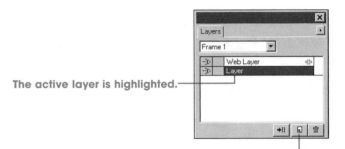

The active layer is highlighted.

7.39 **To add a layer, click the New Layer icon. To duplicate a layer, drag it to the New Layer icon.**

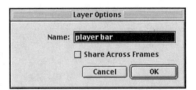

7.40

7.41 **To discard a layer, select it and click the Trash Can icon.**

To hide or reveal a layer, click its "eye" icon.

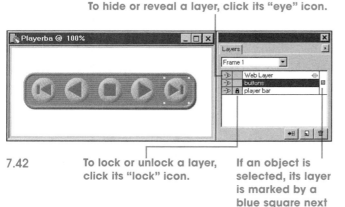

7.42

To lock or unlock a layer, click its "lock" icon.

If an object is selected, its layer is marked by a blue square next to its name.

4. To change to a different layer (7.42), click that layer in the Layers panel or click an object in the Document window that is on that layer.

5. To flatten a layered document, choose Modify→Merge Layers. Each object remains separate and editable but they all move to the bottommost layer, and the other layers, except the Web layer, are deleted.

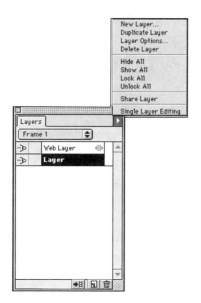

7.43

(T) I P

You also can use the Layers panel Options pop-up menu to perform layer management tasks, such as turning on Single Layer Editing to have edits affect only the active layer (7.43).

(N) O T E

Merge layers to minimize layer bloat and help organize complicated artwork. For example, if you initially created a single button state on multiple layers, merge them and then duplicate that layer. Edit the art on the new second layer to create the second button state. If you want to hide or lock either button state, you have only one layer to deal with. To export, choose File→Export Special→Export As Files and choose Layers to create the files from. Each button state exports as a separate file.

CHAPTER 8

In this chapter you learn how to...

Switch Between Modes

Select Pixels

Transform Pixel Selections

Feather Edges of a Selection

Fill Pixel Areas with Color

Paint Pixels

Apply Effects to an Image Object

Mask an Image with an Alpha Channel

In addition to being a robust Web optimization and vector-drawing program, Fireworks also offers a comprehensive set of tools for painting and editing bitmap images. Bitmaps are composed of pixels—small squares of color like tiles in a mosaic—which are clearly visible at high magnifications. If you currently use Photoshop or another image-editing program to edit scans or paint illustrations, you can easily switch to Fireworks to create your bitmaps.

PAINTING AND EDITING PIXEL IMAGES

To edit pixels in Fireworks, you must be in image edit mode instead of object mode. Although the same tool can be used in either mode, the results are different. If you draw a stroke with the brush tool in object mode, the stroke is a path, which is always editable. If you draw a stroke with the brush tool in image edit mode, the stroke looks the same but it is a bitmap image, which can be edited only on a pixel level.

Fireworks' image mode is similar to using an image-editing program such as Photoshop. Like Photoshop, you can paint and edit on a pixel level, skew or otherwise transform parts of an image, feather or blur the edges of an image, and create and apply alpha-channel masks. Unlike Photoshop, you can also enhance your pixel images with Live Effects, Fireworks' editable 3D glows, bevels, and embossing effects.

Switching Between Modes

Fireworks offers two image-creation modes: object mode for manipulating both vectors and pixel images as objects, and image edit mode for painting and editing pixels (8.1).

Bitmap graphics, such as GIFs, JPEGs, PNGs, and scanned images, open automatically in image edit mode. Layered Photoshop files open in object mode but can be double-clicked to access image edit mode.

1. To edit a bitmap object in image edit mode, double-click it with the Pointer tool (8.2).

2. To convert a selected vector object or objects to a pixel image, choose Modify→Merge Images.

Object mode

Image edit mode

8.1

You can also double-click a bitmap object with the Select Behind or Subselect tool to switch into image edit mode.

8.2

If you prefer to have bitmap files open in object mode, choose File→Preferences→ Editing and deselect Open in Image Edit Mode.

In object mode, pixel images have a rectangular bounding box. In image edit mode, the document is surrounded by a black-and-blue striped border. When you switch back to object mode, any empty space around the selected image is trimmed off.

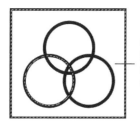

Using a selection tool in object mode switches you to image edit mode with the selected shape surrounded by a moving marquee.

8.3

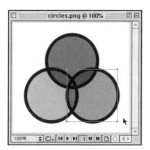

8.4

8.5 **Show/Hide**

3. To switch to image edit mode without selecting an existing object, choose Insert→Empty Image.

4. To switch to image edit mode while restricting the area in which you can paint and edit, use one of the selection tools described in the next section ("Selecting Pixels") to define an area (8.3).

5. To switch back to object mode (8.4), double-click outside the image object with a Pointer tool or click the Stop button at the bottom of the Document window.

(N) O T E

Vector graphics can be converted into pixel images, but can be converted back to editable vector paths only with Edit→Undo.

(N) O T E

Switching to a different layer in the Layer panel Window→Layers (8.5) or hiding the current layer will also switch you back to object mode.

Selecting Pixels

Within image edit mode, you can paint and edit over the entire canvas, or use one of the pixel selection tools to confine your edits to a particular area. Fireworks' pixel selection tools work like their counterparts in Photoshop: Use a Marquee tool to select a geometric area for transforming or feathering its edges (8.6). Use a Lasso tool to trace around an irregularly shaped section of an image and alter or delete it (8.7). Use the Magic Wand tool to select pixels of a specific color or range of colors and substitute a new color (8.8).

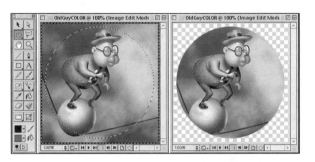

8.6

1. To select an area in an image object, double-click an image-selection tool to access its Tool Options panel.

8.7

   - Marquee tool—Enables you to select a rectangular area of an image object.

   - Ellipse Marquee tool (in the Marquee pop-up group)—Enables you to select an elliptical area of an image object.

   - Lasso tool—Enables you to select a freeform area of an image object.

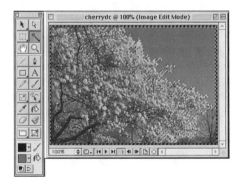

 I P

8.8

To restrain the editable area of a pixel image to the image's boundaries and not the entire document's, choose File→Preferences→ Editing and deselect Expand to Fill Document.

8.9   **If you choose Feather, enter a value in the Amount of Feather field or use its pop-up slider.**

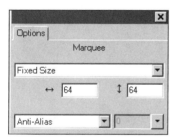

8.10

8.11

- Polygon Lasso tool (in the freeform shapes pop-up group)—Enables you to select a straight-sided freeform area of an image object.

- Magic Wand tool (in the freeform shapes pop-up group)—Enables you to select an area of similarly colored pixels in an image object.

2. In the Tool Options panel, select Hard Edge, Anti-Alias, or Feather in the Edge Type pop-up menu (8.9).

3. If you select a Marquee tool, choose a selection type in the Marquee type pop-up (8.10).

   - Choose Normal to drag selections in which the height and width are in-dependent of each other.

   - Choose Fixed Ratio to drag selections in which the height and width are in a defined proportion to each other. Enter propor-tions in the height and width fields.

continues

 I P

If you select the Magic Wand tool, enter a value in the Tolerance field or use its pop-up slider to set the range of allowable colors the tool will select (8.11). To pick only one color, choose Hard Edge and set the Tolerance to 0.

Selecting Pixels continued

- Choose Fixed Size to drag selections in which the height and width are fixed sizes. Enter measurements in pixels in the height and width fields.

4. To select an area with a Marquee tool, click-drag from one corner of the area to the opposite corner.

5. To select a freeform area with the Lasso tool, click-drag around the shape of the area (8.12).

6. To select a straight-sided freeform area with the Polygon Lasso tool, click corner points for the area. Close the selection by clicking on the selection's starting point (8.13).

7. To add to a selection, hold Shift while using an image mode selection tool (8.14).

8. To subtract from a selection, hold (Option)[Alt] while using any of the image mode selection tools.

9. To deselect a selection and select the rest of the image instead, choose Edit→Select Inverse.

To select an area with the Magic Wand tool, click on a pixel that is the color you want to select.

When you release the mouse, the beginning and end of the dragged shape connect automatically.

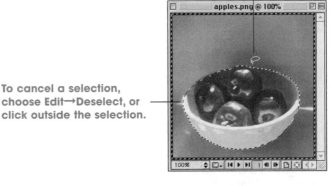

To cancel a selection, choose Edit→Deselect, or click outside the selection.

8.12

The Lasso cursor changes into a lasso with a square when it's over the starting point.

8.13

To automatically add all parts of an image that are similar in color to the selection, choose Edit→Select Similar.

8.14

Transforming Pixel Selections

8.15

Copy and paste a selection before transforming if you do not want to cut a hole in the background.

8.16

8.17

Like vector objects, pixel images can be transformed with the Scale, Skew, and Distort tools and the transformation operations under the Modify menu. In addition to transforming the entire image, any area selected with a pixel selection tool in image edit mode can be transformed (8.15).

Because they are composed of pixels and not paths, bitmap graphics suffer visual degradation when they are transformed. Greater transformations produce more pronounced quality loss.

1. To resize a pixel selection, choose the Scale tool and click-drag a handle (8.16). Double-click to apply the effect.

2. To slant a pixel selection along one axis, choose the Skew tool ⬚ from the Transform tools pop-up and click-drag a side, top, or bottom handle of your selected area (8.17). Double-click to apply the effect.

continues

(N) O T E

To resize a pixel selection numerically, choose Modify→Transform→Numeric Transform. In the Numeric Transform dialog box pop-up, choose Scale to resize by a percentage or Resize to size to a dimension, and enter a value in the Width or Height field. Check Constrain Proportions to scale the width and height proportionally. Click OK.

Exporting a Graphic with the Export Wizard continued

3. To apply perspective to a pixel selection, click-drag a corner handle with the Skew tool (8.18). Double-click to apply the effect.

4. To freely reshape a pixel selection, choose the Distort tool  from the Transform tools pop-up and click-drag any handle. Double-click to apply the effect (8.19).

5. To rotate a pixel selection, choose any transform tool, and then move the cursor outside the selection and click-drag when the circle arrow cursor appears. Double-click to apply the effect.

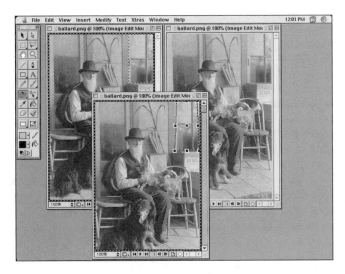

8.18   **Use perspective skewing to straighten out optical distortions in photographs.**

N O T E

To rotate a pixel selection by a degree, choose Modify→Transform→Numeric Transform. In the Numeric Transform dialog box pop-up, choose Rotate and enter a degree in the Angle field or spin the degree wheel. Click OK.

T I P

To rotate the selection around an axis other than its center, drag the center point to a different location, and then rotate. To return the center point to the object's center, double-click the point. Double-click to apply the effect.

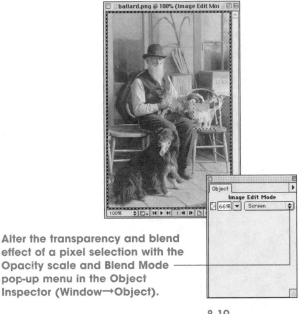

Alter the transparency and blend effect of a pixel selection with the Opacity scale and Blend Mode pop-up menu in the Object Inspector (Window→Object).

8.19

8.20

8.21

6. To rotate a pixel selection by a set amount, choose Modify→ Transform, and then select Rotate 180°, Rotate 90° CW (clockwise), or Rotate 90° CCW (counterclockwise).

7. To flip a pixel selection across an axis, choose Modify→ Transform, and then select Flip Horizontal **(8.20)** or Flip Vertical.

 T I P

*To save a pixel selection for further transformations, copy the selection, click the Stop button at the bottom of the Document window to exit image edit mode, and paste. The selection becomes a separate image object **(8.21)**. When you finish modifying the new image object, exit image edit mode, choose Edit→Select All and Modify→Merge Images to add the object back into the original image.*

Feathering Edges of a Selection

Use feathering in image edit mode to fade or blur the edges of a pixel selection. Feathering incorporates image information from outside the selection marquee, so for feathering to work, the selection must leave enough image area outside of itself for the amount of feathering selected.

8.22

1. To feather the edges of a pixel selection, choose Edit→Feather.

2. In the Feather Selection dialog box **(8.22)**, enter a value in pixels in the Radius field and click OK.

3. Choose Edit→Select Inverse and press (Delete) [Backspace] **(8.23)**.

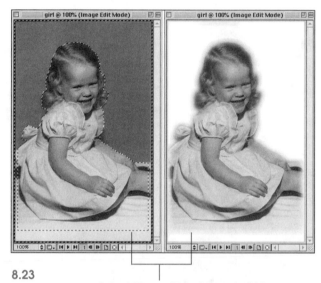

8.23

Select View→Hide Edges to hide
the selection's moving marquee.

I **P**

To trim excess space from a document's canvas after editing, choose Modify→Document→ Trim Canvas. The canvas crops to the outside edge of all the pixels in a document **(8.24)**.

 O T E

Higher radius values in the Feather Selection dialog box require more area left outside the selection for smooth feathering into the background.

8.24

Filling Pixel Areas with Color

8.25

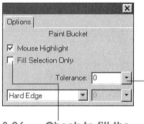

A setting of 0 fills only a solid area of color. Higher settings cause the fill to bleed out into adjoining areas of similar colors.

8.26   **Check to fill the entire selection.**

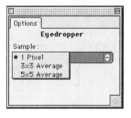

8.27

To fill contiguous areas of color in a pixel image, use Fireworks' Paint Bucket tool. In addition, Fireworks' shape tools can be used in image edit mode for quickly adding bitmapped rectangles, ellipses, polygons, and stars to a pixel image.

1. To fill an area in image edit mode (8.25), double-click the Paint Bucket tool to open the Tool Options panel.

2. In the Tool Options panel (8.26), set the color range to be filled by entering a value in the Tolerance field or use its pop-up slider.

    Select Hard Edge, Anti-Alias, or Feather in the Edge Type pop-up menu. If you choose Feather, enter a value in the Amount of Feather field or use its pop-up slider.

    continues

 I P

To copy a color to use with the Paint Bucket, select the Fill color well in the Toolbox, and then double-click the Eyedropper tool to open the Tool Options panel (8.27). Select a size in the Sample pop-up menu. To match an exact color, choose 1 Pixel. Then click the Eyedropper tool on the color. To sample a blend of pixels, choose 3×3 Average or 5×5 Average, and then click an area. Fireworks averages the colors in the defined radius to create the sample color.

Filling Pixel Areas with Color continued

3. Choose Window→Fill to select a fill type and its attributes in the Fill panel.

4. Choose Window→Object to set the fill's opacity and blend mode in the Object Inspector.

5. Click the Paint Bucket tool on the area to fill it (8.28).

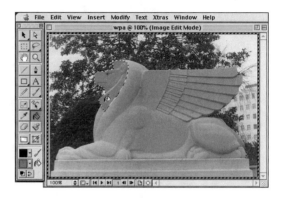

8.28 **To restrict the Paint Bucket fill to only part of an area, select the part before filling it.**

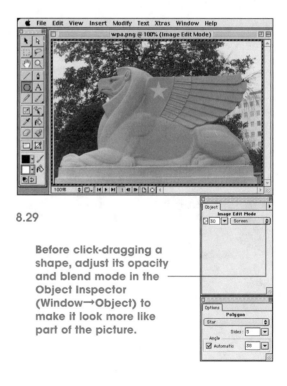

8.29

Before click-dragging a shape, adjust its opacity and blend mode in the Object Inspector (Window→Object) to make it look more like part of the picture.

To paint a simple shape in image edit mode, select the Rectangle, Ellipse, or Polygon tool from the shapes pop-up group in the Toolbox. Double-click the tool to set the shape's attributes in the Tool Options panel. Choose a fill type and its attributes in the Fill panel (Window→Fill). Choose a stroke type and its attributes in the Stroke panel (Window→Stroke), and then click-drag the shape (8.29). Objects created in image edit mode are not editable as vector path objects. They are bitmaps and can be edited only on a pixel level.

Painting Pixels

8.30 **Strokes that are created in image edit mode are not editable as vector path objects. They are bitmaps and can be edited only on a pixel level.**

8.31

Painting in image edit mode is similar to using other image-editing programs, so you can be productive immediately. Like Photoshop, Fireworks includes a Brush tool, for painting brush strokes (8.30); a Pencil tool, for painting and editing single pixels; a Line tool, for painting straight lines; and an Eraser tool, for removing or coloring pixels.

1. To paint in image edit mode, choose stroke attributes in the Stroke panel (Window→ Stroke) (8.31). Select the Brush tool and click-drag to paint.

2. To paint individual pixels or freeform one-pixel-wide lines in image edit mode, select the Pencil tool. Choose a pencil color by double-clicking the Brush color well in the Toolbox or clicking its pop-up palette.

continues

 I P

To copy a color to use with the paint tools, select the Brush color well in the Toolbox, and then double-click the Eyedropper tool. In the Tool Options panel, select a size in the Sample pop-up menu. To match an exact color, choose 1 Pixel, and then click the Eyedropper tool on the color. To blend a group of the pixels, choose 3×3 Average or 5×5 Average, and then click an area of color. Fireworks averages the colors in the defined radius to create the sample color.

Painting Pixels continued

To paint anti-aliased lines, double-click the Pencil tool to open the Tool Options panel (8.32) and check Anti-Aliased. Click in the document to color individual pixels, click-drag to paint freeform lines.

3. To paint straight lines in image edit mode, select the Line tool. Choose Window→Stroke, select a stroke type and its attributes, and then click-drag a line.

4. To erase pixels from an image in image edit mode, double-click the Eraser tool to open the Tool Options panel and set eraser specifications (8.33).

5. Click-drag the Eraser tool to erase (8.34).

O T E

Live Effects, Fireworks' editable 3D effects, cannot be applied in image edit mode. They can be applied only to objects, either image or vector, in object edit mode.

T I P

Use the Object Inspector's Opacity scale and Blending Mode pop-up menu to paint transparent and blended strokes. In image edit mode, set the opacity and blend mode in the Object Inspector (Window→Object). Any new pixels added will blend into the image using these settings.

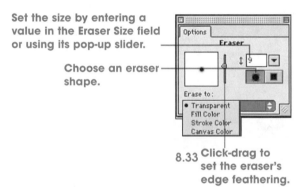

Auto Erase switches the color of an edited pixel from the Brush color to the Fill color when the pixel is clicked with the Pencil tool.

8.32

Set the size by entering a value in the Eraser Size field or using its pop-up slider.

Choose an eraser shape.

8.33 Click-drag to set the eraser's edge feathering.

To erase in a specific area, select the area before erasing.

Set the Eraser tool's opacity to less than 100% for subtle effects.

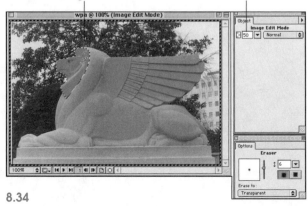

8.34

Applying Effects to an Image Object

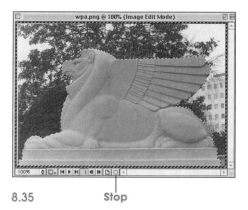

8.35   Stop

To see your selection clearly, click the background image with a Pointer tool and choose View→Hide Selection.

To add a border, select Glow, and set the border's width and color. Set the Opacity to 100% and the Softness to 0.

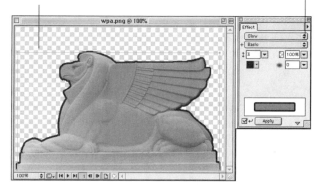

8.36

8.37

Although Live Effects do not work in image edit mode, pixel selections can be modified with Live Effects if they are first converted to image objects. Add glows, embossing, or drop shadows to parts of an image or outline an image object.

1. In image edit mode, select an area (8.35). Choose Edit→Copy.

2. Click the Stop button to exit image edit mode, and then choose Edit→Paste.

3. With the pasted image object selected, choose Window→ Effect, and then choose an Effect and its attributes (8.36).

4. Select the pasted image object and Shift-select the original image object, and then choose Modify→Group.

 I P

Live Effect borders have rounded corners. To create a square-cornered border instead, double-click the Rectangle tool and set the corner roundness to 0% in the Tool Options panel. Click-drag a rectangle in object mode over the image object. Set its fill to None, and its stroke to Basic and Hard Line (8.37). Set the stroke's color and size. Double-click the rectangle to open the Object Inspector, and set the stroke to the outside of the path. Cut the image object, select the border, and choose Edit→Paste Inside.

Masking an Image with an Alpha Channel

Use mask groups to create gradient blends of image objects, so they blend into a background, or mask an image with another image to create the look of a double exposure.

1. To mask an open pixel image with a gradient blend, switch to object mode. Use the Rectangle tool to click-drag a rectangle over the image.

2. With the rectangle selected, choose Window→Fill and select Linear in the Fill Category pop-up menu. Choose White, Black in the Fill Name pop-up menu (8.38).

3. Select the rectangle and the image object, and choose Modify→Mask Group (8.39).

4. To set the background color, choose Modify→Document→ Canvas Color. Choose a custom color by clicking the color well to access the system color picker or the pop-up arrow to use the palette (8.40).

 T I P

To mask out areas of a pixel image, copy the area(s) you want to keep, exit image edit mode, and paste. Select the empty area(s) in the copy with the Magic Wand tool, choose Edit→Select Inverse, and fill the selection with Black. Exit image edit mode, select all, and choose Modify→Mask Group.

The alpha channel masks out any part of the image object it does not cover.

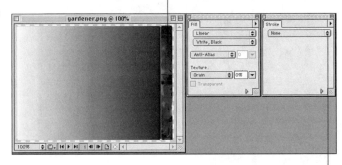

8.38   **Set the rectangle's stroke to None.**

The gradient's white area converts the corresponding image area to transparent, the gradient's black area maintains the image's opacity, and the gradient's gray areas are semitransparent.

8.39

8.40   **To match the canvas to a color in another document, use the Eyedropper tool to click the color you want.**

8.41

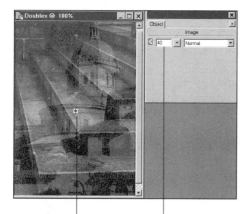

8.42

Instead of switching to the Subselect tool, double-click the mask group's "belly button" to edit the masked image object.

Create a more subtle look by altering the masked image object's transparency in the Object Inspector (Window→Object).

5. To adjust the mask object's gradient range and direction, select the mask group with the Pointer tool. Select the Paint Bucket tool and move the round start handle to change the gradient start point. Move the ending square handle to change its end point (8.41).

6. To edit the mask object's style attributes, select the mask group with the Pointer tool, and then change its settings in the Fill, Stroke, Effect, and Style panels.

7. To edit the masked image object in a mask group, select the object with the Subselect tool (8.42), and then change its settings or use a related editing tool.

 I P

To reverse the masked and unmasked areas of an alpha channel, select the mask with the Subselect tool and choose Xtras→Invert→ Invert. The brightness value of each pixel in the mask converts to its opposite. For example, black reverses to white. However, if the mask is a vector object such as a gradient fill, it converts to a pixel image and is no longer editable as a vector object.

 I P

To make a monochromatic version of a masked image object, create the mask vector object in the color you want the image to be and place it behind the image object to be masked (Modify→Arrange→ Send Backward). With the vector object still selected, Shift-click the image, and then choose Modify→Mask Group.

©HAPTER 9

Rarely are scans exactly what they should be. The scanned image is too large for the Web page it must fit into. Colors veer off to the red side of the spectrum or the blue. Details get lost in the unavoidable degeneration that comes from making a copy of an image. Sometimes, the original image you start from is less than perfect, with creases, stains, and scratches obscuring the image.

FINE-TUNING SCANNED IMAGES

Luckily, Fireworks offers more than just the ability to scan in images. It also offers a complete array of photo-fixing tools to bring your scans closer to perfection.

Using the Crop tool, you can make a scan more visually powerful (and faster loading) by deleting everything but the essential image.

Bring the scanned image back into color balance or create unique visual effects with the more complex color-correcting PhotoOptics Xtras. PhotoOptics Xtras differ from other image-editing tools in that they more naturally mimic traditional camera lenses and darkroom techniques.

Finally, eliminate visual imperfections with the Rubber Stamp tool and Fireworks' Blur and Sharpen Xtras. Use the same tools to cre photo illustrations, painting images of images with the Rubber Stamp adding special effects with Fir

Yc can drag and th beyond space do

Cropping Images

Remove unnecessary visual information from an image object by cropping it. Firework's Crop tool works differently depending on which mode you use it in. In image edit mode, the Crop tool deletes the parts of a selected image outside the crop marquee area but doesn't affect the document's dimensions. In object mode, cropping cuts the document's canvas but not the objects on it.

1. To crop an image object, click-drag with the Marquee tool across the area you want to keep (9.1).

2. Choose Edit→Crop Selected Image to add a crop marquee to the selection.

3. To adjust the crop area, pull the crop marquee handles (9.2). Click-drag inside the crop marquee to move it.

4. To cancel a crop selection without cropping the image, double-click outside the crop marquee.

9.1

You can select areas with other pixel selection tools, but cropping will be done to a rectangle bounded by the outermost pixels of the selection.

9.2

To move the right or bottom side of the crop selection one pixel at a time, press Shift while using the keyboard's arrow keys. To move opposite sides simultaneously, press (Option) (Alt) while using the arrow keys.

T I P

u can also use the Crop tool to make the
as larger than the image by click-
ing a crop marquee inside the image
n pulling the crop marquee handles
he image area. To add the extra
ble-click inside the selection.

9.3

9.4

Cropping the document
instead of the image
makes the document
a window into the
unchanged image.

9.5

5. To crop the image to the selection, double-click inside the selection (9.3).

6. To remove excess space around the cropped image object, choose Modify→Document→Trim Canvas (9.4).

(T) I P

To crop the graphic for export without changing the document, use the Export Area tool *from the Pointer pop-up group in the Toolbox to click-drag a selection. Double-click inside the selected area to bring up the Export Preview window. Exporting only the area defined by the marquee selection does not alter the original document.*

(T) I P

To crop the document instead of an image object, exit image edit mode by clicking the Stop button at the bottom of the Document window. Choose the Crop tool *from the Pointer pop-up group in the Toolbox and click-drag the area to keep. Adjust the crop marquee, if needed, and double-click to crop the document. The objects in the document remain uncropped, but any parts that extend beyond the edges of the canvas are hidden (9.5).*

Color-Correcting Images with PhotoOptics Xtras

Fireworks 2 includes CSI
PhotoOptics, a set of eight filter
Xtras that mimic traditional photographic filters and gels and darkroom color correction (9.6). The
software is not as easy to use as
Photoshop's filters, so if you already
use Photoshop for color correction,
you might not want to switch. The
PhotoOptics set does include a set of
customizable default settings plus
the capability to save multiple custom settings within Fireworks itself.

9.6

Each PhotoOptics filter displays a
before and after thumbnail of the
pixel selection that updates dynami-
cally as you change the settings.

1. To change or add color to a
   specific luminance range in a
   pixel selection (9.7), choose
   Xtras→PhotoOptics→CSI
   GradTone. In the CSI
   GradTone dialog box, click the
   large color swatch to pick a
   color in the system color picker
   or click the Eyedropper button
   to select any color visible (on
   the desktop)[in Fireworks] by
   clicking it.

9.7

 I P

*To shorten the range of colors that are affect-
ed after adding a color to the Gradient Scale,
click the black preset color square [double-
click the color square to access Windows pre-
sets] and click-drag the Gradient Scale to
shorten the new color's range.*

To replace colors instead of colorizing them, click Opacity.

9.8   **To access Windows preset colors, double-click the color swatch.**

To reverse the Gradient Scale's luminance range, click Reverse.

Use CSI HueSlider to quickly colorize a black-and-white image.

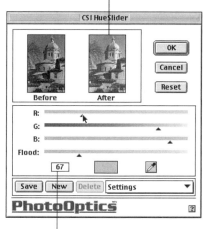

9.9   **When you adjust a color slider, its value from 0 to 255 appears next to the color swatch.**

2. Using the grayscale bar as a guide to which range of colors is changed (the black end represents the darkest colors; the white end represents the lightest), click the black Gradient Scale where you want to add color to the image (9.8). To change the range, drag before releasing. To add another color, select it and click the Gradient Scale again. No color is applied to areas that are left black on the Gradient Scale. Click OK.

3. To color-shift a pixel selection toward a single color, choose Xtras→PhotoOptics→CSI HueSlider. In the dialog box (9.9), click the large color swatch to pick a color in the system color picker or click the Eyedropper button to select any color visible (on the desktop)[in Fireworks].

4. To adjust the color, click-drag the RGB sliders. To adjust the color saturation, click-drag the Flood slider. Click OK.

continues

 **O T E**

GradTone replaces colors based on their luminance, how light or dark they are, not their hue. To replace a particular color in a pixel image, select it with the Magic Wand tool, choose Edit→Select Similar to find the rest of its instances in the image, and then use GradTone to replace the color.

Color-Correcting Images with PhotoOptics Xtras continued

5. To adjust the contrast in a pixel selection, choose Xtras→ PhotoOptics→CSI Levels (9.10). In the CSI Levels dialog box, enter values in the Shadow and High Light fields or adjust their sliders to set the image's tonal range.

6. Adjust the overall exposure by entering a value in the Exposure field or adjust its slider to compensate for levels settings that are too dark or too light. Click OK.

7. To convert a full-color pixel selection into a duotone, choose Xtras→PhotoOptics →CSI Monochrome. In the CSI Monochrome dialog box (9.11), click the large color swatch to pick a color in the system color picker or click the Eyedropper button to select any color (on the desktop)[in Fireworks].

Use the Equalize button to balance the shadow and highlight settings.

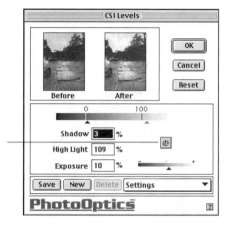

9.10

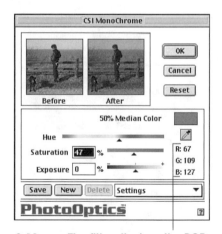

9.11   **The filter displays the RGB values of the median color selected.**

 I   P

To add outlines to a photograph, choose Modify→Document→Canvas Color and set the canvas to black. Select the photograph in object mode, and choose Edit→Clone. With the clone selected, choose Xtras→Other→ Find Edges, and then Xtras→PhotoOptics→ CSI Monochrome. In the CSI Monochrome dialog box, click Reset and OK. Choose Edit→Select All and Modify→Mask Group.

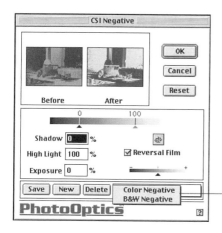

9.12

CSI Negative filter compensates for the orange cast in color film stock.

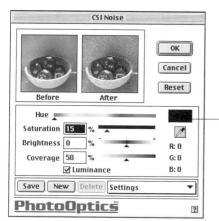

9.13

For color noise, uncheck Luminance and click the color swatch to access the system color picker, or click the Eyedropper button to select any color visible (on the desktop)(in Fireworks) by clicking it. Adjust the noise color by dragging the Hue slider.

8. To adjust the resulting duotone, change the color with the Hue slider, and enter values in the Saturation and Exposure fields or adjust their sliders. Click OK.

9. To convert a scanned negative into a positive image or vice versa, choose Xtras→ PhotoOptics→CSI Negative. In the CSI Negative dialog box (9.12), select Color Negative or B&W Negative from the Settings pop-up menu.

10. To adjust the contrast, enter values in the Shadow and High Light fields or adjust their sliders. To adjust the overall exposure, enter a value in the Exposure field or adjust its slider. Click OK.

11. To add random noise to a pixel selection, choose Xtras→ PhotoOptics→CSI Noise. For brightness noise, check Luminance in the CSI Noise dialog box (9.13).

continues

 I P

If you are exporting a gradient as a GIF and are experiencing visible color banding, add CSI Noise at a luminance setting of 15% saturation (for light color blends, higher percentages for bright or dark color blends), 0% Brightness and 50% Coverage to the gradient, and then blur it with Xtras→Blur→ Blur.

Color-Correcting Images with PhotoOptics Xtras continued

12. Adjust the noise's saturation, brightness, and amount (coverage) by entering a value in their fields or using their sliders. Click OK.

13. To color-correct a pixel selection using a range of camera lens' filters, choose Xtras→ PhotoOptics→CSI PhotoFilter. In the CSI PhotoFilter dialog box (9.14), select a gel or filter effect from the Settings pop-up menu.

If a scanned image's color balance leans too much toward one color, select that color with the PhotoFilter Eyedropper tool, and then subtract that color by reducing its brightness to a negative value.

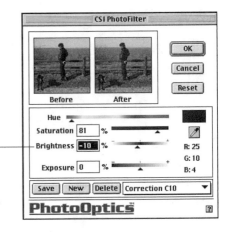

9.14

14. To change the color of the filter, click the large color swatch to pick a color in the system color picker or click the Eyedropper button to select any color visible (on the desktop)[in Fireworks].

15. Adjust the filter's saturation, brightness, and overall exposure by entering values in their fields or using their sliders. Click OK.

9.15

 I P

If you have composited a color image with a solid-color background, blend the image into the background with Luminance noise. In the CSI Noise dialog box, set the Saturation between 10% and 20%, the Brightness to 0%, and the Coverage between 20% and 40%. Check Luminance and click OK (9.15).

9.16

16. To simulate the look of infrared color film, choose Xtras→PhotoOptics→CSI PseudoColor. In the CSI PseudoColor dialog box (9.16), select a filter effect from the Settings pop-up menu.

17. To change the color of the filter, click the large color swatch to pick a color in the system color picker or click the Eyedropper button to select any color visible (on the desktop)[in Fireworks] by clicking it.

18. Adjust the filter's saturation, brightness, and overall exposure by entering values in their fields or using their sliders. To apply the settings, click OK.

Fireworks tints the entire image.   Photoshop leaves any white areas as is.

9.17

(N) O T E

CSI PhotoFilter mimics the effect of traditional lens filters, so it changes the color cast of the entire selected image, including any white areas. Other image-editing applications, such as Photoshop, are unable to do this. When you edit the colors of an image in other applications by adjusting curves, color balance, and so on, any areas that are absolute white remain white and must be colored separately (9.17).

Retouching Images

If your scans or other images are less than perfect, retouch them with Fireworks' Rubber Stamp tool, and the Blur and Sharpen Xtras (9.18). Use the Rubber Stamp tool to clone areas in an image object to fill in missing pieces or cover blemishes. Use the Blur Xtras to soften hard edges and hide dust, scratches, and other artifacts. As a final step, use the Sharpen Xtras to enhance details that got lost in scanning.

9.18

1. To clone a section of an image object, double-click the image to enter image edit mode and double-click the Rubber Stamp tool to open the Tool Options panel.

Use Fixed Source to clone an element or area more than once.

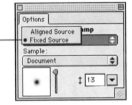

9.19

2. In the Offset from Cursor pop-up menu in the Tool Options panel (9.19), choose Aligned Source to clone from a location that is a set distance from the mouse or Fixed Source to clone from the same location each time you click the mouse.

Ⓣ I P

Use Aligned Source when you want to cover an area in an image by extending an adjacent area over it, such as when you want to fill in a torn corner to match the rest of the background. Use Fixed Source when you want to copy a part of an image and repeat it numerous times in other parts of the image, such as when you want to add more windows to a picture of a building.

9.20   **The Rubber Stamp cursor changes into a crosshairs cursor when (Option)(Alt) is pressed.**

In the Sample pop-up menu, choose Image to sample from the selected image or Document to sample from anywhere in the document.

Set the amount of edge feathering by entering a value in the Edge Softness field or use its pop-up slider.

Set the size of the clone by entering a value in the Stamp Size field or use its pop-up slider.

3. To select the clone source in the image, hold (Option)[Alt] and click the Rubber Stamp tool on the origin area (9.20).

continues

9.21   **Before painting, adjust the Rubber Stamp tool's opacity in the Object Inspector to make the strokes semitransparent.**

 I   P

To paint a vector or image object into another image object, import the source object into the image object document. (Enlarge the document's canvas size, if needed.) Double-click the image object and double-click the Rubber Stamp tool. Choose Document in the Tool Options panel Sample menu. Then (Option)[Alt]-click the source object and click-drag over the image to paint (9.21). Delete the source object after painting.

Retouching Images continued

4. To apply the stamp, move the Rubber Stamp tool to the area to be covered and click or click-drag to clone from the origin to the change area (9.22).

5. To automatically blur a pixel selection, choose Xtras→Blur→ Blur (9.23).

6. To blur a selection by an adjustable amount, choose Xtras→Blur→Gaussian Blur to open the Gaussian Blur dialog box.

7. In the Gaussian Blur dialog box (9.24), set the amount of blur by entering a value from 0.1 to 250 in the Radius field or by using the slider. Higher numbers increase the blur effect. Click OK.

A blue circle indicates the clone source in the image as you apply the Rubber Stamp tool.

9.22

To smooth out a background, choose Xtras→ Blur→Blur More, which automatically blurs a selection by three times the amount of a simple blur.

9.23

Preview the blur's effect as you set it. Click and drag inside the window to scroll the preview image. Zoom in or out.

 I P

To repeat the most recently applied Xtra, choose Xtras→Repeat Xtra.

9.24

9.25

To automatically increase the contrast of adjacent pixels in a selection, choose Xtras→Sharpen→ Sharpen More.

8. To automatically sharpen a selection, choose Xtras→ Sharpen→Sharpen (9.25).

9. To sharpen a selection by adjusting its edge detail contrast, choose Xtras→Sharpen→ Unsharp Mask to open the Unsharp Mask dialog box.

10. In the Unsharp Mask dialog box (9.26), set the contrast amount, sharpening area, and threshold by entering values in the fields or by using the sliders.

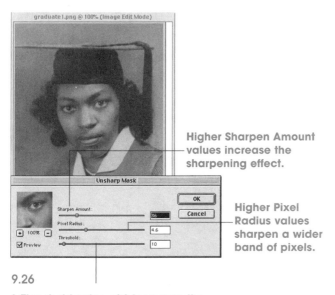

Higher Sharpen Amount values increase the sharpening effect.

Higher Pixel Radius values sharpen a wider band of pixels.

9.26

A Threshold value of 0 increases the contrast of every pixel in a selection.

 O T E

Because the sharpening filters discard image information as they increase the contrast in details, they should be applied last before exporting an image.

CHAPTER 10

In this chapter you learn how to...

Design Custom Brush Strokes

Add Custom Patterns and Textures

Use Third-Party Xtras

If you are a power user, Fireworks offers a variety of ways to customize your tools and supplies. In addition to the basic Options panel choices for setting up your tools and the general application preferences you can set under the File menu, Fireworks also gives you the ability to create your own custom brush strokes, patterns, and textures, and use third-party filters to create unique effects.

CUSTOMIZING TOOLS AND MATERIALS

Designing custom brush strokes involves setting numeric parameters for all the different aspects of the stroke, such as its size, shape, and texture. As you design a stroke, the stroke's preview window updates so that you can fine-tune your choices immediately. After the hard work is done, save the stroke as a style to use in other documents and to share with other Fireworks users.

Add your own patterns and textures, either by creating them from scanned images, vector objects, and image objects, or by copying existing files and saving them as Fireworks PNG files. Convert your custom patterns and textures into seamless tiles to apply to vector and image objects, or use as backgrounds for Web pages.

Some third-party filters are compatible with Fireworks and can be added as Xtras so that you can achieve your favorite effects without switching programs.

Designing Custom Brush Strokes

Fireworks offers a wealth of options for creating custom brush strokes, including settings for brush shape, texture, and randomization. You also can set a stroke's sensitivity for responding to a pressure-sensitive pen. After creating strokes, save them for reuse later.

Stroke panel Options pop-up menu

For a dashed or dotted line, select Random and Dots.

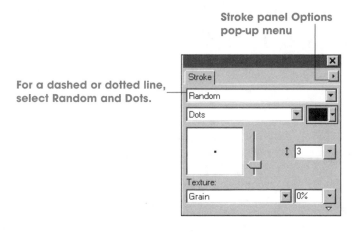

10.1

1. To create a brush stroke, choose a stroke preset in the Stroke panel's Stroke category pop-up menu (Window→ Stroke), and select a brush shape to adapt in the Stroke Name pop-up menu (10.1).

3. Choose Edit Stroke in the Stroke panel Options pop-up menu.

For a dashed or dotted line, set Ink Amount to 100% and Spacing to 300%. Uncheck Build-Up. Set Tips to 1.

4. In the Edit Stroke Options panel, adjust settings and check the results in the Stroke Preview (10.2).

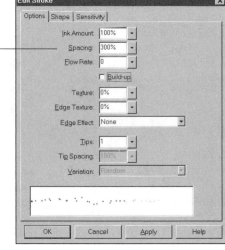

10.2

O T E

Fireworks doesn't offer dotted or dashed lines as standard brush strokes, but you can create your own with the Edit Stroke dialog boxes. There are a few limitations: Dashes do not follow the curve or angle of a line, they orient themselves to the document, so you can make only straight dashed lines; and you must make a stroke style for horizontal dashes and another stroke style for vertical dashes.

For a dotted line, uncheck Square, set Size to 4 for small dots, and set Aspect to 100.

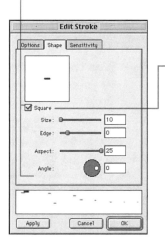

For a dashed line, check Square, set Size to 10, Edge to 0, Aspect to 25, and Angle to 0° for a horizontal dashed line, 90° for a vertical line.

10.3

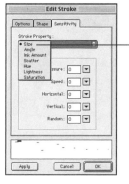

For a dashed or dotted line, choose Size and set all the fields to 0. Repeat with each of the rest of the properties in the Stroke Property pop-up menu.

10.4

5. Adjust settings in the Edit Stroke Shape panel and check the results in the Stroke Preview (10.3).

6. Adjust settings in the Edit Stroke Sensitivity panel and check the results in the Stroke Preview (10.4). Click OK.

7. To save a custom stroke within an open document, select Save Stroke As in the Stroke panel Options pop-up menu, name the stroke in the Save Stroke dialog box, and click OK.

8. To use a saved brush stroke in another document, copy and paste an object that contains that stroke into the new document. The stroke appears in the new document's Stroke Name pop-up menu.

continues

 I P

For a dashed line that follows a path, draw the path with the Pen or Brush tool, and then double-click the Type tool and type a row of hyphens in the Text Editor dialog box. Set size and spacing options and click OK. Select the path and the hyphens with the Pointer tool and choose Text→Attach to Path.

Designing Custom Brush Strokes continued

9. To reuse a custom stroke without copying and pasting, save it as a style. Choose Window→Styles to open the Styles panel. With the object selected, click the New Style button at the bottom of the Styles panel. In the Edit Style dialog box, enter a name for the style and select Stroke Type **(10.5)**. Click OK.

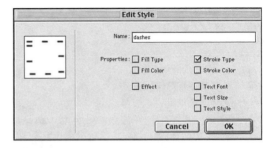

10.5

10. To share a custom stroke with other users, select it in the Styles panel (Shift-click to export multiple styles) and choose Export Styles from the Styles panel Options pop-up menu. In the Export Selected Styles As dialog box, name and save the .stl file, and then distribute it. Other users can import styles by choosing Import Styles from the Styles panel Options pop-up menu **(10.6)**, and then opening the .stl file.

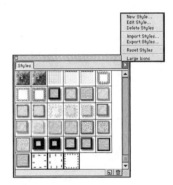

10.6

 I P

Custom strokes can be added to the Stroke panel by saving a document that contains the strokes as Fireworks Defaults.PNG in Fireworks 2\Settings\Presets. (Create a Presets folder if one doesn't exist.) When you relaunch Fireworks, the strokes appear in the Stroke Name pop-up menu. You also can include custom gradient fills and Live Effects in the PNG document.

Adding Custom Patterns and Textures

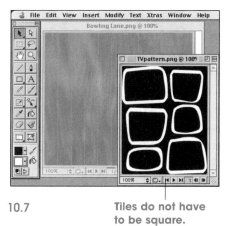

10.7

Tiles do not have to be square.

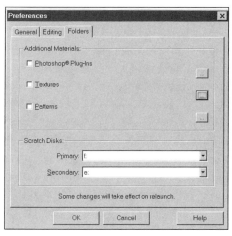

10.8

Create your own custom patterns and textures from scanned images, vector objects, and image objects. Almost any Fireworks PNG file can be used as a pattern. To avoid the appearance of tile edges in objects or pages that use your patterns and textures, touch up the edges of the patterns and textures you create so they blend seamlessly when tiled. If you have Kai's Power Tools' KPT 3 Seamless Welder filter, add it as a third-party Xtra to Fireworks and use it to automatically blend tile edges. If you don't have an Xtra to create seamless tiles, you can make them yourself.

1. Create a pattern or texture in Fireworks using scans, vector objects, or image objects.

2. If your document contains multiple image objects and/or vector objects, choose Edit→ Select All, and then Modify→ Merge Images to create one image object **(10.7)**.

continues

 **O T E**

*The Fireworks 2 CD-ROM contains additional patterns and textures that you can copy into your Fireworks\Settings\Patterns and Textures folders or access directly from the CD-ROM by choosing File→Preferences→ Folders, and then clicking their ellipsis (…) buttons to locate the folders **(10.8)**.*

Adding Custom Patterns and Textures continued

3. If your image is larger than your target tile size, click-drag with the Marquee tool to select the tile area and choose Edit→Crop Selected Image (10.9). Adjust the crop handles, if necessary, and double-click within the crop marquee to crop.

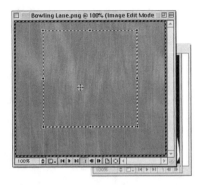

10.9

4. Choose Modify→Document→ Trim Canvas.

5. With the image object selected, choose Edit→Copy.

6. Choose Modify→Document→ Canvas Size. In the Canvas Size dialog box, double the value in the New Size Width field, and then select one of the left side squares in the Anchor diagram (10.10). Click OK.

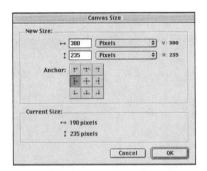

10.10

7. Double-click the object with the Pointer tool to enter image edit mode and choose Edit→Paste, and then click-drag to move the duplicate tile to fill the blank area on the right (10.11).

10.11

8. Choose Edit→Select All, and then Edit→Copy.

Use the keyboard's arrow keys to adjust the duplicate tile's position.

If you overlap the original tile with the duplicate tile, reduce the canvas width to eliminate excess space on the right.

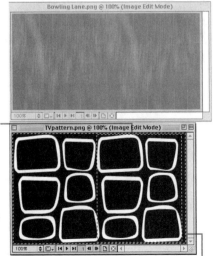

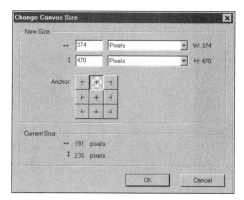

10.12

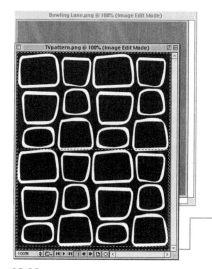

Trim the canvas bottom
to remove excess space
if you overlap the tiles.

10.13

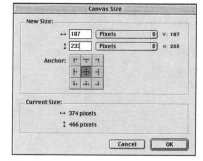

10.14

9. Choose Modify→Document→ Canvas Size. In the Canvas Size dialog box, double the value in the New Size Height field, and then select one of the top squares in the Anchor diagram (10.12). Click OK.

10. Double-click the object with the Pointer tool to enter image edit mode and choose Edit→ Paste, and then click-drag to move the duplicate tile to fill the blank area on the bottom (10.13).

11. Choose Modify→Document→ Canvas Size. In the Canvas Size dialog box, halve the values in the New Size Width and Height fields, and then select the center square in the Anchor diagram (10.14). Click OK.

continues

 N O T E

Fireworks patterns have a size limit of 384×384 pixels. Anything larger won't appear in the Patterns menu. Textures can be any size up to the maximum document size of 5,000×5,000 pixels. However, large file sizes will slow your Fireworks startup time.

Adding Custom Patterns and Textures continued

12. Click-drag the Marquee tool to select the visible tile area and choose Edit→Crop Selected Image (10.15). Adjust the crop handles, if necessary, and double-click inside the crop marquee to trim the tile art to the canvas size.

13. Use image-editing tools (brushes, pencil, rubber stamp, and eraser) to blend away the center seams in the tile (10.16).

14. Save pattern tiles as PNG files in the Fireworks\Settings\ Patterns folder.

Save texture tiles as PNG files in the Fireworks\Settings\ Textures folder.

15. Quit and relaunch Fireworks. Pattern tiles appear in the Fill Name pop-up menu under Pattern in the Fill panel (10.17). Texture tiles appear in the Texture Name pop-up menu.

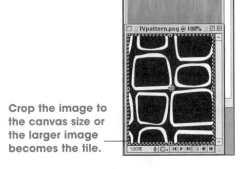

Crop the image to the canvas size or the larger image becomes the tile.

10.15

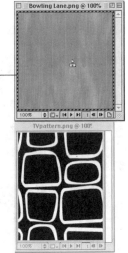

Don't change the tile's new edge pixels or it might not line up correctly when repeated on an object.

10.16

If you have custom patterns and textures created in other programs, open them in Fireworks and save them as PNG files in the appropriate Fireworks Settings folder.

If you want to use a custom pattern or texture as a background tile in a Web page, export the tile as a GIF, JPEG, or PNG.

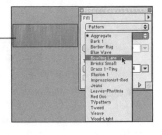

Patterns and textures include a preview swatch.

10.17

Using Third-Party Xtras

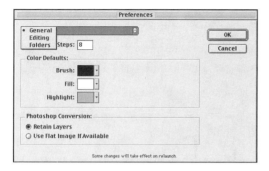

10.18

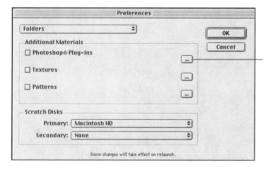

The folder can be located on any drive you are connected to, including CD-ROM drives or on a network.

10.19

10.20

Add familiar functionality to Fireworks with your favorite plug-ins, such as Photoshop filters and Kai's Power Tools. Copy the plug-ins into your Fireworks Xtras folder or set your preferences to target another application's plug-in folder. When you relaunch Fireworks, all compatible plug-ins will be listed in the Xtras menu.

1. To add plug-ins to Fireworks, install or copy them into Fireworks 2\Settings\Xtras.

2. To target an additional folder of plug-ins, choose File→Preferences. In the Preferences dialog box (10.18), choose Folders from the pop-up menu.

3. In the Additional Materials area (10.19), check Photoshop™ Plug-Ins and click the Ellipsis (...) button to locate the plug-ins folder you want to use.

4. Quit and relaunch Fireworks to access the new Xtras (10.20).

 I P

To save space on your hard drive, make (aliases)[shortcuts] from your third-party plug-ins instead of copying them.

CHAPTER 11

Add text to your Web graphics with Fireworks' Text Editor, a separate window containing typographic controls for setting perfect text. As you work, the text in your document automatically updates. With Fireworks' dynamic preview, you can massage your type to achieve the optimal balance between legibility and aesthetics.

SETTING TEXT

In the Text Editor, combine different fonts, colors, point sizes, and other text attributes in the same block of text. As in other professional design applications, you can adjust individual kern pairs for optimal letter spacing, as well as the overall kerning of the text block or any range of characters within it. You can also create superscript or subscript characters within a text block. Use the Object Inspector to increase the legibility of small print onscreen.

After setting text, alter it with fills, strokes, and Live Effects; save its attributes to reuse and share with others; manipulate it with Fireworks' transform tools; attach it to shaped paths; even convert it to vector graphics so you can customize it point-by-point, or turn it into pixel art for editing in image edit mode. With the exceptions of vector or image conversion, text remains editable as text no matter how much you change its visual appearance.

Formatting Text

Fireworks offers a standard set of type attributes, including kerning/tracking (the space between letters) and leading (the space between lines of text). In addition, you can create condensed or expanded type by adjusting the horizontal scaling to squeeze or stretch the letters. Choose from five different type alignments including Justified, which adds space between words and letters to align text on both sides, and Stretched, which stretches the characters to align text on both sides. Change the text orientation to vertical and use the same alignment commands to arrange the text vertically.

1. To add text to a document, select the Text tool, and then click in the Document window (11.1) to display the Text Editor.

2. Choose a font in the Font pop-up menu (11.2).

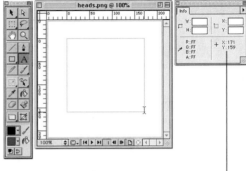

11.1

To make a text block a specific width, click-drag with the Text tool, using the Info panel (Window→Info) to aid in sizing.

To add computer-generated styles—as opposed to font faces—select Bold, Italic, or Underline.

Text Size

To set smooth text, check Anti-Alias.

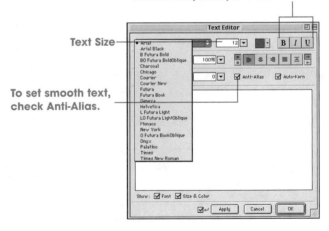

11.2

 **O T E**

The Text Editor displays the text in its specified font, color and point size only. As you type, the text appears in the Document window with all the settings you specified. When you leave the Text Editor, it remembers your text settings for the next text block you create.

Negative values decrease spacing; positive values increase spacing.   **Leading**

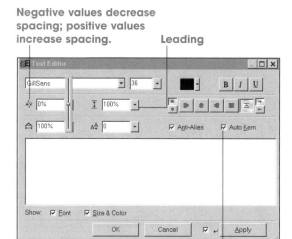

11.3   **To use font-specific kerned character pairs, check Auto-Kern.**

Change text orientation to vertical.

11.4   **Reverse text direction for formatting languages such as Hebrew and vertical Japanese text.**

3. Enter a value in pixels in the Size field or use its slider.

4. Choose a color by clicking the Color well to access the system color picker or by clicking the pop-up Swatches panel.

5. To set tracking, enter a percentage in the Kerning field or use its pop-up slider (11.3).

6. To set leading, enter a percentage in the Leading field or use its pop-up slider.

7. To set text alignment, click the Left, Center, Right, Justified, or Stretched button (11.4).

continues

 I P

Fireworks measures text size in pixels, not points. For onscreen viewing, they are basically the same: 72-pixel text looks like 72-point text. If you print your graphics, however, the text prints at smaller sizes. See Chapter 17, "Using Fireworks Beyond the Web," for more information.

 O T E

Fireworks 2 uses the TrueType fonts installed on your computer and also can handle PostScript Type 1 fonts if Adobe Type Manager 4.0 or later is installed.

Formatting Text continued

8. To set the letters' horizontal scaling, enter a percentage in the Horizontal Scale field or use its pop-up slider (11.5).

9. Type text in the Text Editor window (11.6). To return to the Document window, click OK or press Enter.

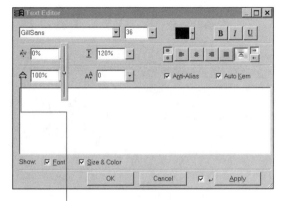

11.5 **Negative values condense letters; positive values expand letters.**

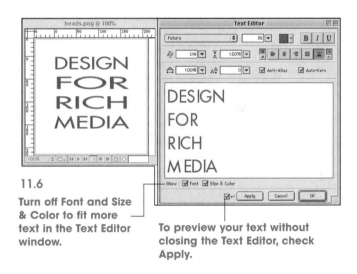

11.6

Turn off Font and Size & Color to fit more text in the Text Editor window.

To preview your text without closing the Text Editor, check Apply.

 I P

To align selected text with a graphic, Shift-click the graphic and choose Modify→Align, and then choose an alignment option from the pop-out menu. For example to center text on a button, choose Center Vertical, and then Center Horizontal with the text and button selected (11.7).

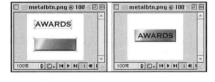

11.7

Saving Text Styles

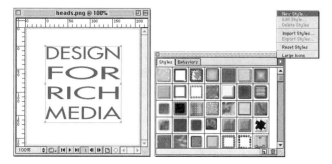

11.8

11.9

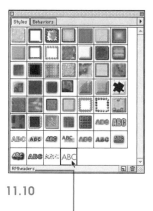

11.10

The style name appears at the bottom of the Styles panel.

Save type attributes as a custom style to reuse later and share with other Fireworks users. Like saving fill, stroke, and Live Effect attributes, you can save type font, point size, and font style in a custom style.

1. To save text attributes as a style, choose Window→Styles. With the text block selected, choose New Style from the Styles panel Options pop-up menu (11.8).

2. In the Edit Style dialog box, enter a name for the style and select which attributes you want to include (11.9). Click OK.

3. To apply a style to a selected text block, choose Window→Styles and click the tile preview for the desired style (11.10).

 I   P

To share a saved type style with other users, select it in the Styles panel (Shift-click to export multiple styles) and choose Export Styles from the Styles panel Options pop-up menu. In the Export Selected Styles As dialog box, name and save the .stl file, and then distribute it. Other users can import styles by choosing Import Styles from the Styles panel Options pop-up menu, and then locating and opening the .stl file. All the styles in the file will be appended to the bottom of the Styles panel.

Editing Text and Text Attributes

Text remains editable in Fireworks PNG files. Any time you want to change or update text, open your master PNG file and select a text block to access the Text Editor.

In addition to editing the text, you can change any of its type attributes. Globally change attributes or change individual letters' attributes. Within a text block, mix fonts, sizes, colors, or any of the other attributes. Create initial caps by changing a letter's font, color, and point size (11.11). Kern letter pairs for precise spacing. Use the baseline shift feature to create dropped caps and superscript or subscript characters.

1. To edit text, double-click the text block. The Text Editor opens with the text selected, ready for editing.

2. To change only part of a text block, click-drag to select text, and then edit the text or apply new type settings.

3. To kern a letter pair, click between the two letters and change the value in the Kern field or adjust its slider (11.12).

11.11

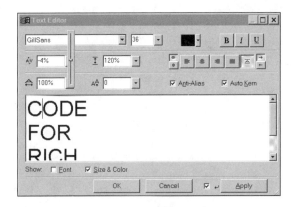

11.12

 I P

To create a succession of text blocks, choose Window→Tool Options and turn off Revert to Pointer in the Tool Options panel. Each time you close the Text Editor, the Text tool remains active.

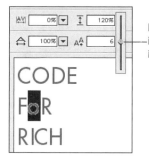

Negative values move text below its baseline; positive values move it above its baseline.

11.13

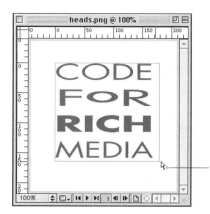

Resizing a text block doesn't change its type specifications. The text reflows according to its alignment specs to fit the new width.

11.14

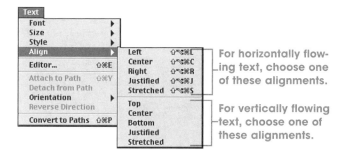

For horizontally flowing text, choose one of these alignments.

For vertically flowing text, choose one of these alignments.

11.15

4. To move selected text above or below its normal baseline, enter a value in the Baseline Shift field or use its pop-up slider (11.13).

5. Resize a text block by click-dragging one of its handles with the Pointer tool in the Document window (11.14).

6. To change the attributes of a selected text block, such as its font, style, size, and alignment, choose the desired item in the Text menu in the Document window (11.15).

Ⓝ O T E

If you open a file that contains fonts not installed on your computer, Fireworks displays a dialog box that says some fonts are missing and substitutes default fonts for them in the file, but it cannot describe which fonts are missing.

Ⓝ O T E

In the Text menus, the current attribute is checked. If no font is checked, either the text block contains more than one font or the font used is not installed on the computer that the text is being viewed on. If no size is checked, either the text block contains more than one size or its point size is not listed on the menu. If no style or alignment is checked, the text block contains more than one of these text attributes.

Applying Style Attributes to Text

The Text Editor sets text with a solid fill, and no stroke or Live Effect. You can change the fill and apply strokes and Live Effects to text in the Document window. If you later change or update the text, the revised text retains these style attributes.

1. To change a selected text block's fill, choose Window→ Fill in the Document window and select new fill attributes in the Fill panel (11.16).

2. To add a stroke to a selected text block, choose Window→ Stroke in the Document window and select stroke attributes in the Stroke panel (11.17).

3. To add a Live Effect to a selected text block, choose Window→Effect in the Document window and select effect attributes in the Effect panel (11.18).

11.16 **The range of a gradient fill applies to the entire text block, not each individual letter.**

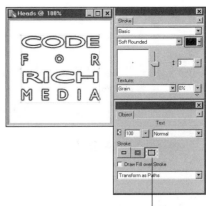

11.17 **Stroke placement defaults to outside the text's paths. To change the stroke's placement, choose Window→Object and select Inside or Centered.**

 T I P

To automate text editing, choose Window→Find & Replace and set parameters for changing text, fonts, or fill, stroke, or Live Effects colors. Search and replace in an individual text block, a document, or a selection of files.

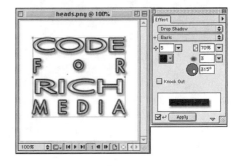

11.18

Setting Small Text

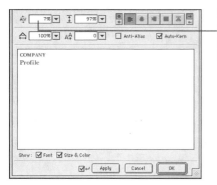

To increase small print legibility, set the text's range kerning to a positive value.

11.19

When changing opacity, keep the combined opacity of the two objects above 100% to keep the text color true.

11.20

Click-drag over the composite and choose Modify→Group.

When adjusting the two copies' opacity, balance visual clarity and color strength.

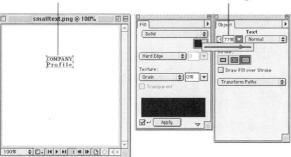

11.21

Anti-aliasing text for the Web usually results in smoother-looking type; however, in sizes under 14 points it often makes text blurry and hard to read. Setting boldfaced, hard-edged text usually solves the problem, especially for sans serif fonts (also known as block lettering). If you find these results less than satisfactory, make a composite of anti-aliased and hard-edged text, and then adjust the combination.

1. Select the Text tool and click in the Document window to display the Text Editor.

2. Set the font, point size, and other type specifications for the small text.

3. Deselect Anti-Alias and enter text in the Text Editor window (11.19). Click OK.

4. With the text selected, choose Edit→Clone.

5. Choose Window→Fill, and then in the Fill panel select Anti-Alias in the Edge of Fills pop-up menu.

6. Choose Window→Object and adjust the Object-Level Opacity slider (11.20).

7. To adjust the opacity of the hard-edged original, click the text with the Select Behind tool to access the bottom copy, and then adjust its opacity (11.21).

Transforming Text

Transform text the same as vector graphics and pixel images, by using the Scale, Skew, and Distort tools and the transform operations. Text transformations offer a couple of extra choices: Text Transformation Method and Remove Transformations.

The two text transformation methods are: Transform Paths, for transforming text like paths with crisp outlines, and Transform Pixels, for transforming text like bitmap images with blurred edges (11.22). Transform Paths is the default method. Use Transform Pixels when you're placing distorted text over bitmap images to make it look like part of the image.

11.22 **Use Transform Pixels over bitmaps.**

Use Transform Paths over flat colors and vector objects.

1. To switch transformation methods, choose Window→ Object, and then choose (Transform Pixels)[Transform as Pixels] from the Text Transformation Method pop-up menu in the Object Inspector (11.23).

11.23

Scaling or otherwise transforming text does not change its text attributes, so you can always return text to its original appearance with the Remove Transformations operation.

11.24

11.25

11.26

2. To resize a selected text block, choose the Scale tool  and click-drag an adjustment handle. Double-click to apply the effect.

3. To slant a selected text block along one axis, choose the Skew tool from the Transform tools pop-up and click-drag a side, top, or bottom handle (11.24).

4. To apply perspective to a selected text block, click-drag a corner handle with the Skew tool. Double-click to apply the effect (11.25).

5. To freely reshape a selected text block, choose the Distort tool from the Transform tools pop-up and click-drag any handle. Double-click to apply the effect (11.26).

continues

(N) O T E

Resize a selected text block numerically by choosing Modify→ Transform→Numeric Transform. In the Numeric Transform dialog box pop-up, choose Scale to resize by a percentage or Resize to size to a dimension, and enter a value in the Width or Height field. Check Scale Attributes to have the text block's fill, stroke, and effects change in size proportionally. Check Constrain Proportions to scale the width and height proportionally. Click OK.

Transforming Text continued

6. To rotate a transform-selected text block, move the cursor outside the text block and click-drag when the circle arrow cursor appears (11.27). Double-click to apply the effect.

11.27

7. To rotate a selected text block by a degree, choose Modify→Transform→Numeric Transform. Choose Rotate in the Numeric Transform dialog box pop-up, and enter a degree in the Angle field or spin the degree wheel. Click OK.

8. To flip a selected text block across an axis, choose Modify→Transform, and then select Flip Horizontal or Flip Vertical.

9. To remove transformations, choose Modify→Transform→Remove Transformations.

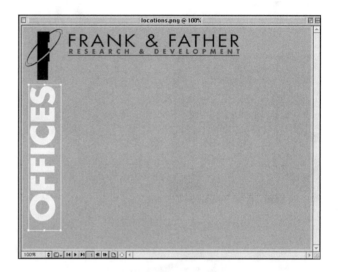

11.28

 I P

To rotate a selected text block around an axis different from the text block's center, drag the center point to a different location, and then rotate. To return the center point to the text block's center, double-click the point. Double-click to apply the effect.

 I P

Quickly rotate a selected text block a set amount by choosing Modify→Transform, and then select Rotate 180°, Rotate 90° CW (clockwise), or Rotate 90° CCW (counterclockwise) (11.28).

Setting Text on a Path

11.29   **To make a half-circle path, select a circle with the Subselect tool, and then hold the Shift key while dragging the Knife tool across its midpoints.**

11.30   **When text is attached to a path, the path's style attributes disappear.**

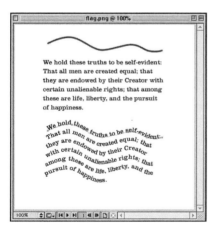

11.31

Text doesn't have to flow in straight lines—it can follow any path you create. Attach text to simple shapes, such as circles, or draw unique paths with the Pen tool to wrap text around. Both the text and the path remain editable.

1. To set text on a path, click-drag or Shift-click the text block and the path, and then choose Text→Attach to Path.

2. To attach text to only part of a path, such as a closed shape, cut the selected path with the Knife tool (11.29).

3. Shift-click or click-drag the text and the edited path and choose Text→Attach to Path (11.30).

(N)OTE

If you attach text to an open path, any text beyond the end of the path moves to a new line that duplicates the shape, length, and alignment of the first line (11.31). If you attach text to a closed path such as a simple shape, any text that doesn't fit on the path is hidden but not discarded. Detach the text from the path and the hidden text reappears. You cannot attach text to joined paths.

Editing Text on a Path

Text-on-a-path remains editable as text and can have style attributes applied to it. In addition to editing type and style attributes, you also can manipulate the path's shape, the text's placement on the path, and its orientation to the path, ranging from the default, which uses the path as the text's baseline, to skewing orientations that distort to follow the path while keeping a vertical orientation.

1. To edit text-on-a-path, double-click it to open the Text Editor. Change the text and its attributes, and then click OK (11.32).

2. To move the text's starting point on a path, select the text-on-a-path and choose Window→Object.

3. Enter a value in the Offset field (11.33).

4. To flip text around the attached path, select the text and choose Text→Reverse Direction (11.34).

Select vertical orientation for text on a vertical path.

Line up text on the path with the alignment buttons.

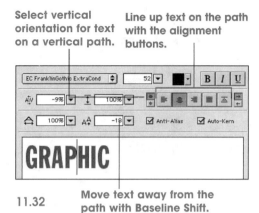

11.32

Move text away from the path with Baseline Shift.

11.33

Use negative values on closed paths or when the text is centered to move the text left.

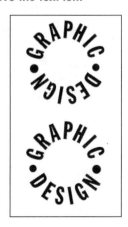

11.34

(T) I P

As a general rule, increase text's overall letter spacing when attaching it to a path to maintain legibility. Then adjust individual kern pairs to fix any gaps resulting from the text's placement on the path. If the text consists of more than one line, increase its leading, also.

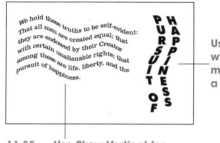

Use Skew Horizontal with vertical text to make text flow along a vertical path.

11.35   **Use Skew Vertical for 3D-looking text paths.**

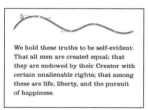

11.36

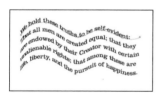

11.37

5. To change the orientation of text on a path, select the text and choose Text➔Orientation, and then choose Rotate Around Path, Vertical, Skew Vertical, or Skew Horizontal (11.35).

6. To reshape a selected text path, break apart the text-on-a-path into its individual objects by choosing Text➔Detach from Path, and then alter the path (11.36).

7. Click-drag or shift-click the text block and the path, and choose Text➔Attach to Path (11.37).

(N) O T E

The default text orientation, Rotate Around Path, makes the path the text's baseline. Vertical orientation lines up the text along the path, but the text remains vertical in relation to the document. Skew Vertical distorts text so that its baseline follows the path while the characters remain vertical. Skew Horizontal, in conjunction with vertical text on a path, distorts text so that the sides of the characters follow the path while the characters remain vertical.

Converting Text to Paths and Images

If you want to edit text with tools not described in this chapter, such as manipulating individual points with the Subselect tool or applying filters, convert the text to vector objects or image objects.

11.38

Text converted to paths becomes a group of vector path objects. Letters with more than one part, such as *i* and *j*, or with enclosed spaces, such as *o* and *p*, become joined objects that can be split apart for further editing, like pasting an image inside a counterspace.

11.39

Edit text converted to paths with any of the object-editing tools, including the Pen, Redraw Path, Freeform, Reshape Area, Knife, and Pointer tools.

1. To convert a selected text block to paths, choose Text→Convert to Paths. The text block converts to a grouped object (11.38).

2. To edit individual letters in the converted text block, choose Modify→Ungroup, and then use the Subselect tool to select individual points in the path objects for editing (11.39).

After splitting an *O*, select the counterspace and use Edit→Paste Inside to insert a copied image.

11.40

3. To split apart joined letters, such as *i* and *o*, select the letter and choose Modify→Split (11.40). To rejoin them, click-drag or Shift-click the parts and choose Modify→Join.

Converted text retains its appearance, but is no longer editable as text, except with Edit→ Undo.

To create outline type, set the fill to None and add a stroke.

11.41

Convert text to image when you want to use filters or paint tools such as the eraser.

11.42

4. To convert a selected text block to image objects, choose Modify→Merge Images (11.41).

5. To edit the merged image, double-click it with a selection tool to access image edit mode (11.42).

 I P

If the ascenders and descenders in a font are cut off, quit Fireworks and open Adobe Type Manager. Select Preserve Character Shapes instead of Preserve Line Spacing. Close ATM and restart your computer. If this doesn't solve the problem or if you aren't using ATM, convert the text to paths and the cut-off areas will reappear. However, the text is no longer editable as text.

CHAPTER 12

Befitting its status as one of the most basic types of interactive Web graphics, setting up an image map in Fireworks is simple. After importing or creating the base art in Fireworks, add hotspots with URL links that direct a browser to different Web pages. Create rectangular, circular, or custom-shaped hotspots, including hotspots that automatically match an object's shape in the base art.

FORMATTING IMAGE MAPS

Use Fireworks' URL Manager to import and organize links into libraries to make assigning URLs efficient. You can avoid the hassle and potential typos of manually adding URLs by using the URL Manager's import feature to copy all the URLs from your site's home page or any other HTML pages.

After adding URLs to the Manager, assign them and other Web attributes to individual hotspots and the overall image. Preview your image map in target browsers directly from Fireworks. Automatically generate client-side and server-side image maps.

When you export an image map, choose from several authoring templates to generate HTML code for adding the image map to a Web page. If you need something more, customize the HTML templates with JavaScript to meet your site's particular requirements.

Drawing Hotspots

Draw hotspots for your URL links over your base art with the hotspot tools in the Toolbox. Hotspots appear as Web objects on the Web Layer in the Layers panel. Lock, move, or hide the Web Layer to edit the image map graphics without affecting the hotspots.

12.1

1. Create rectangular or circular hotspots by click-dragging over the base art with the Rectangle ⬜ or Circle Hotspot tool ⭕ from the pop-up hotspot tool group in the Toolbox (12.1).

2. To create irregularly shaped hotspots, click corner points over the base art with the Polygon Hotspot tool ⬡ from the pop-up hotspot tool group (12.2). Close the shape by clicking its starting point.

3. Click-drag inside a hotspot with a selection tool to move it.

12.2

If a selected hotspot is difficult to see over color artwork, double-click it to open the Object Inspector and click the Hotspot color well to access the system color picker or use its pop-up Swatches palette to change the hotspot's color.

 **O T E**

Click-dragging the Rectangle or Circle hotspot tool automatically opens the Object Inspector, allowing you to set the hotspot's properties.

 I P

To move a selected hotspot one pixel at a time, use the keyboard's arrow keys.

12.3

4. Click-drag a hotspot corner point with the Subselect tool to adjust it (12.3).

5. To see the image map's graphics instead of the hotspots, turn off the Web Layer by clicking its "eye" icon in the Layers panel (12.4) or click-drag the Web Layer to position it beneath the other layers.

12.4

To access the image map graphics while keeping the hotspots visible, lock the Web Layer.

Hide/Reveal Layer

 O T E

Unlike vector shapes, you cannot add or delete points in a hotspot. You can only move points with the Subselect tool to adjust the hotspot's shape.

Adding Automatic Hotspots

Instead of manually drawing hotspots, use your image map to generate hotspots. Fireworks will automatically create hotspots for vector objects, bitmap selections, or text blocks, either one at a time or with multiple selections at once. Change the resulting hotspot's shape and fine-tune its visual mapping, if desired.

1. To create a hotspot in the shape of a vector object or text block, select the object and choose Insert→Hotspot (12.5).

2. To create multiple hotspots at once, select more than one object and choose Insert→ Hotspot. In the dialog box, choose Multiple for separate hotspot objects.

3. To create a rectangular hotspot that covers a marquee selection in image edit mode, choose Insert→Hotspot (12.6).

12.5 **Hotspots can only be straight-sided shapes or absolute circles. If a selection includes curves, but isn't a circle, Fireworks generates either a rectangular or a polygonal hotspot.**

12.6

 I P

Use the Layers panel to create automatic hotspots from selected vector objects by dragging the blue dot next to the active layer to the Web Layer (12.7).

12.7

12.8

12.9

4. To change a hotspot's shape, choose Window→Object and select a shape from the shape pop-up menu in the Object Inspector (12.8).

5. Click-drag inside a hotspot with a selection tool to move it.

6. Click-drag a hotspot corner point with the Subselect tool to adjust it.

 O T E

No matter how you make a hotspot—either by drawing it or creating it automatically—Fireworks places it on the Web Layer. Every Fireworks document contains a Web Layer, which cannot be renamed or deleted.

Ⓣ **I P**

Hotspots are layered in the order in which they are created. Wherever hotspots overlap, the one in front takes precedence (12.9). Use the Modify→Arrange menu to rearrange the order of hotspots after they are created.

Adding URLs to the Document

Typing a URL address for a hotspot link is time-consuming and an opportunity for error. A better strategy, especially when dealing with an image map's numerous links, is to import a list of links for the site from an HTML document, such as the site's home page, that already contains the needed links. Then adding URL links to hotspots is a simple point-and-click operation. By organizing your links into libraries, which you can reuse, update, and share with others, you can ensure consistency within a site.

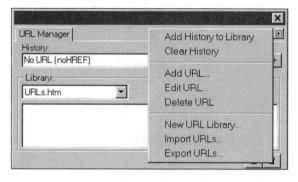

12.10

1. To start a new URL library, choose Window→URL Manager. In the URL Manager's Options pop-up menu, choose New URL Library (12.10).

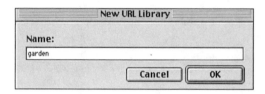

12.11

2. In the New URL Library dialog box, enter a name for the library and click OK (12.11). If the name does not appear as the default in the Library pop-up menu, click the arrow and select it (12.12).

To add a URL manually to a document, enter it here. To save it to the current library, click the + button.

12.12

 I P

URL libraries are stored as HTML documents in Fireworks 2/Settings/URL Libraries. To remove a library from the Library list, remove the file from the URL Libraries (folder)[directory].

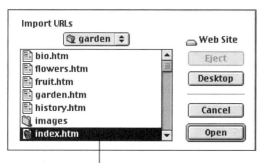

12.13   All the URLs in the selected HTML document are imported into the current library.

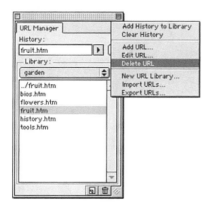

12.14

3. To import URL links from an HTML document into the current library, choose Import URLs in the URL Manager's Options pop-up menu.

4. In the Import URLs dialog box, locate the HTML document and click OK (12.13).

5. Delete a URL from the library by selecting it in the Library list and choosing Delete URL from the URL Manager's Options pop-up menu (12.14).

In addition to adding URL addresses from your HTML documents, you also can add URLs from Netscape Navigator bookmark files or Microsoft Internet Explorer favorites files (Macintosh only).

Assigning URLs to Hotspots

After drawing hotspots and adding URLs to your document, attach the URLs to hotspots. In addition to attaching URLs, you can add alternative text to display while the object is loading or if it's unavailable, and designate a target window or frame for the linked page to appear in.

1. Select a hotspot and choose Window→Object. In the Object inspector, select a URL from the Current URL pop-up menu for the hotspot link (12.15) or enter one manually.

2. In the <alt> field, enter text to display when the object is disabled or unavailable (12.16).

3. To display linked pages in a different browser window or frame, enter the target's name in the Link Target field or select a default in its pop-up menu.

12.15 **You can also select a URL from the History pop-up menu or an open library list.** **Session History**

12.16 **In Internet Explorer, alternative text also appears in rollover balloons.**

 I P

In addition to links libraries, the URL Manager records a temporary history of all the URLs used during a Fireworks session, including URLs already assigned to an open document. To add the session history to the current library, choose Add History to Library in the URL Manager's Options pop-up menu.

Adding Status Messages to Hotspots

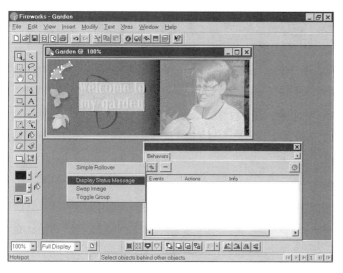

12.17

12.18 **You also can select a message from the pop-up list of the current graphic's status messages.**

12.19

Set a hotspot to display one status message on a mouse-over and another when the user clicks the hotspot.

Change the browser status bar message display for hotspots from the default link information to a custom message using Fireworks' Display Status Message behavior. Add up to three different messages per hotspot: one when the user's cursor moves over the hotspot, one when it rolls off the hotspot, and one when it clicks the hotspot.

1. Select a hotspot and choose Window→Behaviors. In the Behaviors Inspector, click the + button and choose Display Status Message (12.17).

2. In the Display Status Message dialog box, enter text to display in a browser's status bar when the mouse is over the hotspot (12.18). Then click OK.

3. To change the event that triggers a message display from a mouse over to a mouse out or on click, click the event's arrow button (12.19) and select an event.

4. To edit a status message, double-click it. To delete a message, select it and click the – button.

 I P

Use status messages to inform Web surfers of what they will see if they click a hotspot, instead of leaving the status at the default of displaying the linked URL.

Setting Image Map Properties

Before exporting an image map, set its overall properties in the Document Properties dialog box. Depending on which browser versions you are creating your image maps to work with, you can specify whether Fireworks generates HTML code for a client-side or server-side image map or both. Select a default URL for the areas of your image map that are not covered by hotspots so that all parts of the image are clickable. Add a text description that appears in a browser when the image is loading, disabled, or unavailable.

12.20

1. To set image map properties, choose File→Document Properties (12.20).

2. In the Document Properties dialog box, choose client-side, server-side, or both from the Map Type pop-up menu (12.21).

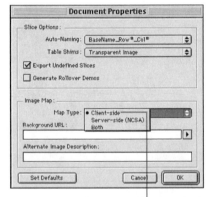

12.21   **Client-side is the default map type and is supported by browser versions 2.0 and later.**

A client-side image map stores its hotspot (MAP) information within its HTML document. Server-side image maps generate two documents, the HTML document and a MAP file, which need to be stored on a server and accessed by a CGI script. The server-side HTML document then needs to be edited to set the URL path to the MAP file's location on the server.

12.22

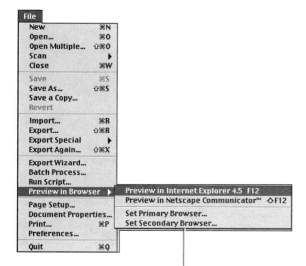

12.23   **Set up an additional preview browser.**

3. To add a link for the areas in the image map not covered by hotspots, enter a URL address in the Background URL field or click its pop-up arrow to access the image map's URL History list.

4. To display a text description in a browser when the image is loading or unavailable, enter the text in the Alternate Image Description field (12.22).

5. To save your settings as the default for future image maps, click Set Defaults. Click OK.

T I P

Background URL links interfere with Display Status Message behaviors in some browsers and are disabled. If you need a background link to work in a browser that doesn't support it, create a hotspot link for the background instead.

T I P

To preview the image map in a browser, define your default browser by choosing File→Preview in Browser→Set Primary Browser. In the Locate Primary Browser dialog box, find and select a browser and click OK. Choose File→Preview in Browser→Preview in [name of your default browser] **(12.23)**.

Exporting Image Maps

When exporting an image map, follow the same procedures you would for exporting other images. Optimize the graphic in the Export Preview window, and then name the graphics file in the Export dialog box and save it to the correct Web images folder (see Chapter 2, "Optimizing Art for the Web," for more information on optimizing and exporting graphics). The only difference is that when you export an image map, Fireworks generates HTML code for it based on the document properties you've set and formatted for the HTML editor you select.

Fireworks' image map HTML contains a link to the exported image, the hotspot coordinates and their Web page links, any attached behaviors, and code to set the Web page's background color to the image map's canvas or matte color.

1. To export an image map, choose File→Export, optimize the graphic in the Export Preview, and click Next **(12.24)**.

2. In the Export dialog box, name the file and select the location where you want to save it.

3. Choose an HTML output style from the Style pop-up menu.

   • Choose Generic for compact, basic HTML code.

   • Choose None to export the image only, no HTML.

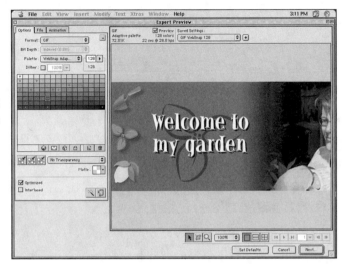

12.24

12.25

Generic HTML style includes all the HTML code for a single Web page.

Dreamweaver Library.lbi style doesn't generate a standalone HTML page and must be placed into an existing HTML page to work.

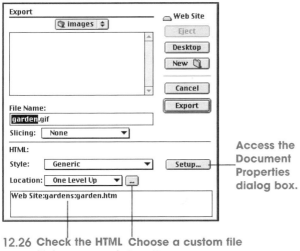

12.26 Check the HTML file's name and path. Choose a custom file location or name.

Access the Document Properties dialog box.

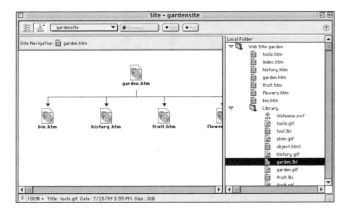

12.27

- Choose FrontPage to create an HTML page formatted to be compatible with Microsoft's FrontPage HTML editor.

- Choose Dreamweaver 2 to create an HTML page formatted to be compatible with Dreamweaver 2 HTML.

- Choose Dreamweaver Library.lbi to create a file that contains just the HTML code for the exported object, not a full Web page (12.25).

4. Select a location for the image map's HTML file in the Location pop-up menu (12.26) and click OK.

ⓣ I P

If you are creating an image map as a Dreamweaver library item, it must be saved in a folder named "Library" located at the site's root level (12.27). (When you choose Dreamweaver Library.lbi, Fireworks prompts you to do this.) Because the pages it links to probably won't reside in the Library folder, the hotspot URLs must include relative path information out of the folder. For example, in the URL Manager, add "../" to the beginning of the URLs attached to a library object to direct a browser to look one level up from the Library directory to find the linked Web page.

Inserting Image Maps into Web Pages

Add a Fireworks' image map to another Web page, using a simple text editor or a Web authoring program to copy and paste the image's link information, map coordinates, and status message JavaScript (if used) from the image map's HTML to the destination file's HTML. The code in Fireworks' image map HTML files contains clear directions for what to copy and paste into other HTML documents.

1. To place a client-side or server-side image map into another HTML document, open the image map's HTML document in a text editor or Web authoring program (12.28).

2. Copy the HTML code between the directions that read "Begin Copying Here" and "Stop Copying Here" (12.29).

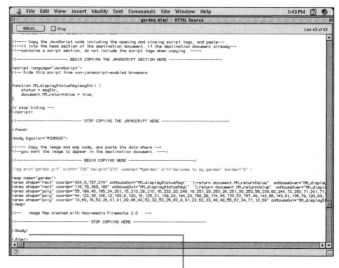

12.28 **When copying and pasting an image map, do not copy its <HTML> or <BODY> tags. The destination Web page's HTML already contains these tags.**

12.29

Copying an image map in a WYSIWYG Web authoring program copies the image only, not the map coordinates. You must access the HTML code to copy and paste the entire image map. If you don't want to deal with code and are using Dreamweaver 2 for Web authoring, export the image map as a Dreamweaver library file, which can be inserted into Dreamweaver pages like an image file.

12.30

12.31

12.32

If the document already contains JavaScript code, don't copy the image map's script tags.

3. Open the destination HTML file and paste the copied code into the document's <BODY> section where you want the image map located on the Web page (12.30).

4. If the image map has status messages, copy the JavaScript code between the directions that read "Begin Copying the JavaScript Section Here" and "Stop Copying the JavaScript Here" (12.31).

5. Paste the copied JavaScript code into the destination document's <HEAD> section before the </head> tag (12.32).

 **O T E**

If you are adding a server-side image map, store the MAP file on the server where it can be accessed by the appropriate CGI script. Then change the HREF tag in the destination HTML file that begins "path_to_map_file…" to the actual path to the image map's MAP file on the server.

Adding Fireworks HTML Templates

Fireworks' HTML output styles are designed for specific HTML editors, but you can add new output styles or edit existing ones to generate custom HTML to meet your site's requirements. For example, if you want Fireworks to generate HTML files with the .html suffix instead of the default .htm suffix, you can easily create templates for that without editing a line of code. If you know JavaScript, you can further customize your Fireworks templates in a text editor or create your own. The styles you create appear automatically in the Export dialog box.

1. To add a new set of HTML output style templates, quit Fireworks and locate a template folder in the Fireworks 2\Settings\HTML Code folder **(12.33)**.

2. Duplicate the folder and rename the duplicate folder **(12.34)**.

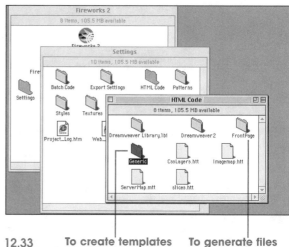

12.33 **To create templates by editing existing JavaScript, select Generic.**

To generate files with the .html suffix, select a templates folder.

(N) O T E

*If you want to change individual properties in Fireworks' HTML output templates, they are written in JavaScript and can be edited in a text editor **(12.35)**. However, if your JavaScript templates contain any errors, Fireworks cannot correct the errors nor can it successfully generate HTML using an invalid template.*

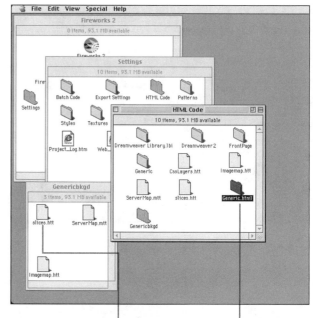

12.34 **To customize templates' JavaScript, edit the folder's files in a text editor. Do not rename the files or move them out of the folder.**

To create .html templates, append .html to the duplicate folder's name.

12.35

3. To use the new HTML output style, launch Fireworks, open an image map file, and choose File→Export.

4. Optimize the file and click Next. In the Export dialog box, name the file and select a save location for the image.

5. Choose the new folder name in the HTML Style pop-up list .

6. Select a save location for the image map's HTML file in the Location pop-up menu and click OK.

If you don't want to change all the URLs in a document, Shift-click only the hotspots you want to update and choose Selection as your search area.

12.36 **To change all the URLs in a document, choose File→Deselect All before clicking Replace All.**

(T) I P

After changing linked pages' file extensions, update their URL references in a document or group of documents by choosing Window→Find & Replace. In the Find & Replace panel, select the search area in the Search In pop-up menu and select URL in the Attribute pop-up menu. Enter .htm in the Find field and .html in the Change To field, and click Replace All (12.36). Find & Replace does not change URLs in libraries in the URL Manager nor does it change a background URL assigned in the Document Properties dialog box.

CHAPTER 13

In this chapter you learn how to...

Create Graphics for Rollover States

Define a Rollover

Add Simple Rollover Interactivity

Swap Images in Rollovers

Create Toggle Group Rollovers

Export Rollovers

Add New Style Templates

Add Rollovers to Web Pages

Although Web graphics with hotspot URL links are more attractive than plain hyperlinked text, they can be just as static. Perk up your Web pages by incorporating interactive rollovers that give visual feedback according to what the mouse is doing.

MAKING A ROLLOVER BUTTON

Fireworks provides everything you need to make rollover buttons. Create up to four different states per button, add a URL link, and assign rollover behaviors to trigger the button's various states. Then export the button, and Fireworks generates the JavaScript and HTML code you need to incorporate the interactive button in a Web page. From there, it's a simple cut-and-paste operation, and you've added rollover interactivity to your Web pages.

Organize button states by using Fireworks' frames. Set up a rollover's interactivity with slice objects. And for precise rollovers, add hotspot objects. Choose one of Fireworks' three types of button behaviors: simple rollover, for individual multistate buttons; swap image, for interlocking multistate buttons; or toggle group, for interdependent multistate buttons.

Add new templates to customize your Fireworks output styles to meet specific needs. Then export your rollovers and insert them into your HTML pages.

Creating Graphics for Rollover States

Fireworks' simple rollovers can be composed of up to four states or modes: the default or up state; the mouse over state, which the button changes to when the cursor is rolled over it; the down state, which is how the button looks on its destination page; and the mouse over down state, which the button changes to when the cursor is rolled over it in the down state.

13.1

Use Fireworks' Live Effects to quickly render 3D button states. Or if you prefer, create unique button art for each state and place the button states on separate frames.

Use Outer Bevel when you want to maintain the object's shape within the button.

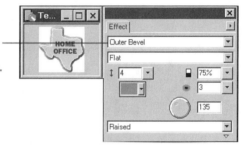

13.2

1. To render rollover states using Live Effects, import or create a vector graphic as the initial button state (13.1).

2. With the vector graphic selected, choose Window→ Effect and select Inner or Outer Bevel. Adjust the settings for the button's default/up state appearance. Leave the Button Preset at Raised (13.2).

 **O T E**

Fireworks uses frames for storing the different button states. Fireworks' frames are like animation cels, not Web page frames. You can view only one frame in a document at a time, like in a flipbook. All the frames in a document are the same size and have the same layer structure as the other frames.

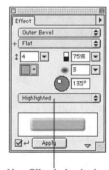

Live Effects include four default button effects to use as button states.

13.3

13.4

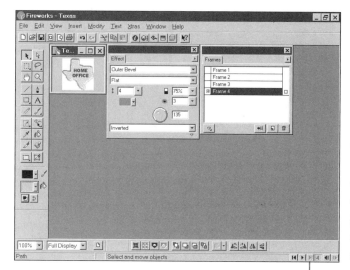

13.5

Use the VCR controls to flip through the frames of a rollover or to play them as an animation.

3. To add a mouseover state, choose Window→Frames, and in the Frames panel, duplicate Frame 1 by dragging it to the New/Duplicate icon at the bottom of the panel.

4. Click Frame 2 to advance to it. Select the vector graphic, and change the Button Preset to Highlighted in the Effect panel (13.3).

5. To add a down state, repeat steps 3 and 4, changing the Button Preset to Inset (13.4).

6. To add an overdown state, repeat steps 3 and 4 changing the Button Preset to Inverted (13.5).

7. Choose Modify→Document →Trim Canvas to crop the document to the button art.

(T) I P

If you created button states in Photoshop on layers, open the document in Fireworks with preferences set to retain layers. (Render masks, grouped layers, and layers with mode effects first.) In the Layers panel, double-click a layer and turn off Share Across Frames in the Layer Options dialog box. Repeat with the rest of the button states. Choose Edit→Select All and click the Distribute to Frames icon at the bottom of the Frames panel.

Defining a Rollover

Rollovers require two things: a trigger that sends a message when the user interacts with it, and a target (or targets) that receives the message and responds. Create triggers and targets with Fireworks' two Web objects: the hotspot and the slice. The differences between the two Web objects are few and simple: Slices can send and receive messages; hotspots can only send messages; but slices can only be rectangles, whereas hotspots can be irregular shapes.

At the minimum, a rollover requires two-state artwork and a slice object. To create a precise rollover trigger for an irregular shape, add a custom-shaped hotspot over the slice (13.6).

Slices differ from hotspots in another way: As their name implies, they cut the base art into individual files on export. Fireworks generates HTML to reassemble the slices into a table when viewed in a browser.

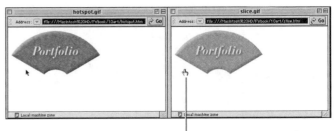

13.6

Without a shaped hotspot trigger, the entire slice area responds to mouse actions.

13.7

 **O T E**

When you draw a slice object, Fireworks automatically figures the rest of the slices needed to generate a table and displays the cuts as slice guides on the art in the Document window. You cannot edit slice guides yourself. When you edit the slice object, Fireworks automatically adjusts the guides.

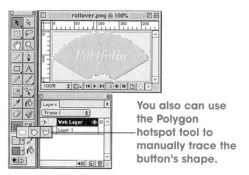

You also can use the Polygon hotspot tool to manually trace the button's shape.

13.8

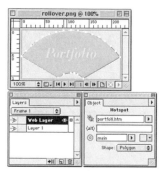

13.9

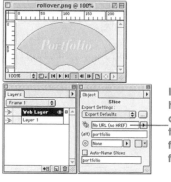

If you are not using a hotspot trigger, enter a URL link and a target window or frame (if desired) for the linked page.

13.10

1. To create a slice object automatically, select a button object in the Document window and choose Insert→Slice (13.7).

2. Adjust the slice object, if necessary, with the Subselect tool.

3. To add a shaped rollover trigger, choose Window→Layers and click the "eye" icon for the Web Layer in the Layer panel to hide the layer. Select the Button object in the Document window and choose Insert→Hotspot (13.8).

4. With the hotspot object selected, choose Window→Object. In the Object Inspector, enter a URL for the hotspot link and a target window or frame (if desired) for the linked page to appear in (13.9).

5. Select the slice object. In the Object Inspector, enter a description in the <alt> field, uncheck Auto-Name Slices and enter a name in the Custom Base Name field below the check box (13.10).

 I P

When creating a file that contains a single slice object, make the slice object cover the entire document so Fireworks doesn't generate unneeded slices.

Adding Rollover Interactivity

After creating art for different button states and adding triggers and targets for URL links, attach a Fireworks' JavaScript behavior to a button to activate its states. For individual rollover buttons, use Fireworks' Simple Rollover behavior. Upon export, Fireworks generates the JavaScript code to swap the button states as a user interacts with the button (see "Exporting Rollovers" later in this chapter for more information).

1. For a precise rollover, select the hotspot object of a multistate button you've created and choose Window→Behaviors (13.11).

2. In the Behaviors Inspector, click the + button and choose Simple Rollover (13.12) from the Add Behaviors pop-up menu.

 **O T E**

For Fireworks Simple Rollover JavaScript to work, place the different buttons states on the first four frames of a document (13.13).

 I P

If you haven't defined a default browser, choose File→Preview in Browser→Set Primary Browser. In the Locate Primary Browser dialog box, select a browser on your hard drive and click OK. Add a second default browser by choosing File→Preview in Browser→Set Secondary Browser.

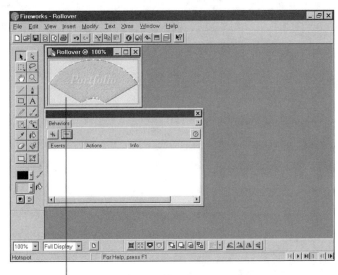

13.11 **For a rectangular rollover, select the slice object instead.**

13.12

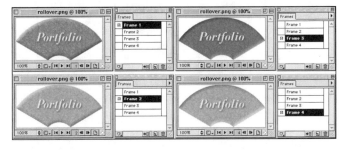

13.13

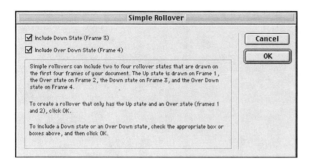

13.14

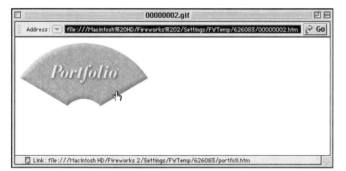

13.15

3. If the button is a three-state or four-state rollover, check Include Down State (Frame 3) and/or Include Over Down State (Frame 4) in the Simple Rollover dialog box (13.14). Then click OK.

4. Choose File→Save. In the Save File dialog box, name the master PNG file and select a location for it. Click Save.

5. Check the rollover in a browser by choosing File→Preview in Browser→Preview in [name of your default browser] (13.15). Then export it. (See "Exporting Rollovers" later in this chapter to export your rollover.)

O T E

Fireworks' Simple Rollover behavior keeps track of a button's down state with a JavaScript "cookie." When you click a button while previewing it in a browser, the cookie tells the browser to display the button's down state and disable the button. If you return to Fireworks without (quitting)[exiting] the browser, and then preview again, the button will remain in the down state. To erase the cookie, (quit)[exit] the browser.

Swapping Images in Rollovers

A slice must be rectangular and can have only one simple rollover trigger. The only way to define a precise rollover for a sliced image is to use a hotspot. If your Web page layout includes irregularly shaped buttons that can't be contained within separate rectangles (interlocking buttons, for example), define the buttons as multiple shaped hotspots over a single rectangular slice. Assign a simple rollover to one hotspot and Fireworks' Swap Image behavior to the others.

1. To create a swap image rollover button set, lay out the default/up button state art for all the buttons as one frame (13.16).

2. In the Frames panel (Window→ Frames), click-drag Frame 1 to the New/Duplicate Frame button to create Frame 2 for the first button's mouse over state (13.17).

I P

Use Swap Image behaviors when you don't want JavaScript "cookies" to track button states. For example, if you want to use text hyperlinks in your site in addition to rollovers, cookies won't be able to track button states correctly. Use Swap Image behaviors instead. You can attach multiple behaviors to the same hotspot, so you can mimic the mouse over and clicked state of a simple rollover.

13.16

To add frames for mouse down and mouse click, choose Duplicate Frame, enter the number of frames you want to add, and select After Current Frame.

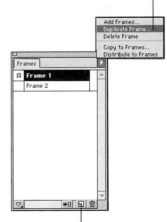

13.17 **New/Duplicate Frame**

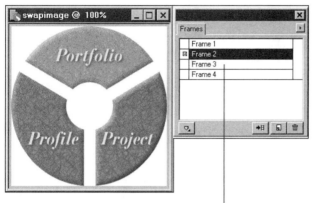

13.18

Repeat if the button has a down and/or on mouse click state, changing its appearance in the next frame(s).

Enter 1 for mouse over, 2 for mouse over and mouse down or on mouse click, or 3 for all three alternate states.

13.19

Repeat if the second button has a down and/or on mouse click state, changing its appearance in the next frame(s).

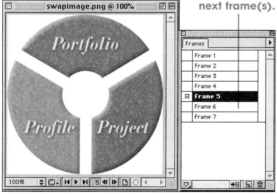

13.20

3. Click Frame 2, select the first button, and change its appearance to its mouse over state (13.18).

4. Select Frame 1 again and choose Duplicate Frame from the Frames panel Options pop-up menu. In the Duplicate Frame dialog box (13.19), enter the number of frames you need for the second button's alternate button states in the Number field or use its pop-up slider. Check At the End for the Insert New Frames choice and click OK.

5. Click the first new frame added and select the second button. Change its appearance to its mouse over state (13.20).

continues

 I P

To keep your file size as small as possible, choose Modify→Document→Trim Canvas to crop the document and the slice to the buttons.

Swapping Images in Rollovers continued

6. Repeat steps 4 and 5 for the rest of the buttons **(13.21)**.

7. Select the Slice tool in the Toolbox 🔲 and click-drag one slice object over all the buttons.

8. In the Object Inspector, uncheck Auto-Name Slices and enter a name in the Custom Base Name field below the check box **(13.22)**.

9. Click the "eye" icon for the Web Layer in the Layers panel (Window→Layers) to hide the layer. Select a button object in the Document window and choose Insert→Hotspot **(13.23)**.

10. With the hotspot object selected, enter a URL for the hotspot link, an <alt> tag, and a target window or frame (if desired) for the linked page in the Object Inspector.

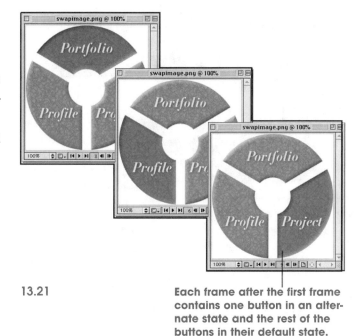

13.21

Each frame after the first frame contains one button in an alternate state and the rest of the buttons in their default state.

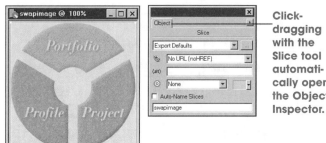

13.22

Click-dragging with the Slice tool automatically opens the Object Inspector.

 **O T E**

To ensure that button rollovers behave realistically, Fireworks' JavaScript preloads all the button states before displaying the button.

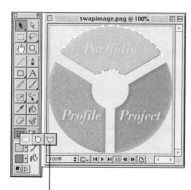

You also can use the Polygon hotspot tool
to manually trace the button's shape.

13.23

13.24

11. Repeat steps 9 and 10 with the rest of the buttons (13.24).

12. Select the first button's hotspot and choose Window→ Behaviors. In the Behaviors Inspector, click the + button and choose Simple Rollover from the Add Behaviors pop-up menu.

13. If the button is a three-state or four-state rollover, check Include Down State (Frame 3) and/or Include Over Down State (Frame 4) in the Simple Rollover dialog box. Then click OK.

continues

(T) I P

Write a list of which frame contains which button's button state to make selecting the source frame in the Swap Image dialog box easier.

Swapping Images in Rollovers continued

14. Select the second button's hotspot object. In the Behaviors Inspector, click the + button and choose Swap Image (13.25).

15. In the Swap Image dialog box, select the frame that contains the second button's mouse over state in the Source of Swap Frame No. pop-up menu (13.26). Then click OK.

16. Repeat steps 14 and 15 if the second button has an on mouse click state (13.27).

17. Repeat steps 14 through 16 for the rest of the buttons.

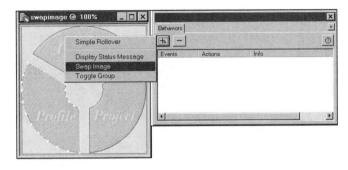

13.25

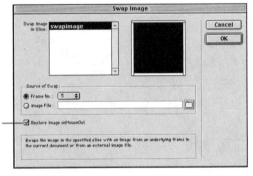

Restore Image onMouseOut replaces the mouse over button state with the default state when the cursor moves off the button.

13.26

 I P

Swap Image behavior doesn't track which button was clicked and should be displayed in a down or clicked-on state. Export the mouse down frames of Swap Image button sets separately by choosing File→Export, selecting a mouse down frame in the Export Preview window, and then exporting it to the same folder you exported the Swap Image button set to. Replace the default Swap Image graphic in each Web page that contains the Swap Image button set with the correct mouse down version for that page. For more information on exporting, see "Exporting Rollovers" later in this chapter.

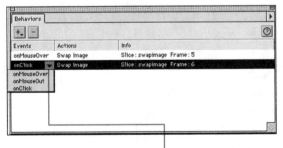

13.27   **Click the second event's arrow button and select onClick to trigger the second button's on mouse click state.**

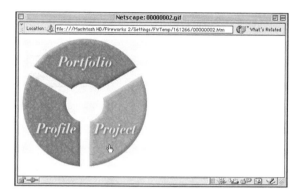

13.28

File Size

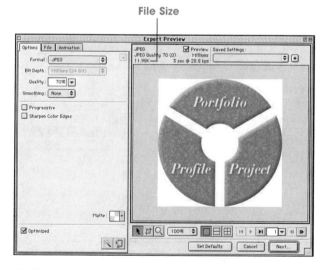

13.29

18. Choose File→Save. In the Save File dialog box, name the master PNG file and select a save location. Click Save.

19. Check the swap image rollover set in a browser by choosing File→Preview in Browser→ Preview in [name of your default browser] (13.28). Then export the rollovers. See "Exporting Rollovers" later in this chapter to export your swap image rollovers.

(T) I P

If load time is an issue, consider using only two-state Swap Image button sets. Swap Image button sets require a separate frame for each button's button state, which increases download time. Choose File→Export to check the estimated file size and download time of all the frames in a JavaScript rollover in the Export Preview window (13.29)*.*

Creating Toggle Group Rollovers

For navigation bars, use Fireworks' Toggle Group behavior, which links a group of related rollovers. When one rollover is triggered, it triggers responses in the other rollovers in the group as well as updating the Web page. For example, when a navigation button is clicked and changes to its down state, a previously clicked button changes at the same time from its down to up state and the Web page changes, also.

1. To create a toggle group rollover, import or create the button states for all the buttons on Frames 1 through 4 (13.30).

2. To create all the button slices at once, select the button objects and choose Insert→Slice. In the dialog box, choose Multiple for separate slice objects.

3. Adjust the slices, if necessary, with the Subselect tool.

Each frame in a toggle group contains one state of all the buttons in the group.

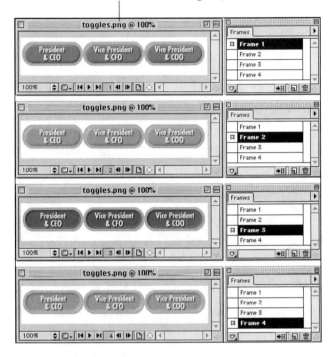

13.30

Slice guides demonstrate how the image will be cut apart when exported.

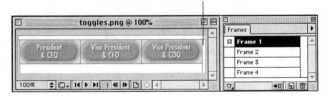

13.31

When slicing, choose View→Guide Options→ Snap to Guides to make it easy to butt slice objects tightly against each other. Fireworks creates separate image files for each slice object and any extra spaces around them, even if the space is only one pixel wide (13.31).

13.32

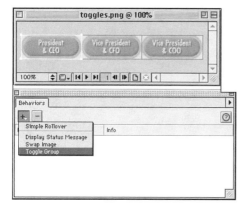

13.33

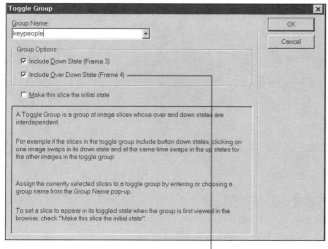

13.34 Over Down in toggle groups appears when the cursor moves over a down-state button.

4. Choose Modify→Document→ Trim Canvas to crop the document and the slices to the toggle group buttons.

5. Double-click a slice object to open the Object Inspector. In the Object Inspector, enter a URL link, an <alt> tag, and a target frame for the linked page to appear in (if desired). Press Enter. Uncheck Auto-Name Slices and enter a name in the Custom Base Name field below the check box (13.32). Repeat with the rest of the slices.

6. Select the first slice object and choose Window→Behaviors. In the Behaviors Inspector, click the + button and choose Toggle Group from the Add Behaviors pop-up menu (13.33).

7. In the Toggle Group dialog box, enter a name for the toggle group in the Group Name field (13.34).

8. If the button is a three-state or four-state rollover, check Include Down State (Frame 3) and/or Include Over Down State (Frame 4). Then click OK.

continues

Creating Toggle Group Rollover continued

9. Repeat steps 5 through 7 for the rest of the slices in the toggle group. In the Toggle Group dialog box, use the pop-up arrow next to the Group Name field to select the same toggle group name for each slice in the group (13.35).

10. Choose File→Save. In the Save File dialog box, name the master PNG file and select the location where you want to save it. Click Save.

11. Check the toggle group in a browser by choosing File→ Preview in Browser→Preview in [name of your default browser] (13.36). Then export it. (See "Exporting Rollovers" next to export your toggle groups.)

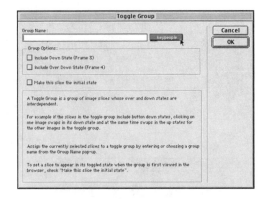

13.35

13.36

 **O T E**

Like simple rollovers, toggle groups use JavaScript cookies to track which button state to display and which button to disable. The cookies can't track hypertext links or other navigation methods used in a frameset. If you want to use multiple navigation methods with Fireworks' rollovers, use Fireworks version 1-style button templates to generate HTML files, which work without "cookies." See "Adding New Style Templates" later in this chapter for more information.

Exporting Rollovers

Export
images ▢
Web Site

Eject
Desktop
New
Cancel
Export

Base Name:
rollover.gif
Slicing: Use Slice Objects ▼

HTML:
Style: Dreamweaver2 ▼   Setup...
Location: One Level Up ▼ ...
Web Site:finearts:rollover.htm

13.37

Export
images ▢
Web Site

Eject
Desktop
New
Cancel
Export

Base Name:
rollover.gif
Slicing: Use Slice Objects ▼

HTML:
Style: Same Directory
One Level Up   ▼   Setup...
Location: ✓ Custom...   ...
Web Site:finearts:rollover.htm

13.38   **Choose Custom or click the ... (ellipsis) button
to select a different location or filename.**

Exporting rollovers is similar to exporting image maps. Optimize the graphic, and then export it. Fireworks generates JavaScript and HTML code for the rollover based on your parameters and saves the resulting HTML page to wherever you designate. When you export a simple rollover, Fireworks generates JavaScript that displays the button in its correct state whether it's placed in a frameset or in multiple HTML documents.

1. To export a rollover, choose File→Export, optimize the graphic in the Export Preview, and click Next.

2. In the Export dialog box, name the file and select a location for it (13.37).

3. Choose an HTML output style from the Style pop-up menu.

4. Select a location for the rollover's HTML file in the Location pop-up menu (13.38).

5. Click Export, and then in the Document window, choose File→Save to save the export settings in the master PNG file.

Fireworks' rollover JavaScript includes browser detection and is compatible with Netscape Navigator and Microsoft Internet Explorer, versions 3.0 and later. In browsers such as Internet Explorer 3, which cannot display all four button states, the JavaScript directs the browser to display the default/up state only. The URL link works correctly.

Adding New Style Templates

If the default HTML style templates don't meet your needs, modify them by editing their JavaScript in a text editor, or download a new template from Macromedia's Web site.

Macromedia updates templates and creates new ones based on customer requests, which are available on their Web site. As a general rule, you need to have the latest version of Fireworks to use the templates.

1. To add new templates, download them from `http://www.macromedia.com/support/fireworks/downloads.html` (13.39).

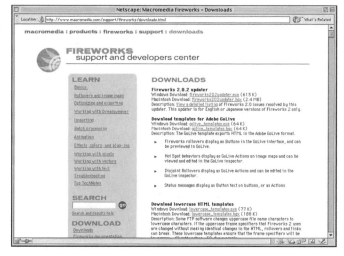

13.39

2. Double-click the (.sea)[.exe] self-extracting archive file(s) on your hard drive to decompress the template folder(s).

3. Drag the resulting template folder(s) into the Fireworks 2\ Settings\HTML Code folder (13.40).

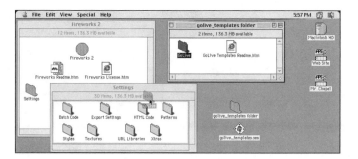

13.40

 **O T E**

Downloadable style templates that are currently available generate Adobe GoLive-compatible HTML, files with lowercase slice names to use with UNIX servers, and Fireworks version 1-style button templates that can be used with the Generate Rollover Demos document property to generate HTML files that work without "cookies."

13.41

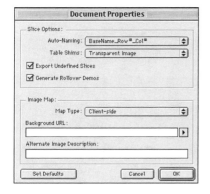

13.42

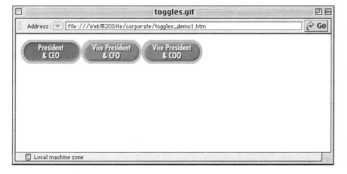

13.43

4. To use a new template, restart Fireworks, open a file and choose File→Export.

5. Optimize the file and click Next. In the Export dialog box, name the file and select a save location for the image.

6. Choose the new folder name, in the HTML Style pop-up list (13.41).

7. If you select FW1-Style Buttons, click the Setup button and choose Generate Rollover Demos in the Document Properties dialog box (13.42), and then click OK.

8. Select a save location for the graphic's HTML file in the Location pop-up menu and click Export. In the Document window, choose File→Save to save the export settings in the master PNG file.

Ⓝ **O T E**

For each rollover or toggle group button that includes a down state, the Fireworks version 1-style button templates export a separate Demo Rollover HTML file. Each resulting [file name]_demo.htm file contains a disabled button in its down state, so that when the page is loaded in a browser, that button is down and the rest of the buttons function normally (13.43).

Adding Rollovers to Web Pages

To add rollovers to HTML documents, use a text editor or a Web authoring program to copy and paste the rollover's JavaScript and image link code into the documents. Fireworks' HTML files contain clear directions for what to copy and paste with one exception: the preload command.

The preload command is within the rollover's <body> tag and isn't clearly separated from the rest of the HTML code as the JavaScript and image link code is. This makes for some tricky cutting and pasting from a rollover's HTML to another document to get the preload command to work.

1. To add a rollover to another HTML document, open the rollover's HTML document in a text editor or Web authoring tool.

2. Copy the JavaScript code from the rollover's <head> section between the directions that say "Begin Copying the JavaScript Section Here" and "Stop Copying the JavaScript Section Here" **(13.44)**.

If the destination document contains JavaScript, don't copy the rollover's script tags. Copy the code between the <script> tags, and paste it in the destination file before the </script> tag.

13.44

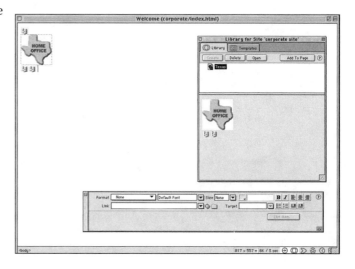

13.45

ⓃOTE

If you plan to reuse your rollovers throughout your site and are using Dreamweaver 2 for Web authoring, export the rollover as a Dreamweaver library file. Then instead of cutting and pasting HTML code, you can drag and drop the library item into a Dreamweaver page **(13.45)**, *and the JavaScript rollover, swap image, and preload code will copy automatically into the Web page. Don't place the rollover on a layer in Dreamweaver—the JavaScript won't copy over.*

13.46 **When copying and pasting a rollover, do not copy its <html> or <body> tags. The destination Web page already contains these tags.**

13.47

3. Open the destination HTML file and paste the copied JavaScript code into the destination document's <head> section before the </head> tag.

4. Copy the rollover's table and map HTML code between the directions that say "Begin Copying the Table Here" and "Stop Copying the Table Here" (13.46).

5. Paste the copied code into the document's <body> section where you want the rollover located on the Web page.

6. Copy the rollover's preload call from the <body> tag beginning with "onLoad="MM_preloadImages(' and ending with the close quote (") before the > at the end of the body tag (13.47).

7. Paste the preload call into the destination document's <body> tag.

 O T E

Fireworks' JavaScript for rollovers preloads the different button states, so when a Web page containing rollovers first loads into a Web browser, all the button states load into the browser's memory before the button is available. This makes the button's highlight state appear immediately when the cursor rolls over the button instead of waiting for it to download.

CHAPTER 14

In this chapter you learn how to...

Lay Out Web Pages

Create a Frameset

Add Layered Graphics As Rollovers and Animations

Import Rollovers and Animations

Prepare Mixed Format Pages for Export

Set Slice Document Properties

Export the Web Page

Swap In External Files

Create a Disjointed Rollover

Export Slices As Multiple Files

Export Cascading Style Sheet Layers

Substitute Files for Slices

Add a Nested Table

Fine-Tune Your Web Page

WYSIWYG Web authoring programs have made designing Web pages easier than coding pages in a non-visual HTML editor, but they still require you to deal with the Web page's structure—its tables, layers, and framesets—before you start arranging elements onscreen. You still have to deal with many technical issues before you get to the art of designing a page.

DESIGNING AND PRODUCING WEB PAGES

Use Fireworks instead for laying out your pages. Fireworks' open canvas enables you to place elements wherever you want onscreen, plus you can move, crop, resize, or otherwise edit the elements all within the same program. Web pages designed and produced in Fireworks can provide a rich visual experience. Because Fireworks lets you optimize each graphic for export individually, you can combine different types of Web graphics in a single file while maintaining their quality.

Design Web pages and framesets in Fireworks, creating graphics within the file or adding art, animation, and rollovers from other sources. Set up a custom page grid, and then lay out a page. Include HTML text areas, mixed graphics types, and GIF animations, and then slice to separate the different file types and add JavaScript behaviors for rollovers. Export each area with its own export settings for optimal quality. When you export the document, Fireworks generates an HTML table that reassembles the pieces so they appear as a seamless page in a Web browser.

Laying Out Web Pages

Set up custom grids for your Web pages to aid in aligning objects on a page and to ensure layout consistency across different Web pages. Set ruler guides to specific pixel distances for accurate layouts. Then create graphics on a Web page directly or import art from other graphics programs and other Fireworks' files, including rollovers and animated GIFs.

1. Choose File→New to create a new document. In the New Document dialog box, enter your Web page's measurements and screen resolution. Select a background color and click OK.

2. To set up a custom grid, choose View→Rulers to display the horizontal and vertical pixel rulers in the Document window, and then click-drag guides from the rulers (14.1).

3. For precise positioning, double-click a guide and enter a value in pixels in the Move Guide dialog box (14.2). After positioning the guides, lock them in position by choosing View→Guide Options→Lock Guides.

Move the zero point by click-dragging from the rulers' top-left corner. Reset it by double-clicking the top-left corner.

Delete a guide by dragging it off the canvas.

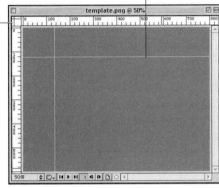

14.1

Guide distance is measured from the rulers' zero point, not the image's top-left corner.

Edit guide color or delete all guides by choosing View→Guide Options→Edit Guides.

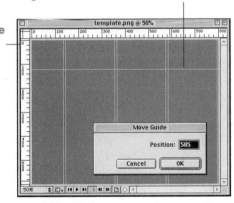

14.2

If you resize your document (Modify→Document→Image Size), any guides you have created in the document also resize.

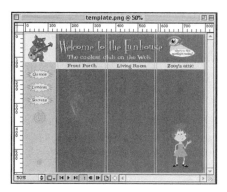

14.3

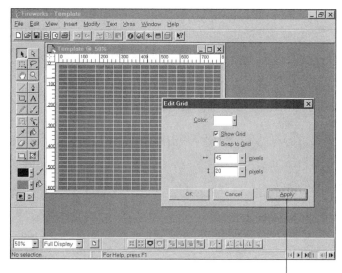

14.4   **Click Apply to proof the grid.**

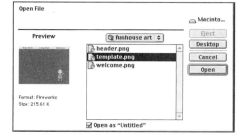

14.5

4. Create the page graphics, including GIF animations and rollovers, in position or import them from other files (14.3). For more information on adding graphics, refer to the relevant tasks later in this chapter.

5. Save the master PNG file (File→Save).

6. To optimize the different areas of the Web page, see "Preparing Mixed Format Pages for Export" later in this chapter.

 I P

To set up a grid of evenly spaced guides in the Web page, choose View→Grid Options→Edit Grid. In the Grids panel, check Show Grid, and then enter measurements in pixels for the horizontal and vertical grid spacing or use their pop-up sliders (14.4). (The smallest grid size is 5×5 pixels.)

I P

If you have elements that repeat across several Web pages, lay out those elements in one document and save. To use the document as a template, choose File→Open and in the Open File dialog box, locate the template and check Open As "Untitled" before clicking Open (14.5).

Creating a Frameset

In addition to creating Web pages, use Fireworks to lay out framesets, Web pages that are divided into frames. You design the frameset in one piece like a Web page, and then use the Slice and Crop tools to select and save individual frames from the frameset. After your frames are all saved, you can reassemble the frame files in an HTML frameset in a Web authoring program.

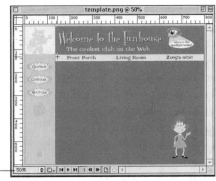

14.6

Fireworks doesn't scroll when you click-drag, so select a page reduction in the Set Magnification pop-up menu that shows the entire area you want to cover.

1. Lay out the frameset as you would a Web page in Fireworks, select the Slice tool in the Toolbox and then click-drag over the first frame area on the Web page (14.6).

2. Adjust the slice if necessary with the Subselect tool.

3. Repeat steps 1 and 2 for the rest of the frames in the frameset.

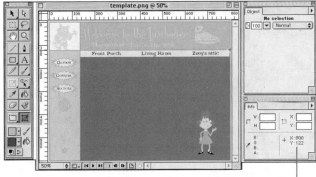

14.7

Pixel coordinates

ⓃOTE

When you draw a slice, Fireworks sets up slice guides for how the entire image will export as slices. Slice guides cannot be adjusted like regular ruler guides; they update as you add, move, or resize slice objects. Fireworks' Slice tool is very accurate: If you leave even one pixel of space between two slice objects, it creates a separate image file for that space. Check slices' X and Y pixel coordinates in the Info panel (Window→Info) **(14.7)**.

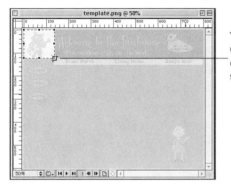

Turn on Snap to Guides to make cropping to the slice easier.

14.8

After cropping, the slice object is no longer needed and can be deleted.

14.9

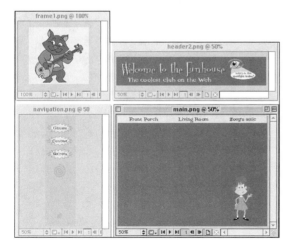

14.10

4. Select the Crop tool in the Pointer tool set in the Toolbox, and click-drag a crop marquee over the first slice (14.8).

5. Adjust the crop marquee, if needed, by dragging its handles, and then double-click inside the selection to crop. Select the slice object with the Pointer tool and press (Delete) [Backspace] (14.9).

6. Choose File→Save As, and enter a name and save location for the first frame's PNG file in the Save Document dialog box. Click Save.

7. Reopen the master PNG file and repeat steps 4 through 6 with the rest of the frames in the frameset (14.10).

8. To optimize the frame files, see "Preparing Mixed Format Pages for Export" later in this chapter.

(T) I P

To find a frame's pixel dimensions before setting up its frameset in a Web authoring program, click and hold the Page Preview icon 🗔 *at the bottom of the Document window. After exporting all the frame files in the frameset, assemble them in a Web authoring program.*

Adding Layered Graphics As Rollovers and Animations

Web pages designed in Fireworks are not limited to static images. If you have created rollovers or animations as layered art in Fireworks or in other compatible graphics programs (14.11), you can import the files and use Fireworks' Distribute to Frames feature to translate the layered graphics to rollovers or animated GIFs.

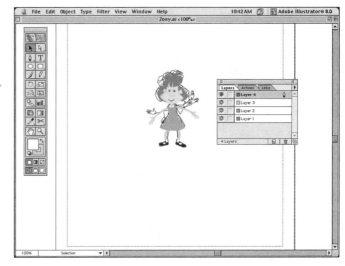

14.11

1. To import layered graphics into an open document and convert them to frames, choose Window→Layers and click the New/Duplicate Layer icon [icon] at the bottom of the Layers panel. Double-click the new layer in the Layers panel and name it in the Layers Options dialog box (14.12). Click OK.

2. Choose File→Import, locate the file in the Import File dialog box, and click Open.

If you are importing a layered vector graphic file from a compatible graphics program, resize the file, if desired, in the Vector File Options dialog box, but ignore layer options. Fireworks cannot convert layers to frames when importing, only when opening a file. Click OK.

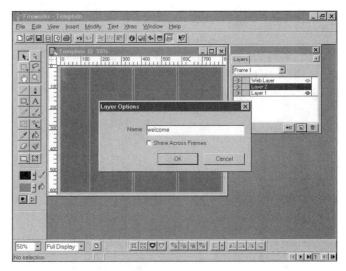

14.12

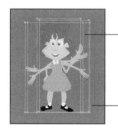

If a vector graphic layer contains more than one object, group those objects before importing.

When importing Photoshop files, each layer is converted to an image object. If a vector graphic layer contains more than one object, group those objects before importing.

14.13

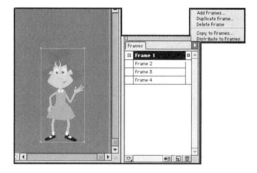

14.14

3. With the empty layer selected, position the angle cursor at the top-left corner of the area where you want to import and click (14.13). Click-drag to move the imported objects, if needed.

4. With the imported objects selected, choose Window→ Frames, and then choose Distribute to Frames from the Frames panel Options pop-up menu to move each object to a new frame (14.14).

5. To prepare the document for export, see "Preparing Mixed Format Pages for Export" later in this chapter.

 O T E

Bitmap file formats you can import include Adobe Photoshop versions 3 and later, BMP, GIF, JPEG, PICT, PNG, TIFF, Targa, and Macromedia xRes LRG. Vector graphic file formats you can import include Adobe Illustrator versions 3 and later, Macromedia FreeHand 7 or 8, and CorelDRAW 7 or 8 (uncompressed).

Importing Rollovers and Animations

Importing an existing Fireworks rollover brings in only the first frame, including its Web layer and any attached behaviors. To add the alternate button states, drag and drop between files instead. Then use the Distribute to Frames feature to automatically create frames for all the button states.

These tactics also work with animated GIFs. However, dragging and dropping is tedious. If the animation has more than a few frames, consider swapping images or substituting files. You also can swap images or substitute files for rollovers. (See "Swapping In External Files" and "Substituting Files for Slices" for more information.)

1. With the destination document open, choose Window→Layers and lock any graphics layers (not the Web layer) by clicking their lock boxes in the Layers panel (14.15). Click the New/Duplicate Layer icon. Double-click the new layer and name it in the Layers Options dialog box. Click OK.

2. Choose Windows→Frames, and select Frame 1 in the Frames panel (14.16).

Lock/
Unlock

14.15   New/Duplicate Layer

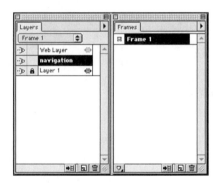

14.16

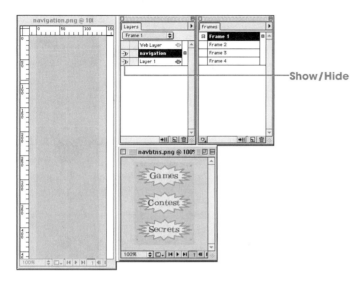

Show/Hide

14.17

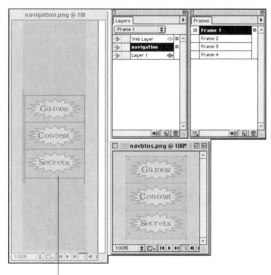

14.18　**Dragging from one document to another places the copied object(s) in the center of the document.**

3. With the empty layer selected in the Layers panel, choose File→Open. Locate the rollover's file in the Open File dialog box and click Open.

4. In the Layers panel, turn off the rollover's Web layer by clicking the Show/Hide icon. If the rollover contains more than one object per frame (for example, text on a button), choose Edit→ Select All and Modify→Group (14.17).

5. Select Frame 2 in the Frames panel, and choose Edit→Select All and Modify→Group. Repeat selecting and grouping with the rest of the frames.

6. Select Frame 1 in the Frames panel. In the Layers panel, turn the Web layer back on. Choose Edit→Select All. Click-drag the graphic and Web objects to the destination document (14.18).

continues

 I　P

Organize your Web page document's slices with color-coding. Use the color well in the Object Inspector to change the color of different types of slices, such as placeholder slices for later file substitution, frameset slices for cropping, and slices that include behaviors. This visual record can make it easier to remember all the tasks you need to do before exporting a page.

Importing Rollovers and Animations continued

7. Return to the rollover document and turn off the Web layer in the Layers panel.

8. Select Frame 2 in the Frames panel. Select the rollover object and click-drag it to the destination document (14.19). Repeat with the rest of the frames in the rollover document.

9. In the destination document, choose Edit→Select All to select the rollover objects and their Web objects. Click-drag them to their desired location (14.20).

10. With the objects still selected, choose Distribute to Frames in the Frames panel Options pop-up menu.

11. To prepare the document for export, see "Preparing Mixed Format Pages for Export" later in this chapter.

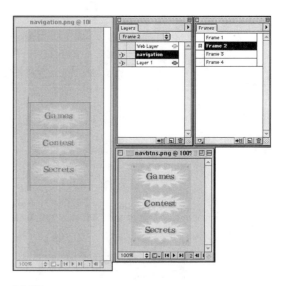

14.19

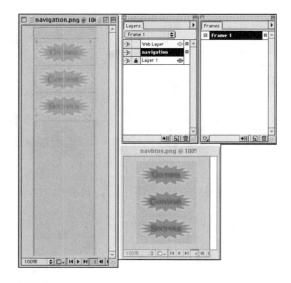

14.20

 I P

Preview the button states or animated GIF using the VCR control buttons at the bottom of the Document window. If a graphic is out of order, click-drag its frame in the Frames panel to its correct position.

Preparing Mixed Format Pages for Export

14.21

You do not have to cover your Web page with slices. Fireworks divides the undefined portions of the page to create a table using as few slices as possible.

14.22

The best Web pages get their message across in a combination of images and words, but the different types of content in these pages require different optimization parameters to download quickly and display correctly. To preserve your document's visual quality, slice it apart to separate different file formats (including HTML text), compression values, or other export parameters. Then use Fireworks' Object Inspector to set custom export parameters for specific slices.

1. To create a slice automatically, select an object in object mode or an area in image edit mode, and choose Insert→Slice (14.21). If you've selected multiple objects, select Multiple in the dialog box.

2. To create a custom slice, select the Slice tool in the Toolbox and click-drag a slice marquee. Adjust the slice as needed with the Subselect tool.

continues

(T) I P

If you are slicing a rollover, make the slice large enough to cover the entire area that changes. Check the slice in all the frames of the rollover and adjust it, if necessary, to cover any effects such as feathering, glows, or drop shadows that are not on the first frame of the rollover **(14.22)**.

Preparing Mixed Format Pages for Export continued

3. In the Object Inspector (Window→Object), select an export preset in the Export Settings pop-up menu (14.23).

To include HTML text, select Text (No Image) in the Export Settings pop-up menu. Then enter text in the text entry box that appears in the Object Inspector (14.24).

To assign multiple slices the same export settings, Shift-click them with the Pointer tool before choosing an export setting.

14.23

 I P

Any slices you do not set export parameters for are exported with the file's default export settings, which you define in the Export Preview and Document Properties dialog boxes.

HTML text doesn't appear in the open Fireworks document. Choose File→ Preview in Browser→Preview in (your default browser) to see it.

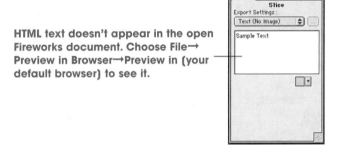

14.24

 O T E

You can format text using HTML tags in Fireworks, although the HTML text window is too small to be practical for more than a few words. If no tags are used, any text entered is exported with HTML text defaults. If there is more text than space for it in the slice, the HTML table cell expands to fit the text, which stretches out the whole table, leaving gaps in other table cells. A better choice is to use the text slice as a placeholder. When you export the Web page, empty text slices translate into empty table cells, into which you can add text in a text editor or Web authoring program (14.25).

14.25

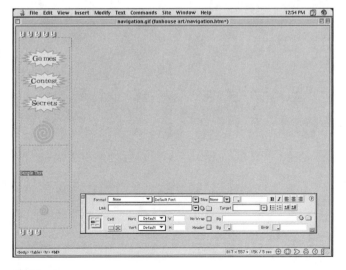

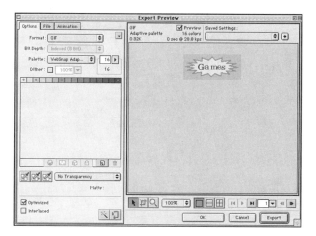

14.26

You can also select a
URL from the URL
Manager's History pop-
up menu or an open
library list.

14.27

4. To set custom export parameters, click the Ellipsis button
   next to the Export Settings
   pop-up menu to access the
   Export Preview. In the Export
   Preview, set the export optimization parameters for the
   slice and click OK (14.26).

5. If the slice links to another
   Web page, enter a URL or
   select one from the Current
   URL pop-up menu (14.27).

6. In the <alt> field, enter text to
   display when the object is disabled or unavailable. Press
   Enter.

7. To display the linked page in a
   different browser window or
   frame, enter the window or
   frame's name in the Link
   Target field or select a default
   in its pop-up menu.

8. To make the slice easy to identify, uncheck Auto-Name Slices
   and enter a name in the
   Custom Base Name field
   below the check box.

9. To add rollover behaviors to a
   slice, see Chapter 13, "Making
   a Rollover Button."

 **O T E**

*Custom names cannot include uppercase char-
acters or special characters, such as "|" and "."*

Setting Slice Document Properties

Before exporting a sliced Web page document, set its overall properties in the Document Properties dialog box. You can choose a naming scheme for the slices and which type of shims Fireworks generates to maintain your table's dimensions. Fireworks uses the document settings when exporting to define unnamed slices and format an HTML table.

Do not check Generate Rollover Demos, unless you choose FW1-Style Buttons for your HTML output style in the Export dialog box.

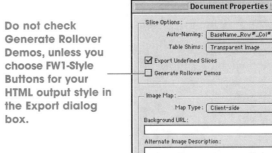

14.28

1. To set a sliced document's properties, choose File→ Document Properties.

2. In the Document Properties dialog box, choose a slice naming style from the Auto-Naming pop-up menu (14.28).

   ● Choose Basename_ Row#_Col# to name sliced graphics by their location in a table, starting with the exported base graphic's filename followed by the slice's row location and column location in a table.

14.29

 **O T E**

Table shims are an HTML trick to prop open table cells that are not filled by a graphic. As a general rule, leave table shims at their default setting of Transparent Image. Transparent shim format adds a 1-pixel-tall row to the top of a table and a 1-pixel-wide column to the right of a table that it fills with a transparent GIF **(14.29)**.

If you select Shims from Image and deselect Export Undefined Slices, Fireworks inserts transparent shims to maintain the table.

14.30

- Choose Row#_Col#_ Base-Name to add the row and column designations before the base graphic's name.

- Choose BaseName_ Numeric to create sequentially numbered sliced graphics files with the base graphic's filename before the number.

- Choose Numeric_ BaseName to create sequentially numbered sliced graphics files with the base graphic's filename after the number.

- Choose BaseName_ Alphabetical to create alphabetically sliced graphics files with the base graphic's filename before the letter.

- Choose Alphabetical_ BaseName to create alphabetically sliced graphics files with the base graphic's filename after the letter.

3. Choose the type of shims you want to maintain your sliced graphics' table dimensions in the Table Shims pop-up menu (14.30).

continues

 **O T E**

The default table shim style, Transparent Image, adds a 1×1-pixel transparent GIF file to your sliced graphics' HTML table, which it uses to prop open cells in the table to maintain its dimensions. Shims from Image uses the graphics in the table as shims to fill the table's cells. No Shims adds no extra files and leaves any empty cells blank.

Setting Slice Document Properties continued

4. To export a graphic for every slice, check Export Undefined Slices. If you want to export only areas covered by slice objects, deselect Export Undefined Slices.

5. To display a text description in a browser when an undefined slice is loading or unavailable, enter the text in the Alternate Image Description field **(14.31)**.

6. To save your settings as the default for future documents, click Set Defaults. Then click OK.

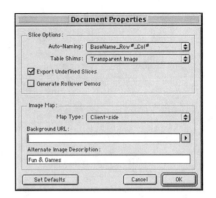

14.31

14.32

(N)OTE

*If you export a graphics file for every slice in your document, you can choose Shims from Image or No Shims. Shims from Image makes the fastest loading file, and No Shims makes the smallest HTML file. However, if your Web page has a complicated slicing scheme, it might not reassemble seamlessly in a browser **(14.32)**. If you choose to export only the slices you have defined, or if you plan to substitute HTML text for some cells in the table, select Transparent Image in the Table Shims pop-up menu to prop open empty cells.*

Exporting the Web Page

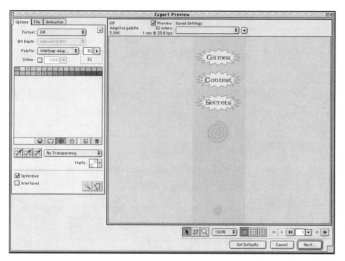

14.33

14.34

After setting custom export parameters for unique areas in your Web page and defining default page parameters, export the page. Each slice exports as a separate graphic by using the custom export parameters and filename assigned to it in the Object Inspector. Slices without a custom name are named according to the Document Properties Auto-Naming setting, and exported by using the default export settings.

Save the graphics files and the HTML file to their final locations on your site. Fireworks generates HTML with relative path links to graphics. If you plan to copy the Web page's HTML into another HTML document, place that document in the same location as the Web page so that the relative path links do not break. For more information on copying Fireworks-generated HTML into other HTML documents, see "Adding Rollovers to Web Pages" in Chapter 13.

1. To export a sliced graphic, choose File→Export, set optimization parameters for the undefined slices in the document in the Export Preview (14.33), and click Next.

2. In the Export dialog box, enter a base name for the undefined slices in the document and select a save location for all the graphics files (14.34).

continues

Exporting the Web Page continued

3. Choose Use Slice Objects to slice the exported image along its slice guides in the Slicing pop-up menu.

4. Choose an HTML output style for the page from the Style pop-up menu.

5. Select a destination folder for the page's HTML file in the Location pop-up menu. If you choose Custom, select a location in the Name HTML File dialog box and click OK **(14.35)**.

6. Click Export, and then choose File→Save to save the export settings in the master PNG file.

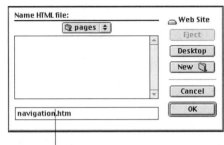

14.35 **Choose Custom when you want to name the HTML file yourself.**

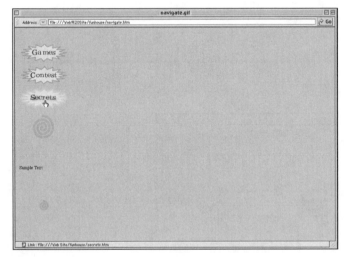

14.36

 I P

Proof the Web page's HTML document by opening it in your target browser(s) (File→Preview in Browser→Preview in [your default browser]) (14.36). If you then make adjustments to the Web page's PNG file, choose File→Export Again. You skip the Export Preview, but can change filenames, locations, or HTML styles in the Export dialog box.

 **O T E**

To export a single selected slice, click the Ellipsis button in the Object Inspector. In the Export Preview, adjust the slice's export parameters, if needed, and click Export. In the Export dialog box, adjust the export settings, if needed, and click OK.

Swapping In External Files

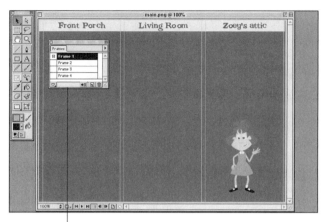

14.37   **If the swap image external file is a rollover, add frames to your Web page to match the number of frames in your rollover.**

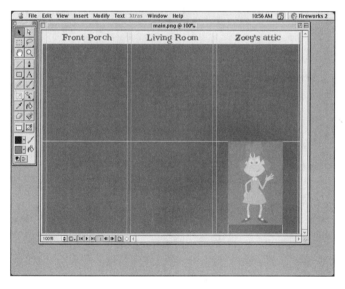

14.38

Importing or creating every graphic in a single file is not the only way to create a Web page in Fireworks. If you are including interactive behaviors such as rollovers, you can create the rollover as a separate file, export the rollover states, and then add a slice object and Swap Image behaviors in the Web page to swap in the rollover's alternate states.

You can design your Web page first and create your external files from sliced areas in the page, or create your external files first and import their first frames into your Web page. Web objects apply to all frames of a document.

1. In the open Web page document, create or import the default art for the first frame of a swap image rollover in position (14.37).

2. Add a slice object by selecting the default art object and choosing Insert→Slice (14.38).

continues

 O T E

If you want to use an animated GIF as a rollover button state, targeting it as an external file is the only way because the rollover behavior works with frames 1 through 4, exclusively. Any additional frames are ignored. Instead, the animated GIF should be an external file that swaps in as a response to a mouse event.

Swapping In External Files continued

3. Double-click the slice with the Pointer tool to open the Object Inspector. Turn off Auto-Name Slices and enter a name in the Custom Base Name field below the check box. Press Enter (14.39).

4. Choose File→Save to save the Web page PNG file.

5. Create art for the swap image rollover states or animated GIF on frames in a separate document (14.40). Choose File→ Save, and then File→Export.

If the slice links to another Web page, enter its link and target information.

Enter text in the <alt> field to display when the object is disabled or unavailable.

Do not give the slice the same name as the external swap image file.

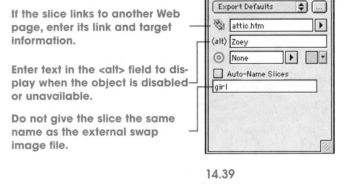

14.39

 **O T E**

Microsoft's IE 4.5 cannot use a Fireworks hotspot trigger to target a swap image change in a slice underneath the hotspot. Use the slice itself instead to trigger a change. Swap Image behaviors function correctly in Netscape Navigator.

 **O T E**

To create art for the swap image using the default art in the Web page, use the Crop tool to click-drag a crop marquee over the default art's slice. Adjust the crop marquee, if needed, and then double-click inside the selection. Select the slice with the Pointer tool and press (Delete)[Backspace]. Choose File→Save As and enter a name and save location for your swap image PNG file (14.41).

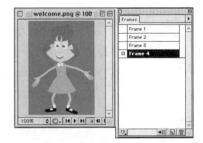

14.40

Don't give the external file the same name as the slice you want to swap it with in the Web page.

14.41

**If the swap image is an animation,
select Animated GIF.**

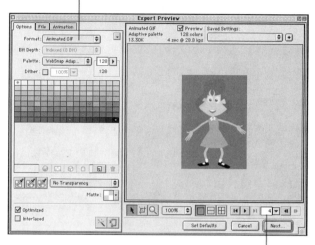

14.42

**If the swap image is a rollover, use the
Current Frame pop-up slider to select
each frame and export it separately.**

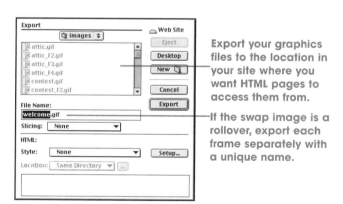

Export your graphics
files to the location in
your site where you
want HTML pages to
access them from.

If the swap image is a
rollover, export each
frame separately with
a unique name.

14.43

6. In the Export Preview window,
set the file's export parameters
and click Next (14.42).

7. In the Export dialog box, enter
a name and select a location for
the exported file. Choose None
in the Slicing pop-up menu
and None in the HTML style
menu (14.43). Click Export.

8. Open the Web page file again.
With the slice selected, choose
Window→Behaviors.

continues

 I P

*If your swap image rollover has more than
one alternate state, instead of exporting them
one at a time, cover the image with a slice
object and assign the Simple Rollover
behavior to it in the Behavior Inspector. In the
Export dialog box, choose Use Slice Objects
in the Slicing pop-up menu and any style
except None in the HTML style menu. Click
Export. You can throw away the HTML document that Fireworks generates, and use the
individual graphics files for your swap image.*

 **O T E**

*Fireworks doesn't preload swap images that
use external files as their source.*

 **O T E**

*Microsoft's Internet Explorer cannot preload
or cache swap image graphics.*

Swapping In External Files continued

9. In the Behaviors Inspector, click the + button and choose Swap Image from the Add Behaviors pop-up menu (**14.44**).

10. In the Swap Image dialog box, click the folder icon under Source of Swap. Find the file you want to swap in the Locate External Swap Image Source dialog box and click Open (**14.45**). Click OK.

11. Choose File→Save, and then File→Export. Set the file's export parameters and click Next.

12. In the Export dialog box, enter a name and select a location for the Web page's exported graphics files. Choose Use Slice Objects in the Slicing pop-up menu and select an HTML template in the HTML style menu. Choose a location for the Web page's HTML document and click Export.

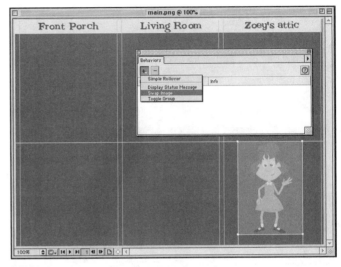

14.44

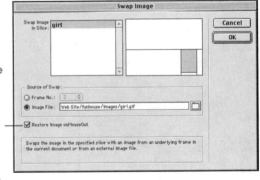

Restore Image onMouseOut reverts the swapped image to its default state when the cursor moves off the button.

14.45

If the swap image is a multistate rollover, choose Swap Image from the Add Behaviors pop-up menu in the Behaviors Inspector for each rollover state. In the Swap Image dialog box, select the external file you want to swap in for each rollover state. Select a different event to trigger the Swap Image behavior for each state by using the event's arrow button in the Behaviors Inspector (**14.46**).

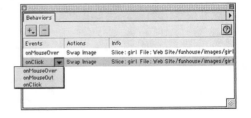

14.46

Creating a Disjointed Rollover

Frame 1

14.47

Frame 2

Check that the target object's frames are positioned correctly and covered by the slice object.

14.48 **If you don't want any visible image as the target object's default state, delete the graphic in Frame 1 after creating its slice object.**

Use Firework's Swap Image behavior to create disjointed rollovers. A disjointed rollover targets changes in other areas in a graphic. A single disjointed rollover trigger can target multiple areas, including itself, for change when a cursor rolls over it. A common use for a disjointed rollover is a navigation bar with a pop-up text graphic that describes a button's linked page when the cursor rolls over that button.

1. To create a disjointed rollover using frames within the Web page, import or create changing graphics on different frames in the Web page (14.47).

2. Select the trigger object and the target object(s) and choose Insert→Slice. In the Fireworks dialog box, choose Multiple.

3. Adjust the slices, if necessary, with the Subselect tool (14.48).

continues

O T E

A disjointed rollover's swapped-in graphic can come from an external file. The external source can be in a different Web format, even an animated GIF. To create a disjointed rollover using external files, create the alternative state(s) and export in a Web format to the images folder in your site. Import one of the files to use as the default image state in the Web page.

Creating a Disjointed Rollover continued

4. If the trigger links to another Web page, double-click it to open the Object Inspector. Enter its link and target information **(14.49)**. Press Enter.

5. Select a target's slice object. In the Object Inspector, set the slice's export parameters, enter a description in the <alt> field, uncheck Auto-Name Slices and enter a name in the Custom Base Name field **(14.50)**. Repeat with any other target slices.

6. Select the trigger's slice object (or hotspot object if used) and choose Window→Behaviors.

 I P

If the swap image trigger is an irregular shape, choose Window→Layers and click the Show/Hide icon  *for the Web Layer in the Layer panel to make the layer invisible. Select the trigger object in the Document window and choose Insert→Hotspot* **(14.51)**.

N O T E

Microsoft's IE 4.5 can use a Fireworks hotspot trigger to target a swap image change in any slice, except one underneath the hotspot. If that slice changes also, use the slice itself instead of a hotspot to trigger changes. Swap Image behaviors function correctly in Netscape Navigator.

14.49

14.50

You can also draw an irregularly shaped trigger with the Polygon Hotspot tool.

14.51

14.52

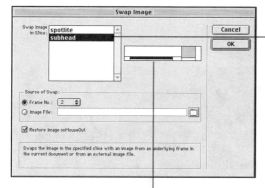

Custom naming slices makes them easier to identify.

14.53 **Select a swap image's target slice in the Slice Preview.**

7. In the Behaviors Inspector, click the + button and choose Swap Image from the Add Behaviors pop-up menu (**14.52**).

8. In the Swap Image dialog box, choose the swap image's target slice by clicking its name in the Swap Image in Slice list (**14.53**).

9. If the target's alternate state is on another frame in the same document, select its frame number in the Source of Swap Frame No. pop-up menu. Then click OK.

continues

 O T E

If the target's alternate state is another file, click the folder icon under Source of Swap in the Swap Image dialog box. Find the file you want to swap in the Locate External Swap Image Source dialog box and click Open.

 O T E

To make the swap image trigger change when rolled over, choose Simple Rollover from the Add Behaviors pop-up menu in the Behaviors Inspector. In the Simple Rollover dialog box, check Include Down State (Frame 3) and/or Include Over Down State (Frame 4) if the trigger is a three-state or four-state rollover button.

Creating a Disjointed Rollover continued

10. To select a different event to trigger the Swap Image behavior, click the event's arrow button in the Behaviors Inspector **(14.54)**.

11. Save the master PNG file (File→Save). Then export it (File→Export). Set the file's export parameters and click Next.

12. In the Export dialog box, enter a name and select a location for the Web page's exported graphics files. Choose Use Slice Objects in the Slicing pop-up menu and select an HTML template in the HTML style menu. Choose a location for the Web page's HTML document and click Export.

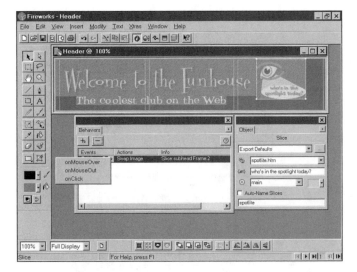

14.54

14.55

 I P

Proof the Web page's HTML document by opening it in your target browser(s) (File→Preview in Browser→Preview in [your default browser]) (14.55).

Exporting Slices As Multiple Files

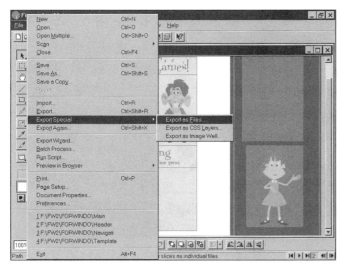

14.56

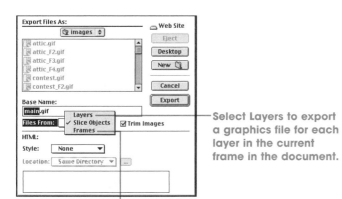

Select Layers to export
a graphics file for each
layer in the current
frame in the document.

14.57 Select Frames to export
a graphics file for each
frame in the document.

If you want to export slices as graphics files only, without generating a file of JavaScript behaviors and an HTML table, use the Export As Files feature. Exporting slices as files exports only user-created image slices, not text slices or any areas in the image file that do not have slice objects attached.

1. In an open sliced document, choose File→Export Special→ Export As Files (14.56).

2. In the (Export Files As)[Export Special-Files As:] dialog box, select Slice Objects in the Files From pop-up menu, enter a base name for any unnamed slices, and select a location for the saved files (14.57).

3. Choose None in the HTML Style pop-up menu and click Export.

 I P

If you want to set export parameters for any slices you have not set individually in the Object Inspector, choose File→Export before exporting as files. In the Export Preview window, set optimization parameters and click Set Defaults.

Exporting Cascading Style Sheet Layers

If you want to use Cascading Style Sheet layers to have precise control over your Web page's layout, export your document with the CSS Layers export option. Set preferences to create CSS layers from frames, layers, or slices. Fireworks generates the HTML, which you can then further customize in a Web authoring program.

1. Choose File→Export Special→ Export As CSS layers.

2. In the (Export Files As)[Export Special-Files As:] dialog box, select the CSS layers' source in the Files From pop-up menu, dialog box, enter a base name for the files, and select a location for the saved files (14.58).

3. Choose CSS Layers in the HTML Style pop-up menu, select a location for the HTML file, and click Export (14.59).

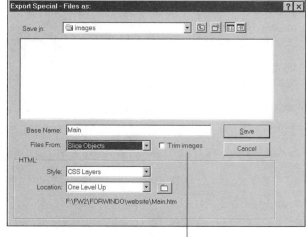

14.58 **To make CSS layers the exact size of the slice objects, deselect Trim Images. To make CSS layers the size of the graphics under the slice objects, select Trim Images.**

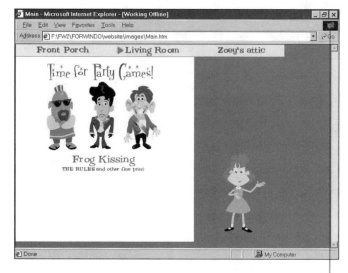

14.59 **Proof the CSS Layers HTML document by opening it in your target browser(s).**

 **O T E**

Fireworks behaviors do not export with the CSS Layers option. Create JavaScript behaviors for the layers in a Web authoring program instead. Style sheets are supported only by 4.0 and newer browsers.

Substituting Files for Slices

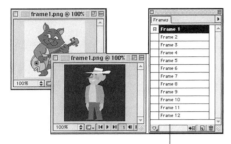

14.60   **To make the graphic an animated GIF, add frames and art to the graphic's exported file.**

If you added animation to the file, choose Animated GIF.

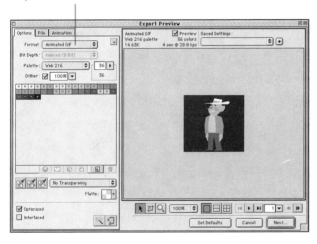

14.61

Update your Web pages by substituting files after exporting. For example, when a sliced area in a page changes, you can export and upload that individual file to your site. Or swap an animated GIF for a still graphic.

1. To revise a graphic in a Web page, open the exported file of the slice you want to update and change the art (14.60). Choose File→Save; do not change the filename. Select a location and click Save.

2. Choose File→Export. Set the new graphic's export parameters in the Export Preview and click Next (14.61).

continues

 T I P

Always use exported graphics files (GIF, JPEG, or PNG) for Web graphics, not Fireworks' native PNG files. Microsoft's Internet Explorer has problems with Fireworks' native PNG files.

 T I P

If the revised graphic is a different file format from the original, reexport the HTML page by choosing File→Export Again. In the warning box that asks whether you want to replace the HTML file, click OK. In the warning box that asks whether you want to replace graphics, click Cancel.

Substituting Files for Slices continued

3. In the Export dialog box, select the same name and location as the graphic being replaced, choose None for Slicing and HTML style, and click Export. In the Replace dialog box, click Replace (14.62).

4. Proof your edited HTML documents by opening them in your target browser(s) (14.63).

If the external file isn't the same size as the slice that targets it, it resizes to fit, resulting in quality loss.

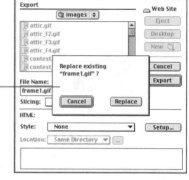

14.62

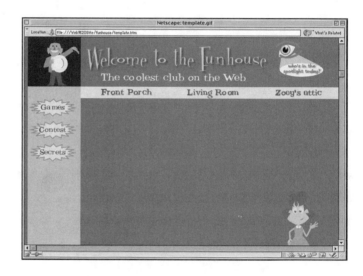

14.63

(T) I P

To substitute an existing rollover or animated GIF file into a Web page, import the file. Only its first frame imports. Cover the frame with a slice. In the Object Inspector, set the slice's export format to GIF, uncheck auto-naming, and give the slice the same name as the substitute file. Export the sliced document to a different folder than the substitute file resides in. Finally, replace the placeholder slice file with the substitute file.

Adding a Nested Table

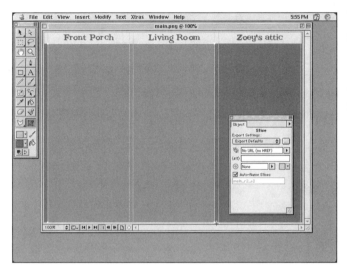

14.64

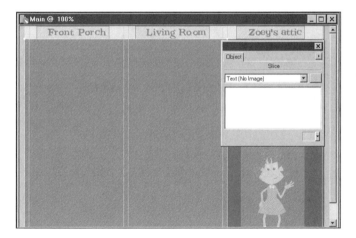

14.65

If you want to include a nested table in your Web page for changing graphics and other information, use a text slice to create the blank table cell in your Web page and the separate nested table file.

1. To add a nested table, click-drag the Slice tool over the Web page where you want the table (14.64).

2. In the Object Inspector, click the Export Settings pop-up menu and select Text (No Image) (14.65).

3. Save the Web page's PNG file (File→Save). Then export it (File→Export). Set the Web page's optimization parameters and click Next.

4. In the Export dialog box, enter a name and select a location for the Web page's exported graphics files. Choose Use Slice Objects in the Slicing pop-up menu and an HTML template in the HTML style menu.

continues

 I P

Choose Text (No Image) in the Object Inspector for any slices you don't want Fireworks to generate a graphic for when exporting a document. Your document will load more quickly in a browser, and you will have fewer image files to manage.

Adding a Nested Table continued

Choose a location for the Web page's HTML document and click Export. Choose File→Save.

5. Proof the Web page's HTML document by opening it in your target browser(s). Return to the Web page's PNG file in Fireworks.

6. Select the Crop tool from the Pointer tool group in the Toolbox and click-drag over the nested table slice (14.66).

7. Adjust the crop marquee, if needed, by dragging its handles, and then double-click inside the selection to crop.

8. Choose File→Save As. In the Save dialog box, enter a different name for the nested table's PNG file and select a save location.

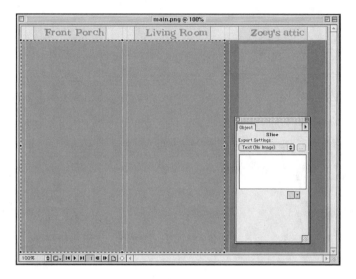

14.66

 I P

Use the Info panel (Window→Info) to line up the crop marquee with the nested table slice when selecting the table to save as a separate file (14.67). Select the slice to register its dimensions and coordinates. Then use the cursor positioning to match the coordinates when using the Crop tool and drag the marquee to the slice's dimensions.

Selected object's dimensions **Selected object's coordinates**

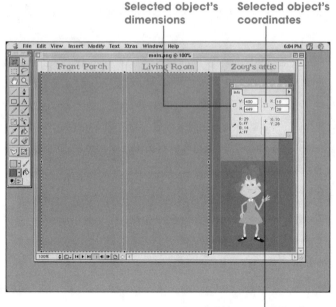

14.67

Cursor coordinates

14.68

14.69

9. Delete the table slice object, and then create the nested table with images, slices, behaviors, and so on, and choose File→Save (14.68).

10. Choose File→Export, set the nested table's optimization parameters, and click Next .

11. In the Export dialog box, select the same save location for the graphics as the Web page's graphics, the same HTML output style for the nested table, and the same save location for its HTML file as the Web page's HTML. Click Export.

12. Proof the nested table's HTML document by opening it in your target browser(s) (14.69). Return to the nested table's PNG file in Fireworks and save it (File→Save).

continues

(T) I P

Choose View→Guide Options→Snap to Guides when drawing multiple slices in a document to facilitate lining up slices and eliminate excess slices that result from leaving as little as a 1-pixel gap between slices.

Adding a Nested Table continued

13. Open the two HTML files in an HTML editor. Copy the nested table's HTML code between the directions that say "Begin Copying Here" and "Stop Copying Here" and paste it into the Web page's HTML in the empty text cell **(14.70)**.

14. If you have any JavaScript code in the nested table document, copy and paste it between the Web page's <head> tags.

If the Web page already contains JavaScript, just copy the JavaScript code in the nested table that differs from the Web page's JavaScript and paste it before the "// stop hiding —>" command.

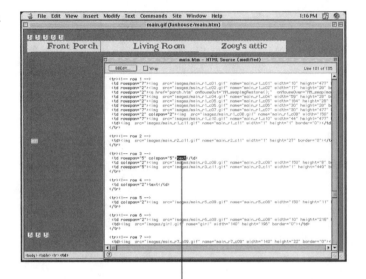

14.70 **Paste the nested table into the text cell.**

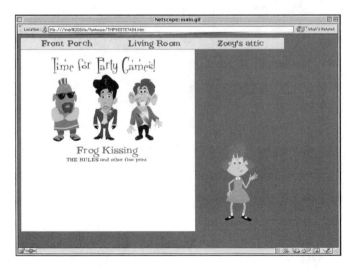

14.71

Proof your edited HTML document by opening it in your target browser(s) **(14.71)**.

Fine-Tuning Your Web Page

Default positioning

14.72   **Absolute-zero positioning**

14.73   Move the transparent pixel row instead of deleting it so that it still holds the table together.

When you export a sliced document, Fireworks generates HTML to reassemble the slices as a seamless-looking graphic in a table. Although this makes for an efficient workflow, if you are less than happy with Fireworks' table defaults—such as the space it leaves between the sliced document and the top-left side of a browser window—or you want to include other media, such as Shockwave (which Fireworks doesn't support), edit the HTML yourself.

1. To edit your Web page, open its HTML document in a text editor or Web authoring tool.

2. To eliminate the default browser offset, insert the following text into the <body> tag: marginwidth="0" margin-height="0" topmargin="0" leftmargin="0" (14.72).

3. To eliminate the 1-pixel gap at the top of the Web page's table, cut the 1-pixel spacing row at the top of the table and paste it at the end of the table just before the </table> tag (14.73).

 O T E

Editing your Web page in a text editor or other Web authoring program is the only way to add other JavaScript code not included in Fireworks' behaviors, or other Web formats, such as Shockwave Director or Flash movies, not supported by Fireworks.

(T) I P

If dotted lines appear on the top and right sides of your uploaded sliced images, their table is missing the shim GIF graphics file. Upload shim.gif to the folder containing the sliced graphics.

CHAPTER 15

In this chapter you learn how to...

Create a Simple Animated GIF

Import Animated Vector Sequences

Export Animated GIFs

Nothing livens up a Web page the way animation does. Animated GIFs are the oldest and most commonly used type of animation on the Web. They require no plug-ins and are compatible with nearly every Web browser.

In Fireworks, animated GIFs can begin life as vector art, bitmaps, photographs, even as existing animated GIFs. Use Fireworks to design, edit, time, and optimize your animated GIFs.

MAKING ANIMATED GIFS

Because animated GIFs are most effective at smaller file sizes, it's important to design them to communicate as quickly as possible. Because they have no sound, they must communicate visually through images and text. And because animated GIFs take time to view, they should offer the viewer a payoff—a point in the animation where it proves to be worth its weight. Because Fireworks is an all-in-one package for creating and optimizing animated GIFs, it frees you to focus on other aspects of creating animated GIFs.

Whether you want moving illustrations, headlines, logos, charts, or ad banners, Fireworks makes creating animated GIFs manageable, and even easy.

Creating a Simple Animated GIF

One of the simplest kinds of animation is the slideshow animation, in which elements on the screen are replaced by other elements. In Fireworks, you can animate images, text, shapes, or even colors.

1. To make a slideshow animation, create a new document.

2. Use Fireworks' drawing and painting tools to create background graphics for your animated GIF. Or choose File→Import and select your background graphic. Click to place the imported graphic on the screen **(15.1)**.

3. Choose Window→Layers and double-click the label for Layer 1. In the Layer Options dialog box, enter a new name for the layer (that is, "background") **(15.2)**. Click OK.

4. To protect objects on the background from being accidentally selected or manipulated, lock the layer by clicking the Lock Layer space **(15.3)**.

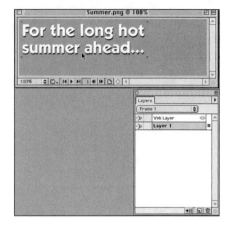

15.1

If the elements on the background layer do not change or move during the animation, choose Share Across Frames.

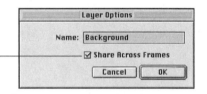

15.2

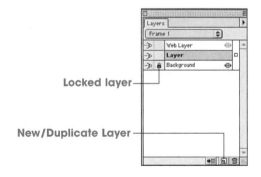

Locked layer—

New/Duplicate Layer—

15.3

 I P

Use layers to organize your artwork and to establish spatial relationships between objects. Using descriptive names for layers makes it easier to remember what is on each layer.

When you import graphics, the cursor changes to an angle. Position the cursor at the upper-left corner of your target area and click to place the artwork.

15.4

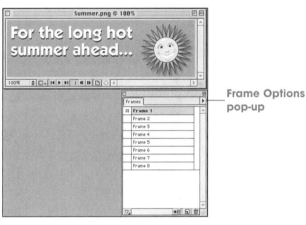

Frame Options pop-up

15.5

5. Click the New/Duplicate layer icon (15.3) to make a new layer for the changing images. Name the layer.

6. Import the changing graphics or create them in Fireworks (15.4).

7. Choose Edit→Select All, and then center the objects one on top of another by choosing Modify→Align→Center Vertically and Modify→Align →Center Horizontally. Drag them into position on the layer.

8. With the changing objects still selected, choose Window→ Frames. In the Frames panel, click the Frame Options pop-up arrow and choose Distribute to Frames. This creates a new frame for each of the individual images (15.5).

continues

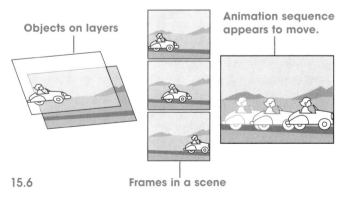

Objects on layers

Animation sequence appears to move.

15.6

Frames in a scene

  O T E

In Fireworks, scenes are made up of layered objects (text and/or graphics). Frames are essentially snapshots of a scene. Each frame shows the changes and movement in the scene since the previous frame. Viewed as a sequence, the differences from frame to frame give the illusion of motion (15.6).

Creating a Simple Animated GIF continued

9. To rearrange frames, click the Frame label of the frame you want to move and drag it to the new position **(15.7)**. Release the mouse button when a dark line appears where you want the frame to be.

Use the VCR controls at the bottom of the Document window to preview the animation.

15.7

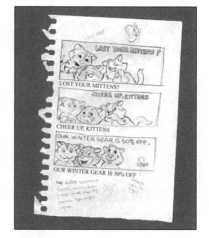

15.8

When using Distribute to Frames, new frames are created for the selected artwork based on their stacking order within the frame. The lowermost object remains on the original frame while the others are distributed in order to new frames.

To save production time, make sketches or storyboards of your animation concepts **(15.8)**. *Even rough drawings can help you visualize and refine your ideas.*

Importing Animated Sequences

15.9

Use the VCR
controls to preview
your animation.

15.10

Although Fireworks has everything you need to make an animated GIF, if you prefer drawing in other programs or you want to repurpose images that were created for other media, Fireworks can open animated GIFs or documents from applications such as FreeHand, Illustrator, Photoshop, and CorelDRAW as animation frames.

1. To open a layered vector file or animated GIF as frames in Fireworks, choose File→Open, locate the file, and click Open.

2. If you are opening a vector file, choose Convert Layers to Frames in the Vector File Options dialog box (15.9).

3. If your sequence contains a background, select the background graphic(s) and choose Edit→Cut.

4. Click the New/Duplicate Layer icon at the bottom of the Layers panel to make a new layer and choose Edit→Paste. Rename the layer and position it at the bottom of the Layers list (15.10).

(N) O T E

When opening an animated GIF, Fireworks automatically separates the document into two layers. The background layer contains non-changing elements and the GIF layer contains all the changing elements. Each frame in the animated GIF becomes a frame in Fireworks. You can edit, add, delete, and rearrange frames as well as optimize colors and change timing.

(N) O T E

When opening a layered Photoshop file, Fireworks sets each layer to be shared across frames. To animate them, turn off the Share Across Frames option for each layer. Then open the Frames window, choose Edit→ Select All, and choose Distribute to Frames from the Frame Options pop-up menu.

Exporting Animated GIFs

After you've made an animation, you'll want to make some additional adjustments to it before saving the final GIF file. Optimize colors, adjust file size, and set timing in the Export Preview window.

1. Choose File→Export to open the Export Preview window.

2. In the Options panel, set the format to Animated GIF (15.11) (see Chapter 2, "Optimizing Art for the Web," for more information).

3. Set the palette and number of colors.

 **O T E**

To make an animated GIF with transparency, either use a transparent canvas or identify colors for transparency in the Export Preview's Options panel (15.12).

Transparent animated GIFs are not supported by all browsers.

 I P

When you choose the Export Options for an animation, Fireworks shows the first frame of the animation and the number of colors in that GIF frame. Changing the format from GIF to Animated GIF polls colors in all the frames and suggests a WebSnap Adaptive palette based on those colors. Experiment with reducing the number of colors and changing the Palette to get the best results.

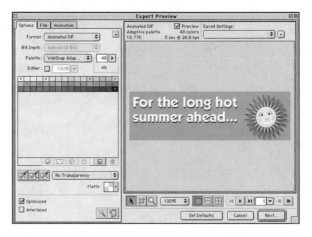

15.11

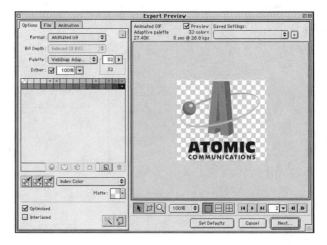

15.12

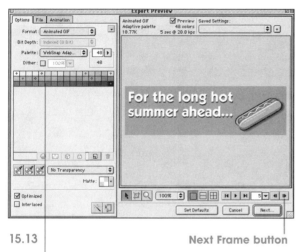

15.13

The Export Preview, unlike the preview in the workspace, shows your animation in the actual color depth in which it will be exported.

Next Frame button

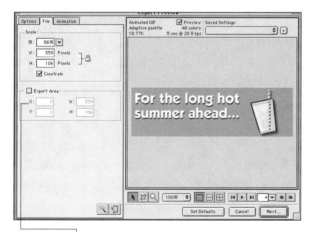

15.14

Fine-tune your cropping by entering coordinates in the Export Area fields.

4. Step through the animation frame-by-frame by using the Next Frame button in the VCR controls (15.13). Check each frame to see that the image is still readable.

5. To scale or crop the animation, click the File tab. In the File panel (15.14), resize the image by entering a percentage in the scale field or use its pop-up slider. Select the Crop tool and adjust the crop marquee handles to trim the image.

continues

**O T E**

The Trash Can pop-up button in the Animation panel reveals a list of disposal methods. These determine how pixels are replaced from frame to frame in your browser. Unspecified yields the smallest animated GIFs possible. It enables Fireworks to choose the method that best suits your needs. Choose None to add a small object to the current frame without disposing of the previous frame. Restore to Background is used when working with a transparent animated GIF to replace the area no longer covered by the object in the previous frame with the background color from the HTML document. Select Restore to Previous when you are animating over an image. This mode restores areas of background that are no longer covered by foreground objects.

Exporting Animated GIFs continued

6. To set frame delays, click the Animation tab to view the Animation panel and select a frame by clicking the frame label **(15.15)**.

7. In the frame delay field, type how many hundredths of a second to pause before the current frame changes to the next. A delay of 200, for instance, pauses the image for two seconds. Press Enter.

8. To hide a frame, press the Hide/Show icon beside that frame in the Animation panel.

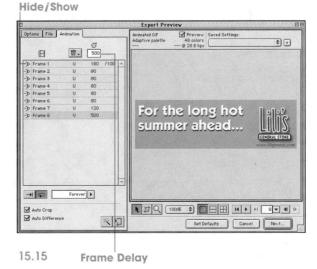

15.15   **Frame Delay**

 O T E

Frames hidden in the Export Preview are not exported in the final animated GIF. Adjustments made in the Export Preview window do not affect the working document.

15.16

(T) I P

*To select noncontiguous frames for export or playback, (Command-click)[Ctrl+click] the frame labels **(15.16)**. To select contiguous frames, Shift-click the frame labels.*

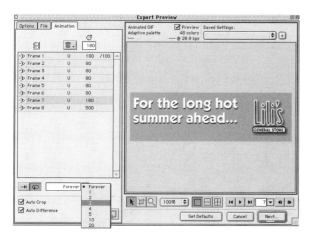

15.17

15.18

9. To set the number of times the animation plays, make a selection from the Number of Loops pop-up menu (15.17) in the Animation panel. A setting of 1 will play the animation once and return to the first frame.

10. Preview the animation using the Play button in the VCR controls. If you want to save the export settings you've made so far without exporting the movie, press Set Defaults and return to the workspace. If you want to export the movie, click Next.

11. In the Export Dialog box, name your animation and select a location for it. Click Export.

12. In the Document window, choose File→Save. In the Save document dialog box, name your working file and select a location for it. Click Save.

 I P

Use scaling to animate objects that appear to move toward or away from the viewer (15.18). Such objects suggest a greater sense of space than those that move only from side to side, up, down, or diagonally.

CHAPTER 16

Fireworks has a number of features to take some of the tedium out of creating and editing animated GIFs. One indispensable feature is the use of Symbols and Instances to help manage and control objects in an animation. With Symbols and Instances, you can make global changes by adjusting a single object.

MAKING BETTER ANIMATED GIFS

Tweening is another useful animation feature in Fireworks. With tweening, you define two or more key positions of an animated action and specify the number of steps between them, then Fireworks generates the frames needed to complete the sequence. By tweening Symbols and Instances, you can animate such attributes as transparency, position, rotation, scaling, and skewing.

Compare and adjust the positions of objects across frames with onion skinning, which lets you view frames before and after the current frame as you work.

Fireworks has all the tools you need to animate in any style or combination of styles you can imagine. Import or draw cartoons or stylized images, scan photographs or use 3-D artwork created in other programs. Make type, shapes, and even clip art jump to life.

Combined creatively, the graphics, text, and animation features in Fireworks can help bring eye-catching, compelling results to any animated GIF. Turn any idea into a memorable experience by using animated text on a path. Fireworks has all the tools you need to make a better animated GIF.

Tweening Symbols and Instances

A Symbol is essentially a master version of an animation object. Symbols can be made up of multiple components or they can be single objects such as shapes or text blocks. A duplicate of a Symbol is called an Instance.

Fireworks' Tween feature automatically animates an object based on key points you define using Symbols and Instances. Although Fireworks currently cannot tween shapes, it can transition an object's Live Effects, position, rotation, opacity, scale, and skewing. Tweening produces in-between artwork in the number of steps you specify.

1. In a new document, create or import a graphic.

2. Select the object and choose Insert→Symbol (16.1).

3. With the Symbol selected, choose Edit→Duplicate to make a copy (Instance) of your Symbol (16.2).

4. Choose Window→Frames. In the first frame of the sequence, position the Symbol where you want your animation to start and the Instance where you want your animation to end.

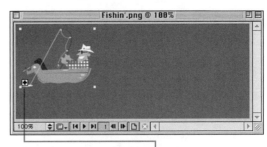

16.1   **A Symbol, indicated by a plus sign in its lower-left corner, can be a single object or several objects.**

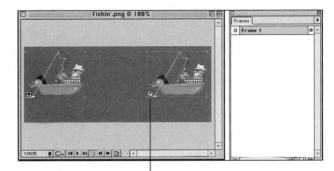

16.2   **An Instance, indicated by a bent arrow in its lower-left corner, is a copy of a Symbol.**

Tweening can be done between a Symbol and an Instance, a Symbol and multiple Instances, or between two or more Instances.

16.3

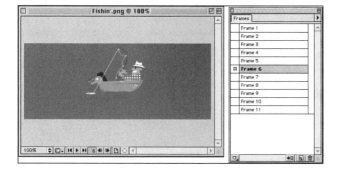

16.4

16.5

5. Shift-select both the Symbol and the Instance. Choose Insert→Tween Instances. In the Steps field of the Tween Instances dialog box, enter the number of steps you want to add between the beginning frame (the Symbol) and the end frame (the Instance) (16.3). Check the Distribute to Frames box and click OK.

6. After a moment, Fireworks generates the new frames, putting the frontmost object (the Instance) on the last frame and distributing the other new Instances in between. Press the Play button on the VCR controls at the bottom of the Document window to preview the animation (16.4).

Ⓣ I P

Symbols enlarge better than Instances. When tweening an enlargement from a small object to a larger object it is best to make the Symbol the larger object and the Instance the smaller object (16.5). To make the tween go from small to large, select the smaller object and choose Modify→ Arrange→Send to Back before tweening.

Editing Symbols and Instances

When you adjust any part of a Symbol, the change is reflected in every Instance made from that Symbol. Changes to an Instance affect only the Instance itself.

1. To alter the Symbol and all its Instances, click Frame 1 in the Frames Panel to go to that frame.

2. Select and edit the Symbol (16.6).

3. To see how Symbol changes affect Instances, step through the movie frames by using the Step button in the Document window VCR controls (16.7).

4. To alter a single Instance, select and edit the Instance (16.8).

5. Using the Document window's VCR controls, step through the movie frames to see how altering an Instance affects the animation.

 I P

Make text into a Symbol instead of duplicating it over the frames of an animation. You then can make global changes when you want to update the text by editing the text in the Symbol. All the text Instances linked to the Symbol automatically update.

 O T E

If you use filters on an Instance, the Instance becomes an image and is no longer attached to the Symbol.

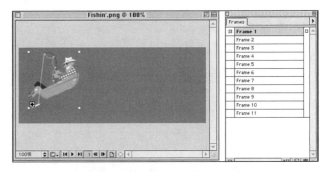

16.6

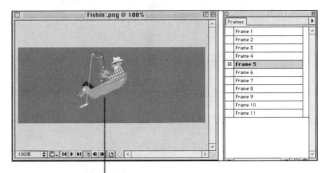

16.7   **The Instances on each frame have changed to match the changes made to the Symbol.**

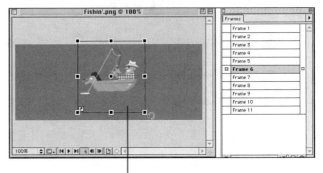

16.8   **Changes to an Instance do not affect the Symbol or the other Instances.**

Adding to Symbols

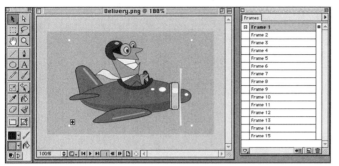

16.9

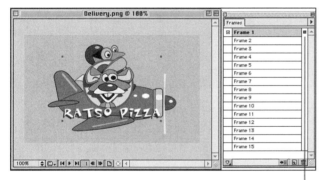

16.10   **When an object in a frame is selected, a blue square appears next to the frame.**

Because Symbols maintain links to their Instances, you can easily change an animation by altering a Symbol. An animated advertisement featuring an airplane, for example, can be customized by adding a logo to the Symbol. That logo would then be a part of the airplane in every Instance made from that Symbol. The Fireworks PNG file of the animation could be reused for a series of ads with different messages by simply altering the Symbol.

1. Open a Fireworks PNG animation that uses Symbols and Instances.

2. Find the Symbol by selecting an Instance in any frame (Window→Frames) and choosing Insert→Symbol Options→Find Symbol (16.9).

3. Create or import a graphic into the document to add to the Symbol (16.10).

4. Resize the new graphic, if needed, and position it where you want it, and then choose Edit→Select All.

continues

 **O T E**

If the Find Symbol option (Insert→Symbol Options→Find Symbol) is grayed out, either you do not have anything selected or the object you have selected is not an Instance.

Adding to Symbols continued

5. Select Insert→Symbol
   Options→Add to Symbol to
   merge the graphic and the
   Symbol (16.11).

6. Use the Document window's
   VCR controls to preview the
   edited animation.

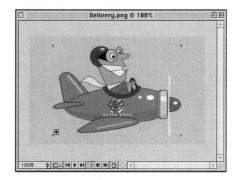

16.11

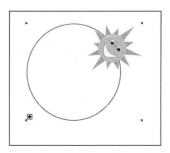

16.12

 I P

*To animate an object that moves in a circle,
draw a circle for the object's path, and make
the circle a Symbol. Choose Edit→Clone to
make an Instance. Rotate the Instance just
under 180° (Modify→Transform→Numeric
Transform). Clone and rotate the new
Instance just under 180° again. Select all,
choose Insert→Tween Instances, enter the
number of frames for the rotation, and check
Distribute to Frames. Position the object you
want to rotate over the circle in Frame 1
(16.12), select all, and choose Insert→
Symbol Options→Add to Symbol (16.13).
Positioning the object in the center of the
circle creates a propeller-like rotation. Finally,
use the Subselect tool to delete the circle.*

16.13   **The Instances on
            each frame have
            changed to match
            the changes made
            to the Symbol.**

Breaking Links Between Symbols and Instances

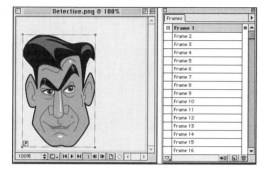

16.14

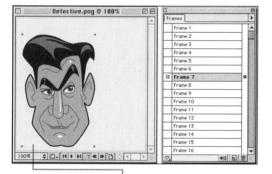

16.15   **The unlinked Instance is now a grouped graphic.**

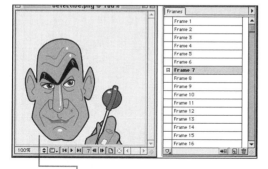

16.16   **The unlinked graphic is no longer controlled by the Symbol.**

Working with Symbols and Instances makes it easy to move and transform an image over time. The capability to alter a Symbol and have that change occur in every Instance made from that Symbol saves time and effort. But when you want to alter an Instance without affecting the rest of the animation, the Break Link feature (Insert→ Symbol Options→ Break Link) enables you to cut the link between an Instance and a Symbol while leaving the links between the Symbol and other Instances intact. The unlinked Instance becomes a grouped, editable copy of the original graphic.

1. Open a Fireworks PNG animation that uses Symbols and Instances (16.14).

2. Select an Instance on one of the frames (Window→Frames) and choose Insert→Symbol Options→ Break Link to make it independent of the Symbol (16.15).

3. Edit the grouped graphic.

4. Preview the animation by using the Document window's VCR controls (16.16).

 **O T E**

When an Instance is unlinked from a Symbol, the unlinked graphic retains the attributes of the Symbol and any manipulations such as scaling or rotation that have been applied to it. Because it is independently editable, you can change any aspect of its appearance.

Creating a Cross Fade

A cross fade is a transition effect in which one image fades into the picture as another fades out (16.17). Cross fades can be used with text, still images, or moving images. Using Layers and the Object-Level Opacity scale makes it easy to create cross fades for your animated GIFs in Fireworks.

16.17

1. Create a new document and choose Window→Layers to open the Layers panel.

2. Make or import a piece of artwork on Layer 1. Select the artwork and choose Insert→Symbol to make it a Symbol (16.18).

3. Click the New/Duplicate icon 🔳 in the Layers window to insert a new layer.

4. On the new layer, make or import a second piece of art-work. Select it and choose Insert→Symbol to make it a Symbol. Visually center it on the first Symbol (16.19).

16.18

(N) O T E

When transparency is added to an animation sequence, through anti-aliasing or object transparency for example, new colors are introduced. Determine for each animation what tradeoffs you are willing to make between performance and image quality. Experiment with palettes, dithering, and color reduction to get the results that best meet your needs.

16.19

16.20

The Current Frame pop-up
enables you to navigate to
any frame in the document
from within the Layers window.

16.21

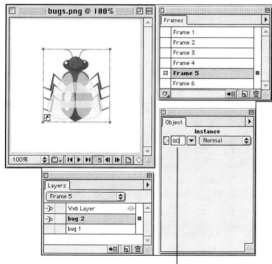

16.22

This renders the selected
Instance at 80 percent
opacity on the current frame.

5. Choose Window→Frames. In the Frames pop-up menu, choose Duplicate Frame and enter 5 in the Number field. Select After Current Frame and click OK (16.20).

6. In the Layers window, click the Hide/Show icon to make Layer 2 invisible in the current frame.

7. Still in the Layers window, choose Frame 6 from the Current Frame pop-up menu (16.21).

8. Click the Hide/Show icon to make Layer 1 invisible. Choose Frame 5 from the Current Frame pop-up.

9. Hide Layer 1 so that you don't accidentally select it, and then double-click the artwork in the Document window to open the Object Inspector.

10. In the Object Inspector's Object-Level Opacity field, enter a setting of 80 (16.22).

continues

 O T E

Crossfading can add a dynamic element to a simple text message using as few as two steps per transition.

Creating a Cross Fade continued

11. Choose Frame 4, hide Layer 1, select the graphic, and then make the opacity 20 percent less than the previous graphic. Repeat for Frames 3 and 2 (16.23).

12. After you've changed Frame 2, show Layer 1 and hide Layer 2. Select the Layer 1 graphic and set its opacity to 80 (16.24).

13. Continue the process for Frames 3, 4, and 5, showing Layer 1, hiding Layer 2, selecting the Layer 1 graphic, and setting its opacity to 20 less than in the previous frame.

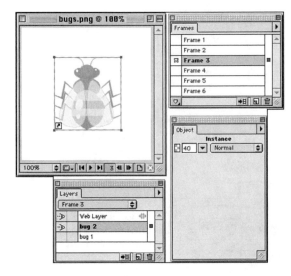

16.23

I P

To create a moving cross fade, use tweening instead of duplicating frames. On the first frame, choose Edit→Duplicate to make an Instance of each Symbol. Position the Symbols where you want the animation to start and the Instances where you want the animation to end. Shift-select both the first Symbol and its Instance, and choose Insert→Tween Instances. Enter the number of steps to add, check Distribute to Frames, and click OK. Repeat with the second Symbol and Instance. Then proceed with steps 6 through 15 to finish the cross fade.

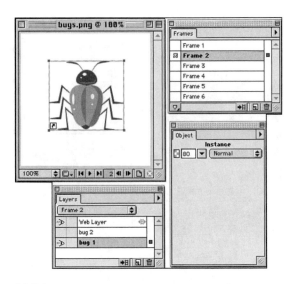

16.24

16.25

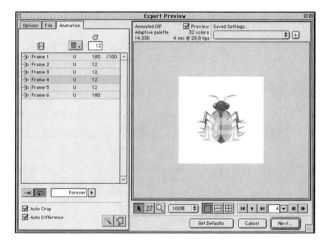

16.26

14. Choose Frame 1 in the Current Frame pop-up in the Layers panel. If Layer 2 is visible, hide it. Be sure that both layers are visible in Frames 2 through 5. In Frame 6, make Layer 2 visible and hide Layer 1.

15. Preview the animation by using the VCR controls at the bottom of the Document window (16.25).

 **N O T E**

Set the cross fade's timing in the Export preview's Animation panel (16.26) by selecting Frame 1 and (Command)[Ctrl]-clicking the last frame, and then enter a long delay value in the Frame Delay field to make the animation hold on the first and last frames. Select Frame 2 and Shift-click the next-to-last frame, and then set the speed of the cross fade by entering a smaller number in the Frame Delay field. Choose a loop setting in the Loop control. Then use the VCR controls in the Export Preview window to preview your animation.

Editing Animations Using Onion Skinning

In traditional animation, onion skinning refers to using tracing paper to create and view an animated sequence. Tracing paper enables the artist to see each drawing in a sequence as well as drawings before and after it. Comparing the differences between drawings, an animator can adjust the artwork to achieve just the right effect in a sequence.

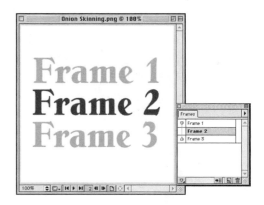

16.27

Fireworks' Onion Skinning feature enables you to view frames before and after the current frame (16.27). Use onion skinning for creating and editing animations frame-by-frame. With Onion Skinning turned on, you can see the differences between objects in a sequence and adjust your animation one frame at a time or all at once.

1. Create or import a graphic to animate and select Insert→ Symbol to make it a Symbol.

2. Position the Symbol where you want your animation to start. Choose Window→Frames, and then duplicate the frame by dragging it onto the New/ Duplicate icon ![icon] at the bottom of the Frames panel (16.28).

3. Click the label for Frame 2. From the Onion Skinning pop-up menu at the bottom of the Frames window, choose Before and After (16.29).

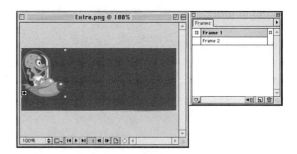

16.28

Beginning and end arrows appear beside the frame before and the frame after the current one.

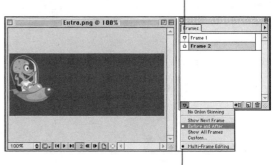

16.29   **Be sure that Multi-Frame Editing is not selected.**

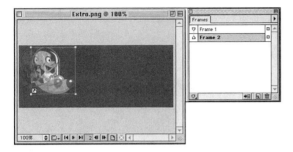

16.30

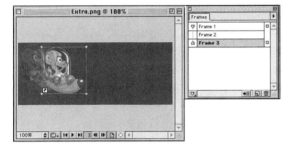

16.31

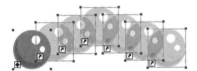

16.32

4. Using the dimmed image of the previous frame as a guide, drag the Instance on Frame 2 to the next location in your animation sequence (16.30).

5. Duplicate Frame 2 and select the label for Frame 3. Click in the Onion Skin column next to Frame 1 to see it as an onion-skinned image.

6. Using the dimmed images as guides, move the Instance on Frame 3 to the next location in your animation (16.31). Duplicate the frame and repeat the process for the rest of your frames.

7. Press the Rewind button in the Document window's VCR controls, and then press Play to preview the animation.

continues

 **O T E**

Onion Skinning anchors on the currently active frame and spans across frames before and/or after it, depending on what settings you assign in the Onion Skinning pop-up.

 I P

For smooth motion, use the same approximate change increment for all the frames in a sequence (16.32).

8. Click the label for Frame 1. In the Onion Skinning pop-up menu in the Frames panel, choose Show All Frames.

9. With all the frames visible, adjust the spacing and location of individual Instances (16.33).

10. Preview the animation again by using the Document window's VCR controls.

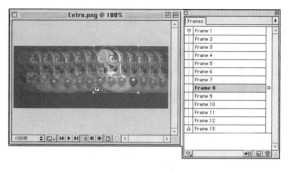

16.33

16.34

 **O T E**

Onion skinning turns off temporarily when you press Play in the Document window's VCR controls.

 I P

To move the entire animation at once, choose Show All Frames and Multi-Frame Editing from the Onion Skinning pop-up menu. Then choose Edit→Select All and drag the artwork to the desired location (16.34).

Animating Text on a Path

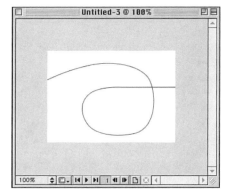

16.35

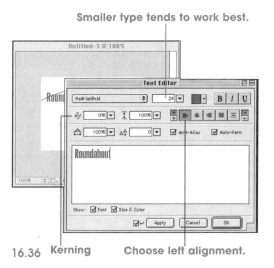

Smaller type tends to work best.

16.36   **Kerning**   **Choose left alignment.**

The Text on a Path feature in Fireworks lets you achieve zippy text animations with a minimum of drawing. Simply create a path for your text to follow, style the text, and attach it to the path. Then move the text along the path. Try this technique with fun fonts, special characters, or dingbats for even more flexibility.

1. In a new document, use the Pen tool to draw a path for your text (16.35).

2. Choose the Text tool and click in the Document window. In the Text Editor, set your type attributes and enter your text (16.36). Click OK.

continues

(T) I P

Avoid tight curves and narrow corners because they can cause odd breaks as your text moves over them.

(T) I P

To make moving text more legible, increase the space between characters by setting the text's range kerning to a positive value.

Animating Text on a Path continued

3. To attach the text to the path, shift-select the text and the path and choose Text→Attach to Path **(16.37)**.

4. Select Window→Frames and in the Frames panel, click-drag Frame 1 onto the New/ Duplicate Frame icon . Select Frame 2.

5. Select the text and choose Window→Object to open the Object Inspector.

6. In the Object Inspector's Offset field, enter a number in pixels for the distance you want to move the text along the path between the two frames, and press Enter or Return to see the results **(16.38)**.

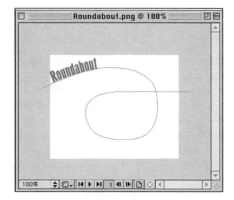

16.37

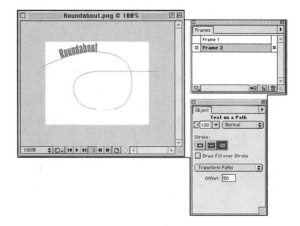

16.38

 **O T E**

When text is attached to a path, the path's style attributes disappear so that the path is invisible in the animation.

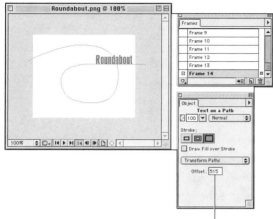

16.39   **Measurements along the text path are relative to the starting point of the text attached to the path.**

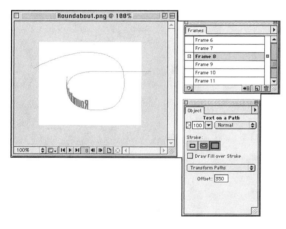

16.40

7. Repeat steps 4, 5, and 6, adding the number you chose in step 6 to the current offset until the text is in its final position (**16.39**).

8. Preview the animation by using the Document window's VCR controls. Adjust the text offset in individual frames as necessary.

To give the text the appearance of moving around a 3D path, select the text and choose Text→Orientation→Skew Vertical (16.40).

In addition to using the text offset to control the movement of text on a path, you can change the speed of the animation by adjusting the frame delay settings in the Export Preview Animation panel. See "Exporting Animated GIFs" in Chapter 15 for more information.

CHAPTER 17

From its inception, Fireworks was designed to address the unique needs of Web designers. Its primary focus is streamlining the process of preparing images to be displayed onscreen in a Web environment.

To best represent images on screen, Fireworks is built around the RGB color model (the model that computer monitors use for display). Because it doesn't fully support the CMYK color model used in commercial printing or offer any color separation controls, Fireworks is not the best application for creating high-end print work. Fireworks does not print PostScript, so text is always bitmapped. It also has no support for spot color, trapping, specifying halftone screens, color separations, or overprinting, features regularly found in print-oriented graphics programs.

USING FIREWORKS BEYOND THE WEB

Although it is not a full-featured print program, Fireworks can still be an effective tool for tasks other than Web development. You can prepare graphics for inserting into desktop publishing applications, and you can also print directly from Fireworks to networked printers. You can use Fireworks output with popular multimedia software, such as Macromedia Director and Flash, or with presentation software such as Microsoft PowerPoint. Fireworks even exports some high-resolution formats and has an internal print function so you can, for example, provide printed support materials for multimedia or Web-based presentations.

Exporting Art for Use in Director and Flash

With Fireworks, you can easily create artwork for Macromedia's Director and Flash. Because vector export is not currently possible from Fireworks, you won't be able to export the clean, scalable vector art for which Flash is known. But both Flash and Director can import a variety of file formats exported by Fireworks, and they both support Fireworks' 32-bit PNGs with alpha channels, which means you can create full-color sprites that blend smoothly into any background (17.1). Plus, Fireworks' frames mimic Director's and Flash's frames, so you can use Fireworks' superior graphics creation tools to design art for inter-activity and animation, lay it out full-screen in frames, and then use slices and Fireworks' extensive export options to produce high-quality graphics efficiently for multimedia.

1. Create or import your graphics into one master file (17.2). Lay out the graphics on the screen as they should appear in the Director or Flash file, using frames (Window→Frames) and layers (Window→Layers) to organize them.

O T E

If you plan to use system standards, such as PICTs with the Macintosh palette or BMPs with the default Windows palette, you do not need to create a custom palette.

Using 32-bit PNGs eliminates halos around silhouetted objects in Director

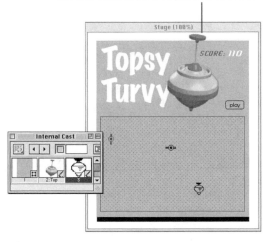

17.1

Set text in Fireworks if you want to use Live Effects to create 3D text effects. Otherwise, add text in Director or Flash to take advantage of their superior compression.

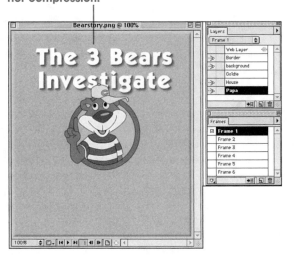

17.2

Options panel pop-up menu **Save Settings**

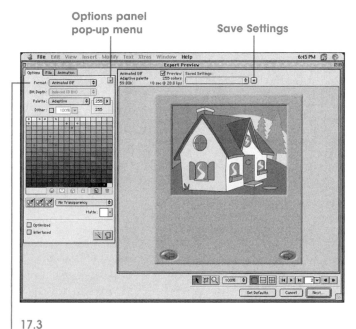

17.3

Use Animated GIF to make Fireworks poll all the frames when creating a custom palette.

17.4

2. To set the custom master palette of the graphics, choose File→ Export. In the Export Preview window, choose Animated GIF as the file format and Adaptive for the palette. Deselect Optimized and set the Number of Colors to the highest number possible (17.3). Choose Save Palette in the Options panel pop-up menu, name the palette in the Export Swatches dialog box, select a location for it, and click Save (17.4).

3. To set the optimization parameters of the graphics, choose Custom in the Palette pop-up menu, and load the saved palette. Then change the file format to GIF and save the settings by clicking the Save Setting button.

continues

 **O T E**

If you are exporting your graphics as 24-bit or 32-bit files, you do not need to include them in a master file for creating a palette. Palettes apply only when you are creating 8-bit or smaller files, such as GIFs, or indexed PNGs, PICTs, and BMPs. For more information on palettes and other export options, see Chapter 2, "Optimizing Art for the Web."

Exporting Art for Use in Director and Flash continued

4. To export a template to use in Director or Flash for arranging the graphics, use the Current Frame slider to select a frame (17.5) and click Next. In the Export dialog box, name the file, select a location for it and click Export.

5. Select the Slice tool and click-drag over areas on screen that contain changing graphics, such as buttons and animations, and other areas that you want to export as single files (17.6); then save as a Fireworks' PNG file (File→Save).

6. Export single static graphics by selecting their slice, clicking the Export Settings ellipsis button in the Object Inspector (Window→Object), and then clicking Export in the Export Preview. In the Export dialog box, name the file, select the exported files folder you set up earlier, and click Export.

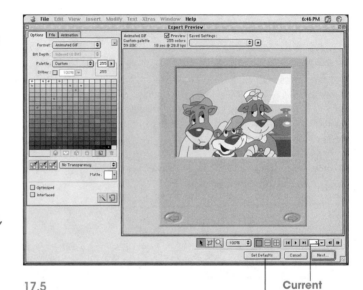

17.5

Current Frame slider

If you don't need a template, click Set Defaults to return to the Document window.

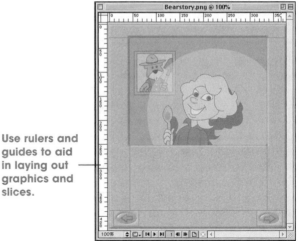

Use rulers and guides to aid in laying out graphics and slices.

17.6

(T) I P

To make importing your files into Director or Flash one-step easy, create a new folder and save only the exported graphics in it.

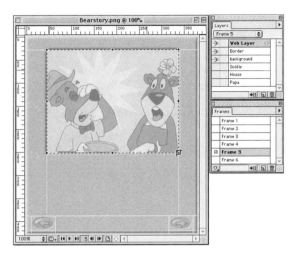

17.7

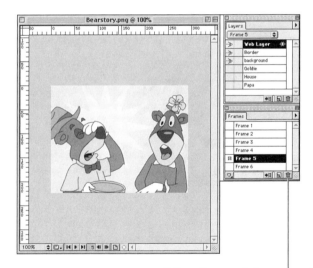

17.8

If the slice contains unneeded
frames, delete them by dragging
them to the Trash Can icon.

7. Export button states, animations, or other changing
   graphics by selecting the Crop
   tool and click-dragging
   over a slice (17.7). Adjust the
   crop handles, if needed, to
   cover the slice exactly, and
   then double-click inside the
   slice to crop the file down to
   the slice only.

8. Delete the slice object (17.8)
   and choose File→Save As.
   Rename the file and save it in
   the same location as the master
   PNG file.

9. Choose File→Export
   Special→Export As Files. In
   the Export Files As dialog
   box, select Frames in the Files
   From pop-up menu, select the
   exported files folder you set
   up earlier, and click Export.

continues

T I P

*If any of your sliced files are animated GIFs,
choose File→Export instead of File→Export
Special→Export As Files, and then choose
Animated GIF in the Export Preview
Options panel. See Chapter 15, "Making
Animated GIFs," for more information on
exporting animated GIFs.*

Exporting Art for Use in Director and Flash continued

10. Open the master PNG file
again (File→Open), and repeat
steps 7 through 9 for any other
changing graphics in the file.

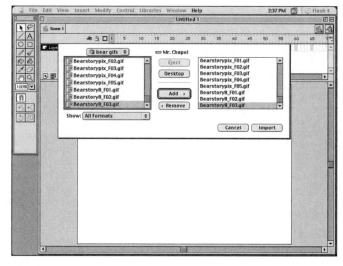

17.9

 **N** O T E

*To import the graphics into Flash after
exporting all the files into a single folder,
launch Flash, choose File→New Movie, and
then choose File→Import. Open the exported
graphics folder, add all the files to the import
list, and then click Import* **(17.9)**.

 **N** O T E

*To import the graphics into Director after
exporting all the files into a single folder,
launch Director, choose File→New Movie,
and then choose File→Import. Open the
exported graphics folder, add all the files to
the import list, and then click Import. In the
Select Format dialog box, choose Bitmap
Image, check Same Format for Remaining
Files, and then click OK. (If any files are
animated GIFs, import them separately and
choose Animated GIF as their format.) In the
Image Options dialog box, select Import
under Palette, check Same Format for
Remaining Files, and click OK* **(17.10)**.

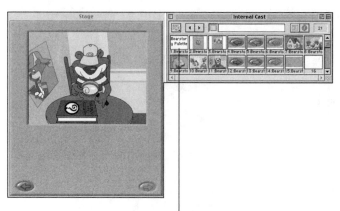

17.10

**All the graphics import into Director
with the same custom palette.**

Exporting Graphics for Other Onscreen Uses

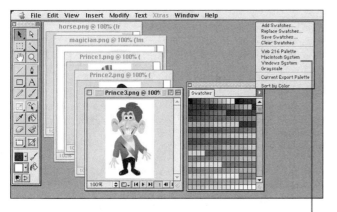

17.11

If you are creating graphics to be used on a Macintosh, use the standard Macintosh palette when creating them. If you are creating graphics to be used on a Windows machine, use the default Windows palette.

If you create graphics for presentations, computer games, software applications, or CD-ROM titles, take advantage of Fireworks' hybrid vector-and-bitmap graphics creation environment, and then optimize and batch process your graphics, all within one program. Your master files retain their editability so that changes and updates are easy. Plus, batch processing for multiple formats can be done directly from your desktop.

1. Create or import your graphics (17.11), and then save them as PNG files in one location.

2. In the Document window, choose File→Batch Process. In the Batch Process dialog box, click the Files to Process … (ellipsis) button to open the Open Multiple Files dialog box, locate the PNG files, click Add All, and then click OK.

continues

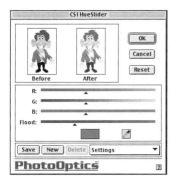

17.12

 I P

If you create pixel images on a Mac to be viewed on a Windows machine, brighten the images before exporting to compensate for the increased contrast in Windows monitors. With the image selected in image edit mode, choose Xtras→PhotoOptics→CSI HueSlider. In the CSI HueSlider window, set the RGB values to 100 and Flood to 75. Click New, name the settings (for example, Windows Brightener) for future reuse, and click Save **(17.12)**. *Then click OK.*

Exporting Graphics for Other Onscreen Uses continued

3. In the Batch Process dialog box under Actions, click the Export ... (ellipsis) button to open the Batch Export dialog box. Click the Export Settings ... (ellipsis) button to open the Export Preview window.

4. In the Options panel of the Export Preview window, choose a file Format, Bit Depth, and Palette type (if selecting 8-bit color depth) (17.13).

5. Click Set Defaults to return to the Batch Export dialog box, set the File Name to Original Name, choose No Scaling, and then click OK.

6. In the Batch Process dialog box, click the Script button to save the script to reuse later. In the Save Script dialog box, name the script and save it in the same location as the PNG files (17.14).

7. To process the batch, click OK in the Batch Process dialog box.

 I P

To process future batches from the desktop, select the .jsf (JavaScript file) file and Shift-click the files you want to process. Drag the selected files to the Fireworks application. Fireworks launches and processes the files. If you are already in Fireworks, choose File→Run Script in the Document window.

For Macintosh graphics, choose PICT and the Macintosh palette. For Windows graphics, choose BMP and the Windows palette.

If you have a preexisting palette, choose Load Palette from the pop-up menu.

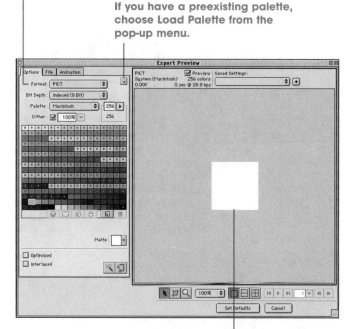

17.13

When batch processing, the Export Preview shows a blank square because it's handling multiple images.

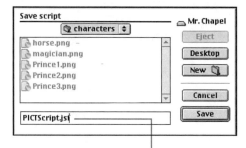

17.14 **If you are preparing art for different platforms, make scripts for each file format.**

Preparing Multiframe Art for Custom Programming

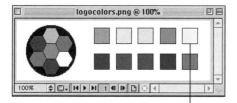

17.15   Turn off anti-aliasing and make all strokes hard lines so that Fireworks doesn't add extra colors to the restricted palette.

If the restricted palette already exists in another program, choose Custom instead of Exact for the palette type, and then locate and load the palette.

Choose GIF, PNG, PICT, xRes LRG, or BMP file format.

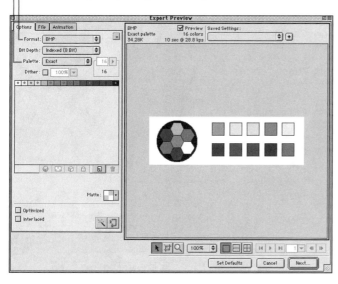

17.16

If you create graphics for use in software titles or interactive CDs, the programmers assembling the product usually have very specific restrictions on how the art should be prepared. In addition to restrictions on file format, palette size, and file naming, they often want multiframe art, such as button states, assembled side-by-side in a single file. You can set up Fireworks as a software graphics production environment by using the Export Preview window, custom palettes, and the Export As Image Well function to provide these files with up to four button states in a single file.

1. To create a restricted palette, create or import a graphics file that contains only the colors in the restricted palette (17.15).

2. Choose File→Export, and in the Export Preview window, select an 8-bit file format (17.16).

continues

ⓝ O T E

Not all palette types can be imported into Fireworks. Photoshop CLUTs (Color Look-Up Tables) and ACTs are compatible. To use a restricted palette from another program that isn't compatible, create a graphic using the palette in the other program and save it as an 8-bit image. Then locate and load the palette from the 8-bit image into Fireworks.

Preparing Multiframe Art for Custom Programming continued

3. Select Exact as the palette type, and save the custom palette by choosing Save Palette in the Options panel pop-up menu. Name the palette in the Export Swatches dialog box, select a location for it, and click Save.

4. Click Set Defaults to return to the Document window. Close the palette document and save it.

5. To use the palette to create graphics, choose Window→Swatches. In the Swatches panel pop-up menu, choose Replace Swatches (17.17). In the Replace Swatches dialog box, locate and load the saved palette.

6. Choose File→New, and in the New Document dialog box, enter the size of a single button state, set the document resolution and canvas color, and then click OK.

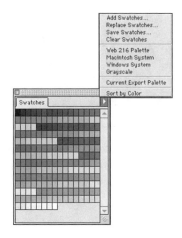

17.17

Do not use anti-aliasing, feathering, gradients, Live Effects, color blends, transparency, or any other operation that results in colors not in the palette when creating restricted-color graphics.

17.18

 T I P

If a graphic contains unwanted colors, choose Adaptive instead of Exact for the palette type, select and lock the restricted colors by clicking on them in the preview window graphic and clicking the Lock icon, enter the number of colors in the Maximum Number of Colors field, and press Enter. For more information on customizing palettes, see Chapter 2, "Optimizing Art for the Web."

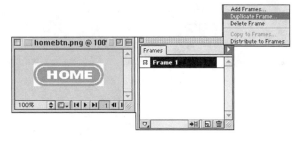

17.19

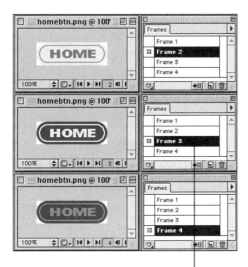

17.20

If you do not have a
fourth button state,
leave frame 3 blank.

Save the export settings for reuse by
clicking the Save Settings button.

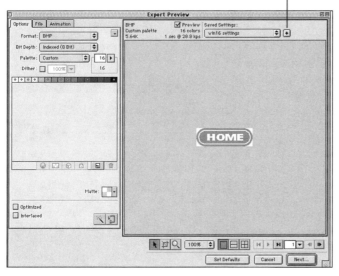

17.21

7. Create the default button state,
using the restricted palette for
all colors (17.18).

8. Add frames for the other
button states (up to four) by
opening the Frames panel
(Window→Frames), and either
duplicating the default button
state or adding blank frames
by choosing that option in the
Frames panel pop-up menu
(17.19).

9. Create the button art for the
additional button states in the
following frames: mouse over
or second button state in
Frame 2, mouse over selected
or fourth button state in Frame
3, and mouse down or third
button state in Frame 4 (17.20).

10. To export the button art,
choose File→Export, and in the
Export Preview window, select
the required file format (17.21).

continues

(N) O T E

*The Export As Image Well feature trans-
poses Frames 3 and 4 upon export, so
reverse the order of Frames 3 and 4 in your
PNG file to have the multistate art appear in
the correct order in the exported file.*

Preparing Multiframe Art for Custom Programming continued

11. Choose Load Palette in the Options panel pop-up menu, locate the palette in the (Replace Swatches)[Open] dialog box, and click Open. Click Set Defaults to return to the Document window.

12. In the Document window, choose File→Export Special→ Export As Image Well. In the Export Files As dialog box, name the exported file per your programmers' specifications, choose Frames in the Files From pop-up menu, choose a location for your file, and click Export (17.22).

17.22

Image Well lays out the button states side-by-side with a 1-pixel red line separating the frames.

I P

If your specs require no space between the button states, open the file and use the Marquee tool to select each button state, and then press the keyboard's left-arrow key to nudge it over one pixel at a time to cover the red line separating the buttons (17.23). Repeat with any remaining buttons. Then choose Modify→Document→Trim Canvas to delete the excess space on the right side of the document. Save the changes by choosing File→Export Again, and clicking Export in the Export dialog box to replace the original Image Well file with the trimmed file. Close the document without saving it.

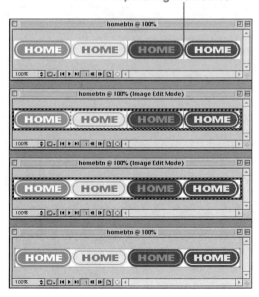

17.23

Preparing Art for Print

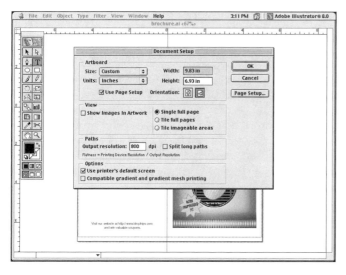

17.24

You can prepare graphics for commercial offset printing in Fireworks if you work within Fireworks' limitations. Because Fireworks is Web-centric, it exports only bitmapped images. Even if you create your graphics as vectors and text, they convert to pixels before printing, which can make text blurry and hard to read. Fireworks also lacks any normal print-specific controls; you can only create a TIFF file, place it in a print-oriented program, and set print controls there **(17.24)**.

Image resolution is another issue: Web image resolution isn't fine enough for print. A printed Web graphic looks pixelated with coarse, visible pixels. Instead, create art at the resolution you need for print, and if you want to reuse it as a Web graphic, downsample it after exporting the TIFF for print.

continues

 **O T E**

Fireworks measures type in pixels, not points like a print program, so printed type size isn't accurate. If you set your resolution to 300 pixels per inch, common for high-quality printing, and set your text size to 72 pixels, your printed text will look more like 24-point type, because the printer compresses the text to less than one-third its screen size. Instead, create high-resolution graphics sans text in Fireworks and add text later in a desktop publishing program or print-oriented drawing program.

Preparing Art for Print continued

1. To create a new document for print, choose File→New in the Document window. In the New Document dialog box, change the width and height measurement units from pixels to inches, and then enter the dimensions for your printed image.

2. Enter the print resolution in the Resolution field set to pixels/inch, and choose a canvas color. Click OK (17.25).

3. Create or import your graphics (17.26).

 **O T E**

Fireworks is a Web graphics program and doesn't support PostScript, so you cannot export EPS (Encapsulated PostScript) files, only TIFFs. TIFF (Tagged Image File Format) is a cross-platform bitmap format that is widely used by image-editing and page-layout applications for high-resolution images. TIFF files can be full-color, indexed color, grayscale, or 1-bit black and white.

 I P

Working with large, high-resolution images is slow. To improve performance, choose File→Preferences and select the Folders option from the pop-up menu. Set your scratch disks to volumes that have a lot of empty space in them. Limiting the number of Undo Steps in the General tab can help, too.

Set the pixels/inch resolution to 1.5 to 2 times the lines/inch of the halftone screen that the image will print at (ask your printer for the screen frequency). For example, for a 150-line halftone screen, set the image resolution to 300 pixels/inch.

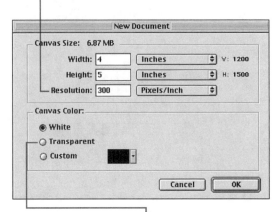

17.25 Choose Transparent if you want to silhouette your graphic.

17.26 If you are using scanned art, scan it at the highest resolution you plan to use.

If your image includes transparency, choose 8-bit or 32-bit TIFF.

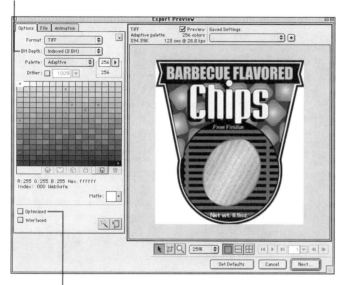

17.27   **Deselect Optimized because file size is not an issue.**

17.28

4. To use specific CMYK colors, double-click the Brush or Fill color well in the Toolbox to access the system color picker, select the CMYK picker (Mac only), define a color, and then click OK. Save the color for reuse by choosing Window→ Swatches, move the cursor to an empty area in the Swatches panel, and click when the cursor turns into a paint bucket.

To create graphics for one-color printing, select Grayscale in the Swatches panel pop-up palette.

5. Save the PNG file, and then choose File→Export. In the Export Preview Options panel (**17.27**), choose TIFF for the file format, and select a color depth:

- Choose 8-bit for indexed color, and Adaptive or Exact palette for a four-color graphic, Grayscale, or Black and White for a one-color graphic.

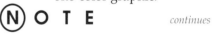

continues

*The Color Mixer offers a CMY color model for creating custom colors. However, colors are measured on a scale from 0 to 255, not as a percentage, and there is no separate black ink channel (**17.28**). To match a specific CMYK color in Windows, open or import an image that contains the color and sample it with the Eyedropper tool.*

Preparing Art for Print continued

- Choose 24-bit for full color.
- Choose 32-bit to include an alpha channel in a full-color TIFF.

6. To retain an image's transparency, click the pop-up arrow next to the Matte color well and select the None icon **(17.29)**.

7. After setting the export parameters, click Export. In the Export dialog box, name the TIFF file, choose a location for it, and click Export.

8. In the Document window, save the PNG file again (File→Save) before resampling the graphic for the Web. (See "Resampling or Resizing an Image" next for more information.)

17.29

 **O T E**

If you are using Macromedia FreeHand for print preparation, you can import Fireworks PNG files directly, without exporting them; however, as in other image editors, only the first frame opens, the image is flattened, and all vector paths and text are converted to pixels **(17.30)**.

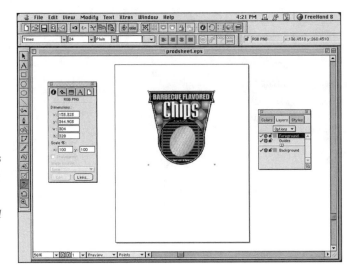

17.30

 I P

When you're creating something for print, proof it on paper, not the screen. As you make changes, print the results to check.

Resampling or Resizing an Image

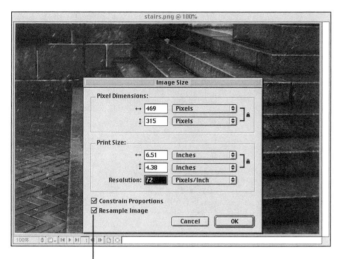

17.31   **To change the image's resolution but not its screen size, turn off Resample Image.**

17.32

If you created a graphic for print and want to use it on the Web, or if you want to resize an image to fit your design, you have to resample the image. Resampling adds or subtracts pixels to a bitmap image to retain image quality when changing its pixel depth. Upsampling to a higher resolution or bigger dimensions adds pixels to the image, making the image blurry. Downsampling to a lower resolution or smaller dimensions eliminates pixels, sharpening details but losing subtle transitions. As a general rule, downsampling is preferable to upsampling.

1. To scale a document or change its resolution, choose Modify→Document→Image Size.

2. To change the image's resolution, check Resample Image in the Image Size dialog box, and enter a number in the Resolution field (**17.31**).

continues

Resampling vector graphics or text results in no image quality loss because they are mathematical paths, not pixel art. However, any part of the paths that contain bitmaps, such as a photographic pattern fill, is affected by resampling (**17.32**).

Resampling or Resizing an Image continued

3. To resize the image **(17.33)**, check Resample Image, and enter a width or height in the Pixel Dimensions field. To resize by a percentage, change the unit of measure in the Pixel Dimensions pop-up menu to Percent, and then enter a percentage. Click OK.

4. Choose File→Save As to keep the original file unchanged **(17.34)**. In the Save Document dialog box, rename the file, select a save location, and click Save.

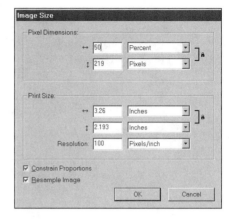

17.33

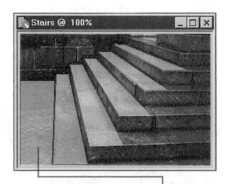

17.34 **When you scale a document, its guides and Web layer objects also resize.**

When resampling pixels to change an image's resolution or dimensions, you can choose one of four different interpolation methods in Fireworks 2.02. The default method, Bicubic Interpolation, offers the smoothest image quality. For softer results, try Bilinear Interpolation or Soft Interpolation, which blur the image, reducing unwanted artifacts but also eliminating sharp details. For a high-contrast result, choose Nearest Neighbor, which resizes images without blurring, but results in jagged edges. To switch interpolation methods, choose File→Run Script, select a .jsf file in the Scaling Options folder in the Fireworks 2 folder, and click Open. The method you choose becomes the default.

Printing from Fireworks

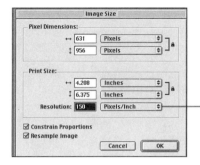

If the printer's resolution is **300 dots per inch,** set the image's resolution to **150 pixels per inch.**

17.35

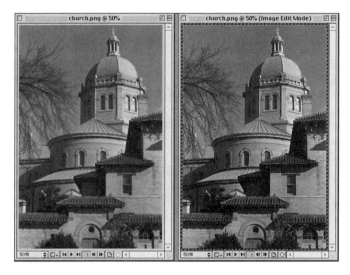

17.36

To print copies of Web graphics, resample your graphics temporarily to a higher resolution using Fireworks 2.02, and then revert them back to their lower, Web-friendly resolution after printing. Vector graphics and text scale smoothly to any size—pixel images suffer some image degradation.

1. To print a Web graphic, save it (File→Save), and then choose Modify→Document→Image Size.

2. In the Image Size dialog box, check Resample Image, and then change the image resolution to half the resolution of the designated printer (17.35). Click OK.

3. To increase the image definition of a selected bitmap graphic, choose Xtras→ Sharpen→Sharpen (17.36).

4. Print the file (File→Print).

5. Choose File→Revert to return the graphic to its Web dimensions before editing the graphic or resaving it.

 I P

Fireworks centers the image on the paper output. To print elsewhere on the page, choose Modify→Document→Canvas Size, and set the canvas size to within your printed page's margins. Then place the graphic on the canvas where you want it to print.

 I P

Download the Fireworks 2.02 upgrade from Macromedia's Web site: `http://www.macromedia.com/support/fireworks/downloads.html.`

INDEX

SYMBOLS

S

S-curve path segments, 103
Saturation blend mode, 125
saturation, CSI PhotoOptics filters, 159
Save Backups dialog box, 57
Save Stroke dialog box, 167
saved palettes, 44
saving
24-bit/32-bit export settings, 48
custom brush strokes, 167
custom palettes, 44
custom patterns, 172
custom textures, 172
effects, 92
eight-bit PNGs export settings, 46
exporting, compared, 29
files, 29
GIF export settings, 39
gradient fills, 96
JPEG export settings, 41
strokes, 88
swatches, 79
text attributes, 179
Scale tool
pixel selections, 139
resizing vector objects, 116
scaling thumbnails, 67
Scan, TWAIN Acquire command (File menu), 16
Scan, TWAIN Source command (File menu), 16
scanned images
color-correcting, 154-159
color-shifting toward single colors, 155
contrast, 156

cropping, 152-153
custom patterns/textures, 169-172
full-color pixel selections, 156
infrared color film look, 159
luminance range, 154
outlines, 156
random noise, adding, 157
scanned negatives, 157
scanning digital images, 16
scenes, 271
Screen blend mode, 124
script tag, 230
scriptlets, 70-71
search and replace (global), 53
Fireworks files, 54, 57
vector files, 59, 62
segments (paths), 102
curved, 103
curves, customizing, 105
S-curve, 103
straight, 102
selecting
color number maximum, optimizing and exporting GIFs, 34
color palettes, eight-bit PNGs, 43
default browser, 203
graphic file formats, 31
layers, 131
objects within groups, 120
pixels, 137-138
selections (pixels)
color-correct with camera lens' filters, 158
color-shifting toward single colors, 155
contrast adjustments, 156

converting into duotones, 156
feathering edges, 142
flipping, 141
luminance range, 154
perspective, applying, 140
random noise, adding, 157
reshaping, 140
resizing, 139
rotating, 140-141
slanting, 139
special effects, applying, 147
transforming, 139-141
shading 3D objects, 127-128
shapes, painting, 144
shaping
hotspots, 197
pixel selections, 140
text, 185
text paths, 189
vector objects, 117
sharing
custom brush strokes, 168
saved type styles, 179
Sharpen, Sharpen command (Xtras menu), 163
sharpening graphics, 163
Simple Rollover dialog box, 217
sites (Web)
Fireworks 2.02 upgrade, 315
Macromedia downloads, 228
regular expressions chart, 55